Developing 21st Century Literacies

A K-12 SCHOOL LIBRARY CURRICULUM BLUEPRINT WITH SAMPLE LESSONS

Mary Jo Langhorne, Denise Rehmke, and the Iowa City Community School District

Neal-Schuman Publishers, Inc.

New York   London

Don't miss this book's companion website!

To access additional lessons, units, guides, bibliographies, strategies, and other library learning tools, go to:

http://www.iccsd.k12.ia.us/
library/curriculum.htm

Published by Neal-Schuman Publishers, Inc.
100 William St., Suite 2004
New York, NY 10038
http://www.neal-schuman.com

Printed and bound in the United States of America.

The paper used in this publication meets the minimum requirements of American National Standard for Information Sciences—Permanence of Paper for Printed Library Materials, ANSI Z39.48-1992.

Library of Congress Cataloging-in-Publication Data

Langhorne, Mary Jo.
    Developing 21st century literacies : a K-12 school library curriculum blueprint with sample lessons / Mary Jo Langhorne, Denise Rehmke, and the Iowa City Community School District.
        p. cm.
    Includes bibliographical references and index.
    ISBN 978-1-55570-752-1 (alk. paper)
    1. School libraries—Iowa—Iowa City. 2. Library orientation—Iowa—Iowa City. 3. Curriculum planning—Iowa—Iowa City. I. Rehmke, Denise. II. Iowa City Community School District (Iowa City, Iowa) III. Title. IV. Title: Developing twenty-first century literacies.

Z675.S3L255 2011
025.567809777'655—dc23

2011031223

Contents

PART I: DESIGNING THE BLUEPRINT

List of Figures

List of Lessons/Units

Preface

May you live in interesting times.
—Chinese proverb

These are indeed interesting times for school libraries in myriad ways. New national standards and initiatives point strongly to a need for school librarians skilled in teaching critical literacies, able to support reading, conversant with technology on many levels, and possessing the leadership skills to work within the professional community. Almost daily changes in technology tools and applications challenge us to learn quickly, and to be adept at helping our "wired" learners be discriminating users of the many tech tools available to them. Support for young and developing readers is imperative, and school librarians have a key role in reading. Ironically, the opportunities afforded by this changing landscape come at a time when many question the need for libraries and librarians.

Today's students will live their entire lives in the 21st century. It is difficult to even begin to imagine the changes in technology and society that will occur during the next 90 years. What is clear, however, is that to survive and thrive in the 21st century, students will need to be skillful readers, critical thinkers, creative and innovative workers, and responsible citizens in a world that will be ever more global. That is our goal as school librarians, and that is the intent of the curriculum blueprint contained in this book.

This curriculum blueprint has resulted from the efforts of the 30 teacher-librarians who serve the Iowa City Community School District (ICCSD). This dynamic and collaborative group has three characteristics in common. They are (1) passionate about reading and sharing books, (2) skillful and enthusiastic about technology, and (3) committed to teaching. The curriculum that they have developed is in place and practiced daily in their libraries. While cognizant of national trends and issues, it is grounded in the reality of today's schools. We hope that this curriculum is both visionary and pragmatic.

Like most curriculum documents, this one is organized around standards, benchmarks, and objectives. Because school librarians have two major areas of responsibility for teaching, the content is also organized into two concept areas: literature and inquiry. These two areas are not independent of one another, but this model helps to frame and describe the school library's teaching program. The school librarian plays a critical role in the reading program of the school, both in supporting classroom reading instruction and in library teaching activities that enrich reading for students through exposure to various types of literature, literary elements, and the work of respected authors. Every student must have the opportunity to become a competent and self-motivated reader. The literature component of this curriculum reflects the long-held belief that skillful reading is fundamental to all types of literacy.

A second underlying belief is that a curriculum that embraces an *inquiry* approach to learning is the best means of developing 21st century literacies. Inquiry may be defined as the process wherein learners access information from a variety of sources, evaluate the information, extract what is needed, and use the information to communicate the results of the search. Inquiry-based learning implies much more than just this process, however. Inquiry requires that students go beyond simply answering questions to exploring topics in depth, thinking critically and creatively, analyzing, transforming, and synthesizing information. In an inquiry-based curriculum, students seek multiple perspectives, work collaboratively with others, use information ethically and creatively, and develop dispositions for learning—curiosity, responsibility, persistence, and independence. Lifelong learners possess these inquiry skills.

This work is intended to provide a model for school librarians who seek to develop and implement a sound library curriculum in their own schools and districts. It must be noted that this is a blueprint only—it is intended as a starting point. The standards, benchmarks, objectives, lessons, and assessments contained herein must be modified to suit the needs and goals of each individual school or district that examines them. Whenever possible the lessons presented should be integrated or coordinated with content-area learning. This guide is K–12 in scope and has been developed as a spiraling model, where librarians at each level can build upon what children have learned in previous grades.

In addition to practicing school librarians, this book will be useful in programs where individuals are pursuing careers in school libraries. It is built upon sound theory, but has the advantage of also being based in practice. It outlines important considerations in school library learning programs: the role of collaboration, the need for careful design of learning activities including assessment, the wise use of technology, and the key role of the library website.

The curriculum acknowledges the realities of life in the schools today: the time crunch, the heavy emphasis on testing, budgetary issues, the challenges of technology, and the presence of fixed schedules. We hope that users of this guide will come away with a sound understanding of how library curriculum is designed and delivered in the schools, how it supports and complements other curricular areas, and the necessity of implementing such a curriculum to enable students to become effective 21st century learners. This curriculum is not perfect; it is not the final answer. It is the product of a group of collaborative librarians who are striving to create a sound library program in these interesting times. The work continues every day.

ORGANIZATION OF THIS BOOK

Part I of this book outlines the building blocks for creating a school library instructional program. Chapter 1 defines 21st century literacies through the lens of major national initiatives including the Common Core and gives an overview of the curriculum development process. Chapters 2 and 3 detail the two major areas of the library's instructional program: reading/literature and inquiry. The literature component, organized around five focus areas, is a particular strength of this book, detailing lessons and activities that may be used to engage students with literature of many types and in differing formats, while improving their proficiency as readers. The inquiry chapter details an expanded view of developing students' skills as critical thinkers and their dispositions as learners while they master the process of locating, processing, creating, and communicating information. Chapter 4 discusses the importance of working collaboratively with teachers and other staff to integrate library instruction with classroom content. Collaboration on many levels is addressed, as are techniques for collaborating in a fixed-schedule environment. A systematic approach to planning instruction using the principle of backward design with close attention to addressing the learning needs of all students is detailed in Chapter 5. This chapter includes an instructional planning tool useful in working with teachers. Chapter 6 discusses the school librarian's role in assessment, with an emphasis on formative assessment as a means of supporting learning and improving instruction. It also outlines a formal assessment model, which may be useful for librarians who work within a fixed-scheduling structure.

Instructional technology and the role of the school librarian in this key area are discussed in Chapter 7. Schools and school libraries could no longer operate effectively without computers and other technologies, and the librarian's expertise in new and emerging technology tools and applications enriches learning opportunities for students. Chapter 8 describes the contribution of the library webpage to curriculum. Just as a library program—including the curriculum, the resources, and the facility—is carefully planned and implemented to enhance student learning and encourage inquiry, the library webpage should reflect this same deliberate attention in its design. A library's physical resources are carefully selected and arranged for greatest accessibility to its users during the school day. Likewise, the library webpage should provide the information, resources, and guidance that users need both during and outside the school day in this digital 24/7 environment.

Part II presents the curriculum blueprint developed in the Iowa City Community School District, including sample lessons and units. Chapter 9 defines and details the ICCSD library program mission, beliefs, standards, benchmarks, and objectives—the structure through which most educators view curriculum in this era of education standards. The library curriculum is represented as a two-part model, one depicting the reading/literature component, the other focusing on inquiry. Beginning in Chapter 10 a selection of lessons and strategies for learning through the library program is presented. These begin with basic lessons on library organization, book selection, book care, and library orientation, and include lessons on types and elements of literature, reading strategies, and literature response. Some of these lessons utilize a SMART Board, one brand of interactive whiteboard, and include SMART Notebook files. These may be modified for other formats, and represent sound integration of technology into instruction.

Sample lessons taught in support of the inquiry portion of the curriculum are presented in Chapter 11. These lessons demonstrate the heavy emphasis placed on reading comprehension strategies, such as using text features, website arrangement, note-taking techniques, and evaluation of information, providing ways for students to develop critical skills when dealing with information. Each lesson includes an assessment tool or suggested assessments.

Although the lessons are presented separately, they are intended to be integrated into or coordinated with classroom units and activities whenever possible. For example, the lesson titled "Using Nonfiction Text Structures to Improve Comprehension" is taught as part of a social studies unit on child labor. Chapter 12 describes units developed collaboratively with teachers and demonstrates how library instruction is integrated with content-area curriculum goals at various grade levels. References at the end of each chapter document sources and also provide a list of resources that may be helpful to those seeking to develop a local curriculum.

WEB CONNECTION

A unique and exciting feature of this guide is the connection to the Iowa City Community School District library website, where many additional lessons, units, guides, bibliographies, strategies, and other library learning tools are accessible to those who have purchased this book. This easy-to-navigate site is updated frequently and will include additional lessons and other content as they are developed and updated by district librarians.

The website is found at http://www.iccsd.k12.ia.us/library/curriculum.htm. The site is organized so that it may be accessed in several ways, including:

1. From a categorized list of lessons arranged by the two major curriculum components. On the site, each topic shown below has a list of lesson links beneath it. (http://www.iccsd.k12.ia.us/library/curriculum/Lessons.htm)

Literature Model	*Inquiry Model*
Orientation	Define the information need
Selection	Locate information
Text Structure	Process information
Types of Literature or Genre	Create and communicate
Comprehension Strategies	Assess product and process

2. From specific benchmarks and objectives:
   http://www.iccsd.k12.ia.us/library/curriculum/Objectives.htm
3. By clicking on the components of the Literature and Inquiry models:
   http://www.iccsd.k12.ia.us/library/curriculum.htm

Additionally, throughout the text you will find the small link icon with an abbreviated URL underneath it (see the sidebar with this paragraph). Since all of the webpages begin with http://www.iccsd.k12.ia.us/library/, the URL is truncated to include just the portion that is unique to the specific page being referenced. You will need to enter *http://www.iccsd .k12.ia.us/library/* followed by the shortened link found under the icon. Once you have bookmarked the site, you will have no difficulty finding the specific tool you wish to access. In some cases where the reference is to a site whose URL is very different, such as a school's webpage or a Google Site, the complete URL will be included in the sidebar.

curriculum.htm

In addition to the current group of teacher-librarians in the Iowa City Community School District, many other individuals now retired or in other places have been involved in the development of this curriculum over a 30-year period. Those individuals are listed at the end of the book in the "About the Authors" section. Special thanks to Janie Schomberg and Sue Harms for their assistance with the preparation of this work. A particular note of appreciation is due to Dr. Jean Donham, former coordinator of the ICCSD library program, and the architect of its success.

We hope that you will find this guide a useful blueprint as you develop and teach your students the concepts and skills essential for 21st century literacies.

PART I

Designing the Blueprint

1

The Curriculum Development Process

Throughout this book, you will find sidebars featuring the small link icon shown here with either a full or abbreviated URL. The full URLs lead to items referenced in the text; the shorter ones are for the ICCSD website that contains actual lessons and other information. The webpages for the short URLs begin with http://www.iccsd.k12.ia.us/library/. Once you have bookmarked the main site, you will have no difficulty finding the specific tool you wish to access.

The more things change, the more they remain the same.
—Jean-Baptiste Alphonse Karr, 1849

WHAT ARE THE 21ST CENTURY LITERACIES?

The media abound with discussions of what students need to learn to be productive workers and citizens in the 21st century. It is clear that in order to thrive in this new century, in which technology will change rapidly and people will change jobs repeatedly, students must possess a variety of skills to enable them to learn quickly, to be adaptable, and to work collaboratively with colleagues who may be thousands of miles away. Students must develop appropriate skills and attitudes to be effective lifelong learners, workers, and citizens.

So, what are these 21st century literacies our schools are charged to ensure that students possess? Literacy has traditionally been defined as the ability to read and write, but true literacy goes far beyond this. The United Nations Educational, Scientific and Cultural Organization (UNESCO) has defined literacy as the "ability to identify, understand, interpret, create, communicate, compute and use printed and written materials associated with varying contexts..." (UNESCO Education Center, 2004). This is an excellent summary of the traditional understanding of literacy and incorporates critical thinking and communication, but remains limited to printed text.

In a 2007 report The Educational Testing Service (ETS) defined 21st century skills as the ability to:

- Collect and/or retrieve information
- Organize and manage information
- Interpret and present information
- Evaluate the quality, relevance, and usefulness of information
- Generate accurate information through the use of existing resources (ETS, 2007)

Other groups, such as the Partnership for 21st Century Skills and the American Association of School Librarians (AASL), have added behavioral goals to these basic skills in using information—the ability to think critically and creatively, engage in inquiry and problem solving, practice ethical behavior in the use of information, and communicate and work effectively with others.

To be literate in this new century, we need to be able to apply traditional literacy skills—the ability to understand, interpret, create, and communicate information—to a wide variety of media, including printed media both on the web and in its traditional form, audio sources, visual media, social media, and other formats we cannot yet imagine that today's students will encounter in their lifetimes. What is common to all of these—and what defines 21st century literacy—is the need for critical thinking, questioning, evaluation, and discrimination in the use of information, whatever its form. Added dimensions, or "dispositions" as they have been labeled by AASL, include creativity, flexibility both in thinking and working with others, self-confidence and initiative, curiosity and motivation. These behaviors are difficult to teach and harder to assess, but are essential for students who will compete on a global level throughout the 21st century.

The Seven Survival Skills for Careers, College, and Citizenship in the 21st Century

1. Critical Thinking and Problem Solving
2. Collaboration Across Networks and Leading by Influence
3. Agility and Adaptability
4. Initiative and Entrepreneurship
5. Effective Oral and Written Communication
6. Accessing and Analyzing Information
7. Curiosity and Imagination (Wagner, 2008: 14–41)

While certainly our digital world has changed the manner in which we find and produce information, the goals described above differ very little from those we have had in school libraries for many years. The tools are increasingly more sophisticated, the speed with which information can be found and communicated increases daily, and the world is shrinking in terms of our ability to communicate and operate globally, but the goals of the school library curriculum remain the same: to "ensure that students are effective users of ideas and information" (AASL and AECT, 1998: 6), no matter what form the information may take and to help them become skillful readers, critical thinkers, and problem solvers.

 *http://www.tonywagner.com/*

DEVELOPING A CURRICULUM FOR 21ST CENTURY LITERACIES

To address these critical 21st century needs, schools must have an effective, dynamic, and up-to-date school library curriculum and program. A sound curriculum does not just happen, but is the result of a planning process that includes:

- a thorough review of the existing curriculum and teaching practices,
- an examination of the standards of relevant national organizations,
- consideration of major national and state initiatives that impact school curricula,
- attention to local content standards and learning goals,
- informing and involving stakeholders, and
- developing local library standards, benchmarks, objectives, lessons, and assessments.

Like many school districts, the Iowa City Community School District (ICCSD) engages in a curriculum review cycle in which each area is evaluated once every several years. Through this process, the library program has been thoroughly reviewed and revised four times over a nearly 30-year period. This cyclical review provides an opportunity to examine all aspects of the program and make needed changes. Of course, change is ongoing, but when the program is under review significant recommendations are made and funding provided for their implementation. A copy of the most recent curriculum review for the Iowa City Community School District library program is found on the website, and further discussion of the process is included in Chapter 9.

 *about/overview.htm*

Whether program evaluation is done at the district level, or is initiated by individual school librarians, such a process is an excellent means of ensuring continuous program improvement, including curriculum development. "A Planning Guide for Empowering Learners," an online tool by the AASL and Encyclopedia Britannica, Inc. (2010), includes a set of rubrics to help librarians and other stakeholders assess the current status of programs and make recommendations for improvement in all areas including evaluation of teaching and learning in the library.

http://www.ala.org/ala/mgrps/divs/aasl/ guidelinesandstandards/planningguide/ planningguide.cfm

   This book provides a blueprint or model for a local curriculum based upon the process described above. However, the library curriculum must be designed to support the overall mission of the local school or district. This is critical, as the ultimate goal is to integrate the library curriculum with that of other areas so that students learn important 21st century literacies in the context of classroom content. The paragraphs that follow summarize national standards and initiatives that were examined by the Iowa City Library Program and incorporated into the development of our own local curriculum document.

National Standards

Two sets of national standards are related closely to school library curricula. The American Association of School Librarians is the major organization representing school library programs at the national level. *Information Power*, published by AASL in 1988 and 1998, has been the most influential document in shaping our curricula over time. In 2009, AASL published new standards that have been reviewed and compared to our local standards. The International Society for Technology in Education (ISTE) also published new standards—the National Educational Technology Standards (NETS)—for student use of technology in the schools (ISTE, 2007). A chart comparing the two sets of national standards with those developed in the ICCSD through the curriculum review process is shown in Figure 1.1 and clearly illustrates the commonalities among them.

AASL
- *Inquire, think critically*, and gain knowledge.
- *Draw conclusions, make informed decisions*, apply knowledge to new situations, and create new knowledge.
- *Share knowledge* and participate *ethically* and productively as members of our democratic society.
- *Pursue personal and aesthetic growth.*

ICCSD
- Read widely both for information and in *pursuit of personal interests.*
- Use *inquiry and critical thinking* skills to *acquire, analyze, and evaluate, use* and *create* information.
- *Seek multiple perspectives, share information* and ideas with others, and use information and resources *ethically.*

NETS
- Demonstrate *creative thinking, construct knowledge,* and develop innovative products and processes using technology.
- Use digital media and environments to communicate and *work collaboratively.*
- Apply digital tools to *gather, evaluate, and use information.*
- Use *critical thinking* skills to plan and conduct research.
- Understand human, cultural, and societal issues related to technology and practice legal and *ethical* behavior.
- Demonstrate a sound understanding of technology concepts, systems.

Figure 1.1. Comparison of AASL, ICCSD, and NETS Standards

American Association of School Librarians: Standards for the 21st Century Learner in Action

http://www.ala.org/ala/mgrps/divs/aasl/guidelines andstandards/guidelinesandstandards.cfm

In adopting its new standards in 2009, AASL took a different direction from that of most conventional curriculum documents. The four AASL standards are:

Learners use skills, resources, & tools to:

1. Inquire, think critically, and gain knowledge.
2. Draw conclusions, make informed decisions, apply knowledge to new situations, and create new knowledge.
3. Share knowledge and participate ethically and productively as members of our democratic society.
4. Pursue personal and aesthetic growth. (AASL, 2009: 12)

These standards imply a commitment to teaching not just skills and strategies for finding and using information, but also what AASL has labeled "dispositions" for learning, including initiative, engagement, persistence, and flexibility. AASL's standards place a strong emphasis on developing thinking and problem-solving skills through the use of an inquiry approach to learning. In addition to the standards and benchmarks included in most curriculum documents, the AASL standards also list the dispositions and responsibilities of learners, including the need for self-assessment in the learning process. These habits of learning define the goal that is well-known to all of us—that of giving students the needed tools to be lifelong learners in order to prepare them for the ever-changing world in which they will be living and working.

The "common beliefs" articulated in the AASL standards document also bear consideration in the design of any school library learning program:

- Reading is a window to the world.
- Inquiry provides a framework for learning.
- Ethical behavior in the use of information must be taught.
- Technology skills are crucial for future employment needs.
- Equitable access is a key component for education.
- The definition of information literacy has become more complex as resources and technologies have changed.
- The continuing expansion of information demands that all individuals acquire the thinking skills that will enable them to learn on their own.
- Learning has a social context.
- School libraries are essential to the development of learning skills. (AASL, 2009: 11)

For many school librarians, the first statement was especially welcome as *Information Power*, long the handbook for school library programs, seemed to give short shrift to the reading portion of the school librarian's job. While technology plays an ever-increasing role, reading is still fundamental to all learning, and the current emphasis in schools on improving reading must be embraced and supported by school librarians. Our reading curriculum, described in Chapter 2, reflects this strongly held belief. Inquiry has been adopted as the framework for our information curriculum described in Chapter 3. The remaining AASL belief statements represent critical considerations in designing a curriculum for the school library, and the last one—"School libraries are essential to the development of learning skills"—is a message we need to continually communicate to stakeholders so that they understand the key role the school librarian plays in the development of 21st century skills. Every state has a designated coordinator to assist with understanding and implementing the AASL standards through its Learning for Life (L4L) program.

International Society of Technology in Education (ISTE): National Educational Technology Standards for Students (NETS)

The National Educational Technology Standards released by ISTE describe skills that students need for success in using technology and information:

http://www.iste.org/standards.aspx

1. *Creativity and Innovation.* Students demonstrate creative thinking, construct knowledge, and develop innovative products and processes using technology.
2. *Communication and Collaboration.* Students use digital media and environments to communicate and work collaboratively, including at a distance, to support individual learning and contribute to the learning of others.
3. *Research and Information Fluency.* Students apply digital tools to gather, evaluate, and use information.
4. *Critical Thinking, Problem Solving, and Decision Making.* Students use critical thinking skills to plan and conduct research, manage projects, solve problems, and make informed decisions using appropriate digital tools and resources.
5. *Digital Citizenship.* Students understand human, cultural, and societal issues related to technology and practice legal and ethical behavior.
6. *Technology Operations and Concepts.* Students demonstrate a sound understanding of technology concepts, systems, and operations. (ISTE, 2007: 9)

The ISTE Standards, both these and the version that preceded them, have been adopted in many areas as state and local technology standards for students. School library programs developing their own standards should carefully consider them. While the earlier version of the NETS was more focused on learning to use technology, these newer standards incorporate the critical thinking, communication and collaboration, and digital citizenship skills common to many of the 21st century initiatives, and are already reflected in school library curricula.

National Initiatives Impacting School Library Curriculum Development

It is important for the school librarian to have a good understanding of the national groups and movements that are impacting education. This serves two purposes: (1) it allows the librarian to participate knowledgeably in curriculum discussions and decisions, and (2) it provides a source of evidence for the integration of library standards and benchmarks into school program curricula.

The Common Core

The Common Core standards are intended to bring a shared focus to the work of schools across the country. The following statements illustrate the strong correlation between library curriculum goals and the Common Core. For example, one of the "Key Design Considerations in the English Language Arts Standards" is:

> To be ready for college, workforce training, and life in a technological society, students need the ability to gather, comprehend, evaluate, synthesize, and report on information and ideas, to conduct original research in order to answer questions or solve problems, and to analyze and create a high volume and extensive range of print and nonprint texts in media forms old and new. The need to conduct research and to produce and consume media is embedded into every aspect of today's curriculum. In like fashion, research and media skills and understandings are embedded throughout the Standards rather than treated in a separate section. (Common Core State Standards Initiative, 2010)

And one of the "Key Points in English Language Arts" states:

> Through reading a diverse array of classic and contemporary literature as well as challenging informational texts in a range of subjects, students are expected to build knowledge, gain insights, explore possibilities, and broaden their perspective. (Common Core State Standards Initiative, 2010)

These are areas where the school librarian's expertise in reading, information tools, and technology provides strong support for curricula. The increasing emphasis on informational text necessitates the development and use of nonfiction print collections as well as a variety of online subscription tools in the library. And, while these goals are listed in the "Language Arts and Literacy" portion of the Common Core, the document makes clear that responsibility for reading, writing, speaking, listening, and language is shared among all subject areas. Collaboration between the librarian and content area teachers is an excellent way to address Common Core goals.

http://www.corestandards.org/

Framework for 21st Century Skills

The Partnership for 21st Century Skills brought together major interests from business, education, and government to create a model for student learning. The group includes corporations such as Microsoft, Apple, Dell, and AOL/Time Warner, as well as key education groups including AASL, the National Education Association (NEA), and the U.S. Department of Education. Many states have become a part of this initiative. Like most curriculum initiatives, the "P21 Framework" developed by the Partnership is centered on mastery of the core subjects—language arts, math, science, and social studies (Partnership for 21st Century Skills, 2004). Supporting this core is a set of themes that are intended to be integrated into the academic areas. These include information, media, and technology skills; creativity, critical thinking, communication, and collaboration; and life and career skills such as initiative, self-direction, and responsibility. These are similar to the "dispositions" of the AASL standards document.

http://www.p21.org/

Local Standards

As a district or school seeks to establish its library curriculum, the standards and guidelines outlined above as well as local curriculum documents should be examined and discussed with a stakeholder group, so that there is broad input and buy-in across the district. A stakeholder group would include school librarians, administrators, parents, curriculum staff, representatives from a local college or public library, and others who would add value to the discussion. Information should be shared and outside experts utilized to raise awareness of trends and issues for the group. Stakeholders provide guidance in developing benchmarks and lessons, as well as advocacy for the need to involve the library program in curriculum planning and delivery across content areas.

After examination and discussion of the initiatives described above, the Iowa City library program adopted three standards for learning in the library:

Students will:

1. Read widely both for information and in pursuit of personal interests.
2. Use inquiry and critical thinking skills to acquire, analyze, and evaluate, use, and create information.
3. Seek multiple perspectives, share information and ideas with others, and use information and resources ethically.

These three standards consolidate the others that were examined in order to focus attention upon the two major areas of the ICCSD library curriculum—reading/literature and inquiry—and on the behavioral aspects of 21st century literacy. These areas are described in detail in the next chapters, along with strategies for successfully designing and delivering instruction to meet the standards.

REFERENCES AND ADDITIONAL RESOURCES

AASL (American Association of School Librarians). 2009. *Standards for the 21st-Century Learner*. Chicago: American Library Association. AASL Standards and Beliefs excerpted from *Standards for the 21st-Century Learner* by the American Association of School Librarians, a division of the American Library Association, copyright © 2007 American Library Association. Available for download at http://www.ala.org/aasl/standards. Used with permission.

AASL (American Association of School Librarians). 2010. *Crosswalk of the Common Core Standards and the Standards for the 21st-Century Learner*. American Library Association. http://www.ala.org/ala/mgrps/ divs/aasl/guidelinesandstandards/commoncorecrosswalk/index.cfm.

AASL (American Association of School Librarians) and AECT (Association for Educational Communications and Technology). 1998. *Information Power: Building Partnerships for Learning*. Chicago, IL: American Library Association and American Association for Educational Communications and Technology.

AASL (American Association of School Librarians) and Encyclopedia Britannica, Inc. 2010. "A Planning Guide for Empowering Learners." American Library Association. http://www.ala.org/ala/mgrps/divs/ aasl/guidelinesandstandards/planningguide/planningguide.cfm.

Common Core State Standards Initiative. 2010. "About the Standards." Common Core State Standards Initiative. http://www.corestandards.org/about-the-standards.

ETS (Educational Testing Service). 2007. *Digital Transformation: A Framework for ICT Literacy—A Report of the International ICT Literacy Panel*. Princeton, NY: Educational Testing Service. http://www.ets .org/Media/Tests/Information_and_Communication_Technology_Literacy/ictreport.pdf.

ISTE (International Society for Technology in Education). 2007. *National Educational Technology Standards for Students, Second Edition*. Washington, DC: International Society for Technology in Education. *National Educational Technology Standards for Students*, Second Edition © 2007 ISTE® (International Society for Technology in Education), http://www.iste.org. All rights reserved.

Partnership for 21st Century Skills. 2004. *Framework for 21st Century Learning*. Washington, DC: Partnership for 21st Century Skills. http://www.p21.org/index.php?option=com_content&task=view&id=254& Itemid=120.

UNESCO Education Center. 2004. *The Plurality of Literacy and Its Implications for Policies and Programmes*. Paris: United Nations Educational, Scientific and Cultural Organization. http://unesdoc.unesco.org/ images/0013/001362/136246e.pdf.

Wagner, Tony. 2008. *The Global Achievement Gap: Why Even Our Best Schools Don't Teach the New Survival Skills Our Children Need—And What We Can Do About It*. New York: Basic Books.

2

The School Librarian's Role in Reading

Throughout this book, you will find sidebars featuring the small link icon shown here with either a full or abbreviated URL. The full URLs lead to items referenced in the text; the shorter ones are for the ICCSD website that contains actual lessons and other information. The webpages for the short URLs begin with http://www.iccsd.k12.ia.us/library/. Once you have bookmarked the main site, you will have no difficulty finding the specific tool you wish to access.

Reading is a window to the world.
—American Association of School Librarians

Whether on the web, in a book, or on an iPad, Kindle, or other e-reader, the ability to comprehend written information is essential both to success in school and in the student's life after school. Clearly, those who read well, and are well read, have a decided advantage in our information-driven world. The ability to understand technical writing, whether found in college textbooks or computer repair manuals, is a critical 21st century skill. Being a skillful reader is essential to lifelong learning. This chapter outlines the dual role of the librarian in the reading program of the school: (1) as a key support person for classroom reading instruction and (2) as a teacher of reading through the library's instructional program.

THE SCHOOL LIBRARIAN AND THE READING PROGRAM

The school librarian is the resources specialist in the school, skilled in the selection and acquisition of learning materials including books, but increasingly expanding to digital formats including online resources. The librarian combines this resources expertise with knowledge of the school's reading program, so that in pairing students with books or collaborating with teachers on classroom reading activities, materials can be suggested that not only reflect high standards of quality and support the curriculum, but also address the reading needs of students at a given level. This is a complex task, since within any given classroom or group of students, reading abilities and interests vary widely.

One example of how the school librarian in the Iowa City Community School District (ICCSD) supports classroom reading instruction is found in Figure 2.1. School libraries contain excellent books that provide an authentic means to teach and reinforce various reading strategies taught in the classroom. Comprehension strategies is the term applied to a specific set of skills that students are taught as they learn to read: predicting, questioning, inferring, visualizing, synthesizing, making connections, monitoring, and summarizing. The list shown in Figure 2.1 includes recently published library books that will be useful for teachers who are focusing on helping students learn the strategy of inferring. Teachers know that these will be good books that kids will enjoy, but also that they will be "on target" for reinforcing the strategy. Suggested books for each of the comprehension strategies are found on the website. This site was developed in Google Docs and all ICCSD librarians are able to

http://sites.google.com/a/iccsd.k12
.ia.us/books-and-reading-strategies/

edit and update the lists as new titles are identified that complement classroom reading goals. This is only one of many areas where the librarian works closely with teachers to assure that the library's collection will contain materials that support and enhance curricula, and that teachers are aware of these materials.

The school librarian's responsibility for selecting and maintaining a diverse library collection that closely reflects the school's curricula and student demographics is critical if students and teachers are to find the books and other resources they want and need in the library. School librarians' broad knowledge of materials also enables them to assist with learning and resource differentiation, providing materials at different reading levels, in different formats, and reflective of different learning styles.

SCHOOL LIBRARIES AND READING: THE RESEARCH

An abundance of research supports the importance of school librarians and libraries in reading achievement. The work of Stephen Krashen has shown that frequent access to a large quantity and

ICCSD **Books and Reading Strategies**
Iowa City Community School District

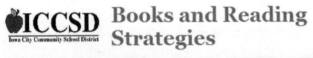

This is a no-frills and ever changing spot to find books to use when teaching specific reading strategies.

Depending on which strategy you're teaching, click on the tab above. The language used throughout this site is not exhaustive. There is much to teaching reading strategies effectively, and the process cannot be summarized into a few points like I tried to do. The bullet points are a way to remind you of some of the language used throughout the district. As always, please read the books first to be sure it will be right for your group of students.

Inferring

- interpretations
- conclusions
- connect background knowledge to specific clues
- how do we decide something when it's not clearly stated?
- book clues + our clues = inference

Brown, Peter. *The curious garden.* New York: Little, Brown, 2009.

Frazee, Marla. *The boss baby.* New York: Beach Lane Books, 2010.

Fucile, Tony Cherie. *Let's do nothing!* Somerville, MA: Candlewick Press, 2009.

Hegamin, Tonya Cherie. *Most loved in all the world.* Boston: Houghton Mifflin, 2009.

Karas, G. Brian. *Young Zeus.* New York: Scholastic Press, 2010.

Lowry, Lois. *Crow call.* New York: Scholastic, 2009.

Mortensen, Greg. *Listen to the wind: The story of Dr. Greg and the three cups of tea.* New York: Dial Books, 2009.

Pinkney, Jerry. *The lion and the mouse.* New York: Little, Brown, 2009.

Rawlinson, Julia. *Fletcher and the springtime blossoms.* New York: Greenwillow Books, 2009.

Scanlon, Liz Garton. *All the world.* New York: Beach Lane Books, 2009.

Stampler, Ann Redisch. *Rooster prince of Breslov.* Boston: Clarion Books, 2010.

(*Source:* https://sites.google.com/a/iccsd.k12.ia.us/books-and-reading-strategies/.)

Figure 2.1. Sample from *Books and Reading Strategies*

variety of good books improves students' reading ability—the more books available, the more students read; the more they read, the better they read (Krashen, 2004). The Curry Lance impact studies in Colorado and 18 other states have shown that the quantity and quality of library collections, and the presence of professional library staffing, are consistently related to higher student achievement as measured by standardized reading tests (Scholastic Library Publishing, 2008). Another important piece of Krashen's research is the clear evidence that children of poverty have far fewer books in the home and less access to good reading material. This deficit extends to computer access; while students from more affluent homes generally have newer computers and high-speed Internet access available to them at home, disadvantaged children often do not. This makes the school library—where books and technology are readily available—especially important in leveling the playing field for those most in need of reading assistance.

> **Classroom Collections**
>
> Many teachers maintain collections of books in the classroom to provide students with immediate access when they need something to read. This "just in time" access is important and efficient. The school library can provide such collections on a rotating basis in collaboration with teachers. Making the classroom collection a part of the overall resources of the school allows for greater sharing and refreshing of the books in the classroom library. It also provides for greater accountability for materials purchased with school funds and a means of checking out and keeping track of materials.

The school librarian's role in developing readers is complex and multifaceted in an environment where there is a growing realization that all teachers PK–12 must help students become effective, capable, and critical readers and consumers of information. This belief is reflected in the national Common Core, which calls for reading instruction to be integrated into all subject areas (Common Core State Standards Initiative, 2010). The school librarian must be an active member of the building literacy or reading team, and play a leadership role in helping to assure that all children have the opportunity to learn to read well.

THE LIBRARY READING AND LITERATURE CURRICULUM

The school librarian's work with elementary children, especially in the early grades, includes teaching how to use the library and sharing good literature to promote reading. The national "Put Reading First" initiative (Armbruster, Lehr, and Osborn, 2001) describes five major areas of reading instruction in the early elementary grades: phonemic awareness, phonics, fluency, vocabulary, and text comprehension. These areas as well as the comprehension strategies described above are elements

http://www.nichd.nih.gov/publications/ pubs_details.cfm?from=&pubs_id=226

that the school librarian can build upon in library lessons. Students in many elementary schools have scheduled classes with the school librarian. The library literature curriculum developed in the ICCSD is used during such scheduled classes, but can also be adapted to use in flexibly scheduled programs. Regardless of the schedule, this curriculum should be used in communication and collaboration with the classroom teacher, so that reading instruction taking place in the classroom can be revisited and reinforced in library lessons.

While the school librarian will not provide direct formal instruction in all of these reading areas, there are many ways the skills may be reviewed and reinforced in the library curriculum:

- Literature activities such as read-alouds, the use of ABC books, rhymes, text with alliteration, and large-format books are used to develop phonemic awareness and reinforce phonics skills being stressed in the classroom.
- Reading with a partner, reading with an adult, Readers' Theater, and the use of audiobooks or e-books for read-alongs are common library activities that contribute to fluency. Fluency increases as students begin to choose and read books in a variety of types of literature at the appropriate level to support and develop their skill as readers.

- The sharing of good literature in library classes is a natural and effective way to build vocabulary and often adds a fun dimension to lessons as new words are encountered and defined. Again, students' individual reading builds vocabulary—the more they read, the more words they encounter and learn.
- Developing comprehension skills is a significant component of library literature (and inquiry) lessons and one where the librarian does significant explicit instruction. This area is one of the five components of the ICCSD library literature curriculum, described in the next section. Through guided interaction with good literature, students learn invaluable lessons in visualizing, making connections, summarizing, synthesizing, recognizing bias and point of view, and evaluating what is read. These understandings form the basis for critical thinking, for not accepting all information at face value, and for constructing meaning out of sometimes-conflicting perspectives; these are all key comprehension strategies that are necessary to enable students to effectively engage in inquiry, solving problems and creating new knowledge.

Literature Model

The model shown in Figure 2.2 illustrates the five components of the ICCSD literature curriculum. The model provides a means of thinking about the elements of the curriculum, but lessons and units frequently combine several of the parts. And, again, it is important to remember that inquiry is also a part of reading activities and lessons; indeed, children's literature provides an excellent means of helping students uncover big ideas and be actively involved in their own learning. From the website, you can access lessons and other content for each of these areas by clicking on the relevant section of the model or from the "lessons" page. The literature lessons presented in Chapter 10 are arranged in categories that include each element of the model as well as traditional areas of instruction such as library organization and book care.

 *curriculum.htm*

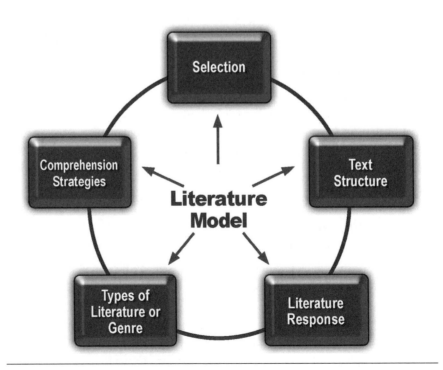

Figure 2.2. Literature Curriculum Model

Selection

Students who are active readers must be able to select reading materials based upon personal interests and appropriateness. School librarians support effective selection through active reading guidance. Lessons that teach children to select "just right books" begin in kindergarten and continue throughout the elementary grades. Booktalks at all levels PK–12 allow the librarian to share new literature, and literature in support of various curriculum objectives, with students to motivate student reading. Booktalking is an important tool in developing readers, and school librarians should study and practice the art of booktalking in order to effectively fill this important role. The reading guidance role of the school librarian extends to the sponsorship of book fairs, family literacy nights, whole school reading activities, displays, participation in state book award programs, and other events that promote reading and the selection of appropriate materials. Through reading guidance, the librarian develops a unique long-term relationship with students as they progress through the grades. This provides an ongoing opportunity to nurture students as they develop their reading interests and abilities and gain confidence in selecting their own reading materials.

> **How to Give an Effective Booktalk**
> - Know your audience.
> - Talk about books you really like.
> - Show the book; tell the title and the author.
> - Find something "catchy" to start out with—the "hook" that will grab students' attention.
> - Describe main characters.
> - Summarize a part of the action that will interest students.
> - Do *not* tell the entire story, especially the ending.
> - Speak slowly and clearly.
> - Maintain eye contact with students.
> - Use humor.
> - Script it and practice ahead of time (but don't read—talk!).
> - Keep it brief—2–4 minutes per book.
> - Use sticky notes to help you remember names and important events.
> - Let your passion for books and reading show.
> - If possible, buy or borrow multiple copies so that students can check out wanted books immediately.

Collaboration with local public libraries to involve students in summer reading programs promotes continued reading by students when school is not in session. Summer reading lists provided to students and accessible from the library website are another effective reading guidance tool. In later grades, book clubs and book discussions continue to promote the enjoyment of literature. Technology provides many excellent ways to share and discuss books through podcasting, reading blogs, online book clubs, and online reviews written by students.

bibliographies.htm

Comprehension Strategies

Many K–12 library curriculum benchmarks are directed at teaching and improving student comprehension. These include skills such as making connections to background knowledge, using illustrations and other visual elements, predicting, summarizing, and using mental images and questions to understand text. This component may be incorporated into read-alouds and the sharing of literature as students activate background knowledge, make predictions about what will happen in stories, participate in small or large group discussions, paraphrase, and use strategies such as FQR (Fact/Question/Response) and other activities that help them construct meaning from text. The use of effective questioning strategies is critical to developing comprehension skills. Questions such as "I wonder why…" lead students to think more deeply about what is being read. The teaching and practice of note taking includes the comprehension strategies of defining importance, summarizing, and synthesizing. This is especially important as students work with nonfiction text and begin to do inquiry assignments.

Text Structure

This portion of the curriculum engages students in understanding how narrative and expository text work. Students examine the traditional literary elements—character, plot, setting, point of view, and theme—and examine text structure and features in both fiction and nonfiction. Again, the study of literary elements and story structure provide endless opportunities to develop students' skills in analyzing, comparing and contrasting the actions of characters, examining cause and effect, discussing meaning, and developing visual literacy skills by analyzing illustrations. Understanding text features—headings, captions, sidebars, visuals—is critical to the understanding of information being presented in books and in digital formats including reading on the web.

Textual Elements That Aid Comprehension

Text Structures

Description
Sequence
Cause and Effect
Problem/Solution
Compare and Contrast

Text Features

Headings
Fonts
Captions and Labels
Graphics—tables, charts, graphs
Sidebars
Photographs
Borders, boxes

Types of Literature or Genre

The study of types of literature provides opportunities to share a variety of literature with children and introduce them to genres with which they may not be familiar. Students are exposed to a variety of types of literature including nonfiction, biography, historical fiction, science fiction, fantasy, realistic fiction, graphic novels, folklore, and poetry during lessons taught in elementary library classes. These lessons help students broaden their reading interests and provide additional opportunities to gain skill in understanding text, analyzing ideas, comparing and contrasting, and engaging in group activities centered on particular literary forms. The powerful ideas found in picture books provide a springboard for meaningful discussions that stimulate higher-level thinking in students.

Nonfiction as a type of literature has an important place in our schools. There is increasing emphasis on using nonfiction trade books in reading instruction, since nonfiction or informational reading is what most of us engage in as we do our jobs or seek answers to questions in our daily lives. Many students prefer nonfiction to "storybooks." Reading nonfiction can help students develop a sense of wonder and a desire to know more about real people, places, and events—this is authentic learning. Nonfiction now being published takes advantage of digital publishing techniques to create attractive and engaging books that address children's interests in a wide range of topics and are available at all reading levels.

Literature Response

Various activities for engaging students with literature are included in this portion of the curriculum, including literature circles, guided reading, and Readers' Theater.

Author Study

One of the most commonly used literature response activities is author study, which engages students with the body of work of a single author or illustrator. Author study provides an excellent vehicle for comparing and examining themes, writing, and artistic style over time. Students come to understand that authors are people like them who base their stories on real-life experience. Librarians prepare author study curriculum units using the following model.

Part 1: Research the Author or Illustrator. Biographical information about the author/illustrator is provided with a particular focus on information that influences the writing or art. A list of sources of further information that can be used for student research is also prepared. The ready availability of websites about the author, or those maintained by many children's and young adult authors, make this step easy and exciting for children.

Part 2: Analyze the Body of Work. A listing of all of the author's work is provided with an analysis of specific elements that characterize the work.

Part 3: Application: Lessons and Activities. Specific titles to be studied by students are chosen on the basis of curriculum goals, suitability for the age level, and availability. Discussion questions and activities to acquaint students with the author's work are outlined.

The ideal culminating activity for an author study is a visit by the author to the school. Through a partnership with a local bank, the Iowa City library program brings an author to speak to students at a given grade level in all schools each fall. Individual buildings also schedule author appearances. Parent groups, school foundations, local service groups, and other avenues may be found to sponsor author visits. Prior to these visits, an author study curriculum should be prepared and used across the district in the grade level designated for the visit. This is best done as a collaborative project between school librarians and classroom teachers, based upon the belief that prior to any author visit, students must have sufficient knowledge of the author or illustrator's work in order to fully appreciate and participate appropriately in the visit. Author visits are events that students remember for a long time, and they spark an increased interest in both reading and writing. If it is impossible to arrange an "in-person" author visit, there are numerous means for students to engage with authors virtually; again, preparation is key.

A sample author study is included in Chapter 10 of this guide and several studies are available on the website.

curriculum/lessons.htm

Collaborative Collection Development

In support of the literature curriculum, elementary school librarians in the ICCSD work as a team to annually identify the "best of the best" new titles for each type and element of literature. Each librarian is assigned an area of responsibility, researches the area, and chooses two books for K–2, two for 3–4, and two for 5–6. He or she booktalks the selected titles to the whole group during district meeting time. The new titles are added to a web-based bibliography. This is a rigorous and deliberate process, and while librarians are certainly free to make their own selections, most usually purchase the titles recommended by their colleagues in this collaborative collection development process. These lists are also used to refresh the literature being used in library lessons. The guidelines for the process described above as well as the bibliography of the titles selected over the past five years are included on the website. The link on the right will guide you to the lists from the last several years presented

bibs/curricularbibs.htm

as annotated bibliographies. There is also a cumulative bibliography accessible from that page. This bibliography is in an Excel spreadsheet, and can be sorted by author, type of literature, grade level, and other ways. While it may work best in larger districts, the sort of collaborative project described above might well be done by regional groups or by individual school librarians working together in support of common goals.

READING AND THE SECONDARY SCHOOLS

Reading promotion continues to be an important responsibility of the secondary school librarian. Many of the reading promotion and comprehension strategies described above are useful at the secondary level as well. Book groups, all-school reads, state book award programs, and frequent booktalking are among many reading promotion strategies common to secondary schools. Once again, it is critical that the library collection includes materials at many levels and in many formats—audiobooks, graphic novels and manga, and e-books, as well as good fiction and nonfiction—and on many levels so that students will find things that they want to read, hear, or view in the library.

The librarian and other faculty and staff model enthusiasm for reading to motivate kids to follow their example. Using social media to promote reading provides another means to couple students' appetite for technology with the need for them to be skillful readers. Digital books are becoming widespread. Matching students' enthusiasm about technology with the ability to read via e-books will have a great motivating effect on reading, and the fact that e-books can use features such as live links to explanatory materials or dictionaries to define unknown words adds value to the use of these tools.

Librarians also collaborate with teachers to identify relevant titles for literature-based units. An example of this is "Ideas in Conflict." The booklist shown in the sidebar was developed by high school librarians to serve as a springboard for the research in this unit. Librarians booktalk these titles to help students select a book and the book leads students to identify questions to become a part of their research.

All school librarians support and promote reading through activities such as the following:

- Maintaining engaging and attractive collections of books and other media for different ages, abilities, and interests
- Creating inviting displays of resources to encourage use
- Using the school website to promote new resources
- Organizing author visits and other opportunities for viewing, listening, and writing
- Sponsoring book clubs and book discussions
- Giving booktalks in the library and classrooms
- Providing reading guidance for students
- Helping students find websites at an appropriate reading level

---

Ideas in Conflict: Compelling Literature

Alvarez, Julia. *In the Time of the Butterflies.*
Bagdasarian, Adam. *Forgotten Fire.*
Bardach, Janusz. *Man Is Wolf to Man.*
Beah, Ishmael. *A Long Way Gone.*
Chang, Iris. *The Rape of Nanking.*
Dalai Lama. *Freedom in Exile.*
Ehrenreich, Barbara. *Nickel and Dimed.*
Gourevitch, Philip. *We Wish to Inform You that Tomorrow We Will Be Killed with Our Families.*
Grossman, David. *The Yellow Wind.*
Gutterson, David. *Snow Falling on Cedars.*
Hosseini, Khaled. *A Thousand Splendid Suns.*
Jiang, Ji-Li. *Red Scarf Girl.*
Kahf, Mohja. *The Girl in the Tangerine Scarf.*
Kidder, Tracy. *Mountains Beyond Mountains.*
Kielburger, Craig. *Free the Children.*
Kozol, Jonathan. *The Shame of the Nation.*
Kuklin, Susan. *Iqbal Masih and the Crusaders Against Child Slavery.*
Marlowe, Jen. *Darfur Diaries: Stories of Survival.*
Nazario, Sonia. *Enrique's Journey.*
Seierstad, Asne. *The Bookseller of Kabul.*
Ung, Loung. *First They Killed My Father.*
Wilentz, Amy. *Martyrs' Crossing.*

READING AND THE INTERNET

Most of the reading curriculum described earlier in this chapter is taught in scheduled classes at the elementary level. However, components of the program are also taught and reinforced in the secondary schools, often as a part of inquiry units. In the secondary schools, students turn increasingly to the Internet for information, and this is an area where secondary school librarians can provide significant reading support and instruction. Clearly today's students are comfortable and proficient in manipulating technology for quick access to text messages, Facebook, and other social networking tools. But doing in-depth research on the Internet is different from the rapid "in/out and move on" that students usually practice when using social media. How to address the somewhat different set of skills required to read deeply on the web is a significant question for educators working to assure that students are capable readers. Reading on the web differs from reading traditional print sources in a number of ways:

- We tend to skim, scan, and skip through websites.
- Distractions such as ads, links, pictures, and sidebars can deflect attention from content.
- There is little consistency in website formatting and organization.
- Information is intermingled with ads, pop-ups, and other devices.
- The authority of website developers may be difficult to determine.

In addition, websites that might be found in a simple Google search may be beyond the reading levels of many students. Also, the amount of information on a single computer screen can be overwhelming, including text and graphics as well as advertising, live links to related information, sidebars that may or may not be relevant, moving images, and more. These distractions cause us to lose the flow of the information, which is critical to comprehension. The ability to discern what is relevant and important from all of the busyness of the screen is a key skill set, requiring analysis, critical viewing, decision making, and continuous questioning. Like most reading skills, these need to be taught explicitly. This is another area where the school librarian can work with teachers to assure that students understand the skills and strategies needed to evaluate and extract relevant information from digital sources. An example of this is a lesson titled "Navigating Websites without Getting Lost," which appears in Chapter 11.

Much has been written recently about the importance of "deep reading," the ability to engage with complex text to garner important ideas, evaluate evidence, and synthesize important content— these are essential skills for critical thinkers and lifelong learners (Wolf and Barzillai, 2009). The Anchor Standards in the national Common Core include several goals for students in this area, including:

- Read closely to determine what the text says explicitly and to make logical inferences from it; cite specific textual evidence when writing or speaking to support conclusions drawn from the text.
- Determine central ideas or themes of a text and analyze their development; summarize the key supporting details and ideas.
- Delineate and evaluate the argument and specific claims in a text, including the validity of the reasoning as well as the relevance and sufficiency of the evidence.

Deep reading requires us to concentrate, focus, and reflect on content for a sustained period of time to develop meaning. This reinforces the need for continued use of print materials with their more linear organization, fewer distractions, and predictable text features as students are developing deep reading skills. Such materials allow students to focus on content and on making meaning from what is being read. Providing diverse collections of nonfiction materials for student reading exposes students to complex text and ideas while they explore topics of interest to them. Traditional sources of information—books, journal articles, and encyclopedias—still have a strong presence in our libraries, whether accessed in hard copy or electronically. Such material allows students to develop reading skills in a more linear medium than most Internet sites provide.

Specific strategies to aid student comprehension of complex text are taught in conjunction with library literature and inquiry activities. This begins with read-alouds in the early grades where students listen to and discuss the key ideas in good literature and progresses to inquiry units where reading comprehension skills are developed through the use of various strategies such as graphic organizers and attention to text features. Such activities require students to slow down, think, and reflect on what is being read, and are areas where the school librarian contributes directly to student reading development. Explicit teaching of such strategies improves reading comprehension whether in print or digital formats.

REFERENCES AND ADDITIONAL RESOURCES

AASL (American Association of School Librarians). 2009. *School Librarian's Role in Reading Toolkit*. American Library Association. http://www.ala.org/ala/mgrps/divs/aasl/aaslissues/toolkits/slroleinreading .cfm.

Armbruster, Bonnie B., Fran Lehr, and Jean Osborn. 2001. *Put Reading First: The Research Building Blocks for Teaching Children to Read*. 3rd ed. National Institute of Child Health and Human Development. http://www.nichd.nih.gov/publications/pubs_details.cfm?from=&pubs_id=226.

Common Core State Standards Initiative. 2010. "About the Standards." Common Core State Standards Initiative. http://www.corestandards.org/about-the-standards.

Fisher, Douglas, William Brozo, Nancy Frey, and Gay Ivey. 2007. *50 Content Area Strategies for Adolescent Literacy*. Upper Saddle River, NJ: Pearson.

Harvey, Stephanie, and Anne Goudvis. 2000. *Strategies That Work: Teaching Reading Comprehension to Enhance Understanding*. Portland, ME: Stenhouse.

Krashen, Stephen. 2004. *The Power of Reading: Insights from the Research*. Portsmouth, NH: Heinemann.

Scholastic Library Publishing. 2008. *School Libraries Work!* New York: Scholastic Library Publishing. http://listbuilder.scholastic.com/content/stores/LibraryStore/pages/images/SLW3.pdf.

Wolf, Maryanne, and Mirit Barzillai. 2009. "The Importance of Deep Reading." *Educational Leadership* 6, no. 6: 32–37.

3

Inquiry in the School Library Program

> Throughout this book, you will find sidebars featuring the small link icon shown here with either a full or abbreviated URL. The full URLs lead to items referenced in the text; the shorter ones are for the ICCSD website that contains actual lessons and other information. The webpages for the short URLs begin with http://www.iccsd.k12.ia.us/library/. Once you have bookmarked the main site, you will have no difficulty finding the specific tool you wish to access.

I think, at a child's birth, if a mother could ask a fairy godmother to endow it with the most useful gift, that gift would be curiosity.

—Eleanor Roosevelt

In his bestseller, *The World Is Flat*, Thomas Friedman states, "Give me a kid with a passion to learn and a curiosity to discover.... Curious, passionate kids are self-educators and self-motivators.... They will always be able to learn how to learn" (Friedman, 2007: 314). This idea of curious, motivated learners perfectly describes the goal of inquiry-based learning.

Inquiry in the school setting is defined as engaging students in investigating and developing their understanding of significant topics or issues through a process of accessing, evaluating, creating, and communicating information. Inquiry includes information literacy, but it goes beyond that process to incorporate the dispositions Friedman praises—curiosity and motivation—as well as others, including critical thinking, persistence, responsibility, creativity, and a willingness to work with others.

Standards 2 and 3 of the Iowa City library curriculum state that students will:

- Use inquiry and critical thinking skills to acquire, analyze and evaluate, use, and create information (2).
- Seek multiple perspectives, share information and ideas with others, and use information and resources ethically (3).

> "Guided inquiry creates an environment that motivates students to learn by providing opportunities for them to construct their own meaning and develop deep understanding. This approach engages all students, not just those who have already shown that they are academically inclined." (Kuhlthau, 2007: 6)

The inquiry portion of this curriculum guides students in developing the skills and dispositions to be lifelong learners and thoughtful, responsible citizens. Again, it must be emphasized that the inquiry curriculum and the literature curriculum are not independent of each other. Inquiry learning is a part of reading lessons and units, and reading competently and critically is a part of inquiry; these two program elements include and complement each other.

ENGAGING STUDENTS IN LEARNING

In *Inquiry-Based Learning: Lessons from Library Power*, Carol Kuhlthau presents a brief summary of what we know about how children learn, including the following:

- Children learn by being actively engaged and reflecting on that experience.
- Children learn by building on what they already know.
- Children learn through social interaction with others. (Donham et al., 2001: 2–4)

These three ideas are central to inquiry-based learning. Students need to be involved in their learning, and in designing their learning through developing questions that engage them, motivate them, and keep them focused on a goal. The library is an ideal setting to couple content-area goals with projects that pique students' interest and involve them in their own learning by making connections with their own lives or with topics in which they have an interest. Learning must be an active process.

Consider the study of a particular war in U.S. history such as the Iraq conflict. An historical event is usually presented to students as a series of dates and facts (the beginning of the invasion, the fall of Saddam Hussein, key battles). But it is also a fertile area for engaging students in significant questions while they are learning about the war and its impact—"What was the effect of the war on life at home? How do protest movements start? Are they effective? What are the lasting effects of the war on Iraq as a country? What was the long-term impact of the war on the United States?" Resources in many formats including video footage of actual events are readily available on YouTube and other sources for teaching and learning. Many students will know, or know of, an Iraq war veteran or family member whom they could interview. The questions that students ask in this process are what are truly important; they may or may not be answered fully, but the engagement and learning comes from igniting students' curiosity about events and issues.

> "Once you have learned how to ask relevant and appropriate questions, you have learned how to learn and no one can keep you from learning whatever you want or need to know." (Postman and Weingartner, 1969)

Other examples may be found in elementary school curricula, taking advantage of students' curiosity about the world around them to explore topics in earth science, social studies, and other areas. Many regions of the country have been subject to severe flooding and tornadoes in recent years. Disasters are common topics of study in earth science, and the local focus as well as students' own direct knowledge of these events are natural motivators. With the background knowledge they already possess, students can generate significant questions about natural disasters and their aftermath: "Should people be allowed to build homes in the floodplain? Should the government be able to evict people from homes in areas that are prone to flooding? Should we try to change the course of natural waterways to gain land for development?" Figure 3.1 is a guide used in the New York City Schools to help students develop questions by exploring what they wonder about. Children always have questions, and this method provides a vehicle to help them develop researchable questions.

http://schools.nyc.gov/Academics/ LibraryServices/Standardsand Curriculum/default.htm

When we ask students questions that have simple or pat answers—"What are the products of Uruguay? What were the names of the characters? When did the war begin and end?"—it is easy for them to simply "copy and paste" and operate only at the recall level. If we ask questions that engage students in real thinking about issues that interest them, the results of research will be deeper and more original. Inquiry learning supports the idea that students should be able to propose and answer their own questions, using a strategy such as Ogle's (1986) widely used K-W-L method—"What do I Know? What do I Want to know? What did I Learn?" The goal is to unite content-area standards and benchmarks with students' own interest and experience. The content-area goals *must* be taught, but the means of learning can vary widely, as can the ways in which students demonstrate their learning.

> "Answer the question. Then, question the answer." (Bush, 2010)

I Wonder...
Topic: _____   _____   _____
I wonder what _____   _____   _____
I wonder how _____   _____   _____
I wonder why _____   _____   _____
I wonder if _____   _____   _____
I wonder when _____   _____   _____
I wonder who _____   _____   _____
I wonder where _____   _____   _____

New York City Information Skills Benchmark 2:2

Figure 3.1. "I Wonder" Chart Used to Develop Questions in Inquiry Activities

The work of Willard Daggett and the International Center for Leadership in Education (2011) supports inquiry-based learning. Their "Rigor and Relevance Framework" is well-known and used in designing instruction by many schools across the country. Rigor might be defined as a curriculum that is multifaceted, challenging, and personally engaging for students. A relevant curriculum requires students to explore complex, real-world topics. Rigorous and relevant learning is student centered rather than teacher centered, requiring students to think, to work, and to solve problems. Both rigor and relevance can be consciously incorporated into inquiry learning, as students explore real issues and real problems and construct significant questions about them. Students, rather than teachers, are the workers in such projects.

COLLABORATION IN LEARNING

Kuhlthau's third point (cited earlier), "Children learn through social interaction with others," offers another avenue where inquiry can address students' learning styles and needs. A number of years ago, University of Minnesota researchers David and Roger Johnson published and did workshops across the country on cooperative learning (Johnson and Johnson, 1988). They described the common situation in schools where students are placed in competition with one another to see who is "best," rather than working cooperatively and taking an interest in one another's learning as well as their own. Cooperative work, or working in teams, is the predominant model in the workplace. The ability to work collaboratively is cited as a necessary 21st century skill in all of the initiatives discussed in Chapter 1 that have helped to shape this curriculum. Inquiry learning provides an ideal vehicle for students to work in teams. We all know the enthusiasm and good ideas that can be generated by a group of people brainstorming and working respectfully together toward a common goal. Ground rules and responsibilities need to be clear for such group work (and must be taught), but it is a part of an inquiry learning program—perhaps not for every assignment, but often enough so that students feel comfortable and capable working in learning groups. Flexible library arrangements lend themselves to group work, and a team approach to learning enables librarians and teachers to support students as they work through the inquiry process.

Ground Rules for Group Work

1. *Everyone* communicates, cooperates, and contributes.
2. Come prepared.
3. Stay on task; be productive.
4. Listen carefully.
5. Show respect for others' ideas.
6. Select a facilitator who summarizes accomplishments and assignments.

CREATING AN ENVIRONMENT FOR INQUIRY

School libraries are central to inquiry learning. The library climate is one that encourages exploration, investigation, and risk-taking. There are several dimensions to this climate for inquiry in the library:

1. *The physical space and arrangement of the library.*
   - The library is a welcoming, user-friendly environment.
   - Library spaces support multiple activities and learning styles including small group, whole class, and individual work.
   - Clear signage, self-help guides, pathfinders, and other tools help students locate and access information.
   - The environment reinforces learning goals.
   - Library spaces are reserved for teaching and learning.
2. *Resources and technology to support inquiry.*
   - There is ready access to information tools in many formats—print and digital.
   - Current online database tools that are related to curricula help support the research process.
   - The librarian is knowledgeable about resources and people in the community who can provide learning support for students.
   - Policies are developed with enhanced access in mind.
3. *Staff who support inquiry learning.*
   - All library staff strive to maintain good relationships with students.
   - Library staff are helpful, positive, and approachable.
   - Professional development keeps librarians' skills "cutting edge."
   - Librarians know the curriculum, and work with teachers to move assignments toward inquiry-based learning.
   - Library staff understand their role in guiding students engaged in inquiry—that of advisor or mentor, not answer provider.

THE INQUIRY MODEL

Over the past 25 years, a number of information search process models have been developed by school library leaders including Barbara Stripling and Judy Pitts (1988); Michael Eisenberg and Robert Berkowitz (1990); Marjorie Pappas and Ann Tepe (2002); Julie Tallman and Marilyn Joyce (2006); Carol Kuhlthau (2007); and others. These models identify discreet stages in the inquiry process. Such a model is useful in planning instruction with teachers, because it allows them to see the stages and better understand the skills students need to complete each of them. It is useful in incorporating an inquiry approach into assignments, because inquiry strategies can be addressed at each stage. And, it is useful in supporting learning, because assessments can be built into each stage of the model to monitor students' progress.

Getting Started with Inquiry

- Discuss inquiry-based learning with your administrator and gain his/her support.
- Find a willing teacher to work with you to plan and teach one inquiry-based unit; publicize your success.
- Each time you plan with teachers, ask them to consider how higher levels of thinking can be promoted within the lesson.
- Always evaluate the questions students are being asked to research: Are they big, engaging, open-ended questions that require investigation or simply fill-in-the-blanks?
- If you use an information search process model, determine small steps to incorporate inquiry principles into each stage.
- Change one element of an existing unit—a different product, group work instead of individual, or having students generate their own questions.
- Be patient; don't overwhelm teachers. You may need to take small steps, but keep moving forward!

The model used in the Iowa City Community School District is shown in Figure 3.2. It is based upon the work of those noted above, but has evolved over the years to more clearly represent our own local program goals and teaching methods.

This five-stage model outlines the steps for helping students locate, use, process, create, and communicate information as they engage in inquiry learning. It must be noted that while the model we use appears to be a linear, step-by-step progression, the reality is that the inquiry process is

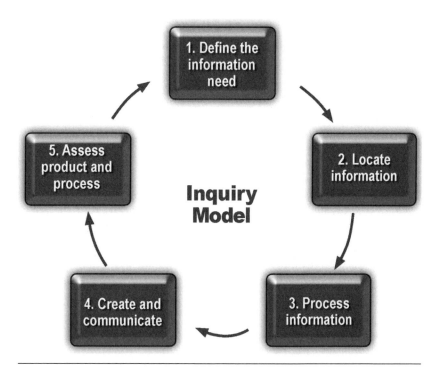

Figure 3.2. Inquiry Curriculum Model

much more complex. With the assistance of the librarian or teacher, students may find themselves going back and forth between stages of the model, modifying their questions, expanding or limiting their searching, and changing and refining conclusions. Students need to know that this is all right, that the "messiness" inherent in inquiry is a normal and natural thing.

Define the Information Need

In the first component of the model, attention is focused on gaining a clear understanding of the problem to be solved. Often, the teacher may assign topics, but through collaborative planning the teacher and librarian can discuss learner goals for both content and process and arrive at ways to involve students more in determining the issues to be researched. This is the time to discuss inquiry and the importance of including challenging and engaging work that will involve students in critical thinking and problem solving. Chapter 5 describes the need to identify the "big ideas" or essential understandings for a unit of study, and this is the time to decide upon those.

The K-W-L strategy described earlier is useful here, as students are guided toward questions and issues in which they have a real interest. This can be a time-consuming process, likely involving a conversation with each student, but when the librarian and teacher work as a team this responsibility can be shared. Finding an area within the project parameters in which the student has a genuine interest will greatly improve motivation and the quality of the final product.

Locate Information

Librarians have always been skilled in helping students locate information, the second stage of the model. In locating information, it is important to help students understand what type of information tool is best for a given need so that they can develop an efficient plan for their research. The library contains abundant resources, including books, video and other nonprint materials, as well as a wealth of digital tools, both free on the Internet and through subscription services. Teaching students effective strategies for using these tools is an important component at this stage. Effective searching techniques—using text features to locate relevant information and applying evaluation criteria such as authority and relevance to sources—will be a part of the instructional responsibilities of the librarian. Lessons illustrating this are found in Chapter 11 and on the website. At this stage, frequent checking for understanding should occur and may be done through the use of exit cards, examining the student's list of sources, discussing sources used, and by other means. This is also a time when the topic or question under investigation may shift a bit due to new information discovered, or a lack of relevant or appropriate information on the original topic. Letting students know that such changes are okay and are a natural part of research can greatly reduce their anxiety. Again, it is important to remember that this a recursive, not linear, process.

Process the Information

Once sources are found, knowing what to do next is often a difficult step for students. Students need specific instruction in efficient ways to extract and record information that they judge to be relevant to their search. At this stage, students compare information from different sources, look for trends and patterns, and begin to draw conclusions. This is a time to review reading comprehension strategies with students, such as predicting, summarizing, and making connections. If students are working in groups, the conversations they engage in here will be excellent learning experiences. The teacher and librarian can structure these conversations so that they take place at key times for all students. This is a critical step, requiring the student to engage in high-level thinking and evaluation skills.

Ethical use of information is also stressed at this stage. As students select the information to be used, instruction or reminders about recoding bibliographic information, quotation rules, and the necessity of crediting sources are needed. The librarian must continue to work closely with students during this time. We cannot assume that our job has ended once the information has been found. This is a key time for the "sitting down beside" style of assessment described in Chapter 6.

Create and Communicate Results

This is the important stage of synthesis. The student or group will organize their information into a logical sequence and create a product. Products can take many forms and need not be the same for all individuals or groups. Again, explicit strategies to aid this organization should be taught. Outlining, whether done the old-fashioned way or through the use of a software tool such as Inspiration is still an important skill. Librarians remain involved in this stage of the project, introducing tools that may be used as products. Students may be taught to use Web 2.0 tools such as Animoto, or other presentation software. The librarian may also teach proper citation skills or the use of a bibliography maker such as NoodleBib. If students are provided a rubric or checklist giving the specific criteria upon which the project will be evaluated, they can self-assess and make corrections at this point as they complete their project.

Assess the Product and Process

At the assessment stage, the student, teacher, and librarian reflect upon what went well and what could be improved in both the product and process of the inquiry activity. Requiring students to reflect and self-evaluate are important components of this step. If the project has been done in a group, self-assessment should be done both by the group and by each individual. Rubrics and other assessment tools may be used productively at this stage. This last stage is too often ignored in favor of just an evaluation by the teacher of the project. This is the stage when a great deal of learning can take place in the form of, "What can I do better next time?" and provision for this process should be made when the unit is planned. This self-evaluation and reflection is essential in helping students gain confidence in their own ability to conduct investigations and to learn how to learn.

Clearly, inquiry-based learning is a time-intensive process. It can be difficult to persuade teachers to allocate sufficient time, given the many demands they face in the classroom. The question must be, "What is the most important information for students to learn?" We cannot create independent, lifelong learners using the traditional teacher-centered read/recite/review/test approach. Critical thinking, like most things, is learned through practice, and inquiry-based assignments provide a perfect vehicle for such practice.

REFERENCES AND ADDITIONAL RESOURCES

Bush, Gail. 2010. "On CORE: Vision and Values Through the School Library." Iowa Association of School Librarians Conference, Des Moines, Iowa, April. 12.

Donham, Jean. 2010. "Deep Learning through Concept-Based Inquiry." *School Library Monthly* 27, no. 1: 8–11.

Donham, Jean, Kay Bishop, Carol Collier Kuhlthau, and Diane Oberg. 2001. *Inquiry-Based Learning: Lessons from Library Power*. Worthington, OH: Linworth Publishing, Inc.

Eisenberg, Michael B., and Robert E. Berkowitz. 1990. *Information Problem-Solving: The Big Six Skills Approach to Library and Information Skills Instruction*. Norwood, NJ: Ablex.

Fontichiaro, K. 2009. "Nudging toward Inquiry: Re-Envisioning Existing Research Projects." *School Library Monthly* 26, no. 1: 17–19.

Friedman, Thomas. 2007. *The World Is Flat: A Brief History of the Twenty-First Century*. New York: Farrar, Straus and Giroux.

Harvey, Stephanie, and Harvey Daniels. 2009. *Inquiry Circles in Action*. Portsmouth, NH: Heinemann.

International Center for Leadership in Education. 2011. "Rigor/Relevance Framework." International Center for Leadership in Education. Accessed June 28. http://www.leadered.com/rrr.html.

Johnson, Roger T., and David W. Johnson. 1988. "Cooperative Learning: Two Heads Learn Better Than One." *In Context 18*, Winter. http://www.context.org/ICLIB/IC18/TOC18.htm.

Kuhlthau, Carol C. 2007. *Guided Inquiry: Learning in the 21st Century*. Westport, CT: Libraries Unlimited.

New York City Department of Education. 2010. Information Fluency Continuum. New York City Department of Education. http://schools.nyc.gov/Academics/LibraryServices/StandardsandCurriculum/default.htm.

Ogle, Donna. 1986. "K-W-L: A Teaching Method that Develops Active Reading of Expository Text." *The Reading Teacher* 39, no. 6 (February): 564–570.

Pappas, Marjorie L., and Ann E. Tepe. 2002. *Pathways to Knowledge and Inquiry Learning*. Greenwood, CO: Libraries Unlimited.

Postman, Neil, and Charles Weingartner. 1969. *Teaching as a Subversive Activity*. New York: Dell.

Stripling, Barbara. 2008. "Inquiry: Inquiring Minds Want to Know." *School Library Media Activities Monthly* 25, no. 1: 50–52.

Stripling, Barbara, and Judy Pitts. 1988. *Brainstorms and Blueprints: Teaching Library Research as a Thinking Process*. Englewood, CO: Libraries Unlimited.

Tallman, Julie I., and Marilyn Z. Joyce. 2006. *Making the Writing and Research Connection with the I-Search Process*, 2nd ed. New York: Neal-Schuman.

4

Developing the Library Instructional Program

> Throughout this book, you will find sidebars featuring the small link icon shown here with either a full or abbreviated URL. The full URLs lead to items referenced in the text; the shorter ones are for the ICCSD website that contains actual lessons and other information. The webpages for the short URLs begin with http://www.iccsd.k12.ia.us/library/. Once you have bookmarked the main site, you will have no difficulty finding the specific tool you wish to access.

The importance of collaboration for educators and teacher-librarians is in its potential to positively affect student learning.

—K. A. Acheson and M. D. Gall

Today's teachers are under tremendous pressure to ensure student success, usually as measured by standardized test scores. Yet, the 21st century skills literature strongly promotes the idea that we need to enable students to work at levels far beyond the knowledge and comprehension that are usually measured by such tests. Students must engage in higher-level thinking, in questioning, in considering multiple perspectives, and in working collaboratively with others to solve real problems. They need to develop their skills in accessing, evaluating, creating, and communicating information through relevant, authentic projects that require critical thinking and problem solving. The school librarian is well suited to work with teachers to help students develop such inquiry skills. How this instruction happens may differ from school to school, depending upon curriculum, teachers, scheduling, and other issues, but school librarians must work within the existing structures to find ways to integrate 21st century skills into student learning experiences.

Inquiry learning is not just another new bandwagon or initiative added to the school librarian's duties. It is simply a better way of thinking about the long-held belief that students must engage with information, compare and contrast points of view, question what they find, and draw conclusions based upon evidence. An excellent article inaugurating a series in *School Library Monthly* is titled "Nudging Toward Inquiry: Re-Envisioning Existing Research Projects" (Fontichiaro, 2009). The idea is that we do not need to start all over again, but rather to take existing assignments and modify them to reflect deeper questions, better products, and greater student involvement, taking small steps to bring about changes in assignments over time. This "evolution, not revolution" philosophy is the way change generally occurs in education, and is much easier to sell to busy teachers than the "We need to completely redo our assignments" approach. Strategies for moving toward inquiry were outlined in the previous chapter.

COLLABORATION AND THE LIBRARY INSTRUCTIONAL PROGRAM

Collaboration with classroom teachers has long been recognized as the best way for school librarians to deliver instruction, so that students learn information and technology skills as they learn classroom content—"just in time" for them to be used and practiced to achieve curriculum goals. Collaborative teaching works best when the school librarian has a flexible schedule, so that he or she is available to work with classes whenever the teacher wishes to bring them to the library. This is the situation in most secondary schools.

Collaboration in this context has been defined as the teacher and school librarian working together to:

1. *identify* what students need to know about accessing, evaluating, interpreting and applying information;
2. *plan* how these skills will be taught and how they relate to content-area learning;
3. *co-teach* so that students learn the skills when they need them to accomplish a specific task and
4. *assess* the students' *process* as they work with information as well as the end *product* of their research. (Donham and Rehmke, 2002: 3; emphasis added)

Classroom teachers and the teacher-librarian engage in collaborative planning to develop curriculum that effectively integrates inquiry and the use of library resources with content-area objectives. For example, students learning about world regions in social studies might do so via an activity wherein they pose and answer significant questions about each region through the use of print and electronic research tools. The study of child labor, a topic of definite interest for young people, might provide a vehicle for exploring the economies of various countries. The popular animals unit might be reframed to explore larger issues such as extinction or the effects of global warming. The teacher brings to the planning process knowledge of subject content and student needs; the librarian contributes a broad knowledge of the inquiry process as well as resources and technology tools. Together they share an understanding of teaching methods and a wide range of strategies. When collaborative planning is employed, inquiry and 21st century skills can be effectively integrated into the classroom curriculum and serve as a medium for learning content. Collaboration energizes the planning process, as multiple perspectives and ideas are brought to bear upon designing learning for students.

COLLABORATING ON A FIXED SCHEDULE

Although flexible scheduling of the school librarian's time is widely accepted as the preferable method to ensure that students have access to the library when needed, the reality is that in many schools the librarian teaches scheduled classes to students, providing prep time for teachers. This is especially true at the elementary level. Most school librarians value this time, especially with children in the younger grades, as it allows them to get to know students, learn their reading abilities and interests, and develop a relationship with them that extends over several years while the students complete elementary school. Even with a fixed schedule, however, time can be found for collaborative projects and library instruction can be coordinated with classroom learning. The elementary schedule shown in Figure 4.1 for an elementary school of about 400 students shows ample time for collaborative teaching on Tuesdays, Wednesdays, and Thursdays, and these slots could be combined with the scheduled class times shown if the librarian is working with that particular teacher. For example, the flex time shown on Tuesday mornings might be used to introduce a research activity that third-grade students could continue during their scheduled time on Wednesday. Students could continue their work during flex time on Friday. This could be repeated each week while the unit progressed. When the third-grade unit ended, the time would be available for other classes. A fixed schedule requires cooperation and careful planning, but it can be made to work to provide time for in-depth units.

There is a definite difference between coordination and collaboration, but both of these can be accomplished on a fixed schedule. The librarian can coordinate with the classroom teacher to

Morning Library Schedule					
Monday 8:35	8:45 4th W	9:25 4th S	10:05 Flex	10:30 5th/6th L	
Tuesday	8:35 Flex			10:15 1st J	10:55 Flex	11:20 6S/R Check Out
Wednesday	8:35 3rd R	9:15 3rd V	9:55 3rd L	10:35 Flex	
Thursday	8:35 Flex	9:15 2nd K	9:55 2nd :	10:35 2nd B/W	11:15 5C Check Out
Friday	8:35 Flex			10:30 5/6th G	11:20 6B Check Out

Figure 4.1. Elementary Library Schedule Showing Fixed and Flex Schedule Times

reinforce reading strategies being taught in the classroom and to prepare students for upcoming inquiry activities. Technology tools and skills that may be needed for upcoming assignments can be taught during library classes, then used and reinforced during class projects. Collaborative inquiry activities can be planned that use some of the students' scheduled library time to develop skills in using library materials, and then build on this instruction during flexibly scheduled times when the teacher and librarian work together in the library in collaborative units.

Regardless of the schedule, all teaching done by the librarian can incorporate inquiry learning goals—questioning, critical thinking, reflection, and self-assessment.

CREATING A CLIMATE FOR LEARNING AND COLLABORATION

Not all teachers are comfortable with the idea of collaboration with the school librarian. In buildings where a collaborative culture is not yet in evidence, the librarian may need to work on developing relationships with teachers that will ultimately result in collaboration. This can be done in a number of ways:

1. *Create an environment in the library* that encourages use and makes people want to be in the library. This includes a number of elements:
   - organizing library space to maximize access,
   - maintaining current, attractive resources and technology,
   - creating a welcoming, user-friendly environment,
   - providing clear signage, self-help guides, and pathfinders,
   - developing policies that enhance access, and
   - maintaining a positive, approachable demeanor.
2. *Select and maintain a collection of resources*, technology, and services appropriate to meet the needs of the students and curriculum. Solicit teachers' input and anticipate their needs for new curriculum. Be sure they are aware of materials that directly support their curriculum and interest areas.
3. *Be involved in the life of the building* as a whole, serving on curriculum and other committees. Be a visible leader.
4. *Promote the value of collaboration* with administrators, teachers, and parents. Articulate a vision for the library program and communicate it to others. Be aware of and use the Curry Lance impact studies and other national research that shows the positive impact of school library media programs and collaboration with teachers on student achievement (Scholastic Library Publishing, 2008).
5. *Target new teachers* and those new to the building and help them in as many ways as you can; they will remember when you ask them to collaborate with you.
6. *Offer workshops for teachers* on new materials and technology tools that will be useful in their teaching.
7. *Engage in professional development activities* to keep yourself on the cutting edge and excited about library programs and 21st century literacies.
8. *Be persistent*—It will not all happen in the first few months, or even the first few years, but your efforts will pay off, and the dividend will be a library program that is recognized as essential to learning in your school.

THE ROLE OF THE ADMINISTRATOR

The school principal and other administrators are critical advocates in developing the library's teaching and learning program. Administrators are well aware of the national initiatives that promote 21st century learning and inquiry. They may be less aware of the school librarian's role in providing learning experiences for students in these areas. You may need to help them understand this role by demonstrating your skill in technology and the design of learning activities. This may be done through conversations with administrators, inviting them to observe teaching and learning in the library, offering to present inquiry and technology in-service to staff, and working on building and district curriculum and technology committees. A supportive principal is your best ally in achieving program goals.

Administrators and curriculum coordinators at the district level can also support collaboration and inquiry-based learning by sponsoring integrated curriculum writing projects, where a team of teachers works with a team of school librarians to develop units that incorporate inquiry and 21st century skills into curriculum content. Such a process would be highly consistent with the philosophy of the national Common Core—integrating media, technology, and reading into all content areas. A seventh-grade unit called "Invisible Invaders: Infectious Disease Research Project"—jointly developed as a district-level project by science teachers and librarians—is included in Chapter 12. It includes both content-area benchmarks and assessments, and library and technology benchmarks and assessments.

PEER COLLABORATION/PROFESSIONAL LEARNING NETWORKS

If you work in a multilibrary district, you already have a professional network for collaboration in lesson and materials development. In Chapter 2, we described the collaborative collection development project that is used by Iowa City's elementary librarians that results in a bibliography of the "best of the best" titles in genres and other library teaching areas. Lesson design provides another avenue for useful collaboration and sharing of ideas, and technology facilitates this process. Peer collaboration in lesson design may have started with an e-mail from one librarian asking, "Does anyone have a good lesson for teaching kids to locate books on the library shelves?" Posted responses went to all of the librarians so the lessons could then be used or modified for their own setting without everyone having to reinvent the same instruction. This has been formalized now, so that lessons are posted on the district website. Even if you are alone in your school or district, there are always "job-alikes" out there with whom you can initiate a formal or semiformal sharing of teaching materials via electronic discussion groups, Google Docs, or other means. Some states have agencies that facilitate regional professional gatherings for teacher-librarians. Professional association conferences provide another good *curriculum/lessons.htm*  place to identify collaborative colleagues. Building such a professional learning network to collaborate with peers is an excellent way to overcome the feeling of isolation that occurs because most of us are the only librarians serving our schools. It also provides a means to lessen the workload by sharing responsibilities with other librarians.

OTHER TYPES OF LIBRARIES

Communication and collaboration with other types of libraries is another way to build a professional network. Many school librarians work with their colleagues in public libraries to promote summer reading programs, help young children obtain library cards, and provide alerts when assignments are given that may result in students coming to the public library for assistance. Recently, there has been increasing attention paid to collaboration among secondary school, community college, and four-year college and university libraries to address the issue of whether students have the necessary skills in research methods to be successful in higher education institutions. The work of David Conley (2005) has underscored the need for research skills and critical thinking skills among students. Academic librarians and school librarians share similar teaching and learning goals. Informing administrators and other educators of the needs identified by higher education can help us make the case for a greater commitment to inquiry and collaboration in our school library programs.

REFERENCES AND ADDITIONAL RESOURCES

Acheson, K. A., and M. D. Gall. 2008. *Techniques in the Clinical Supervision of Teachers*. New York: Longman.

Conley, David T. 2005. *College Knowledge: What It Really Takes for Students to Succeed and What We Can Do to Get Them Ready*. San Francisco, CA: Jossey-Bass.

Donham, Jean, and Denise Rehmke. 2002. *Collaboration: Building Synergistic Partnerships for Instruction*. McHenry, IL: Follett Software.

Fontichiaro, K. 2009. "Nudging toward Inquiry: Re-Envisioning Existing Research Projects." *School Library Monthly* 26, no. 1: 17–19.

Scholastic Library Publishing. 2008. *School Libraries Work!* New York: Scholastic Library Publishing. http://listbuilder.scholastic.com/content/stores/LibraryStore/pages/images/SLW3.pdf.

5

Planning for Learning in the Library

Throughout this book, you will find sidebars featuring the small link icon shown here with either a full or abbreviated URL. The full URLs lead to items referenced in the text; the shorter ones are for the ICCSD website that contains actual lessons and other information. The webpages for the short URLs begin with http://www.iccsd.k12.ia.us/library/. Once you have bookmarked the main site, you will have no difficulty finding the specific tool you wish to access.

> *Begin with the end in mind.*
> —Stephen Covey

"Teacher-librarian" is the official title for those individuals who operate school library programs in Canada, and now in several U.S. states, including Iowa. This is an apt appellation, as it clearly defines the dual role of the school librarian—first as a member of the professional teaching staff in a building, and second as a librarian with a broad knowledge of resources and technology, and how they may be used to support learning. School librarians are skilled teachers, with expertise in curricula and instruction, who can provide leadership in overall curriculum development. Like most successful endeavors, good teaching requires careful planning. While this guide and the accompanying website provide sample lessons and units that may be adapted for your own needs, it is essential that you engage in a deliberate planning process of your own, especially when collaborating with teachers. A process for planning is outlined below.

BACKWARD DESIGN

In their well-known work, *Understanding by Design*, Grant Wiggins and Jay McTighe (2005) suggest that we employ a system of "backward design" when planning instruction, beginning by clearly articulating what we want students to know at the end of the instructional unit or lesson. This model is highly effective in designing inquiry learning activities. Wiggins and McTighe describe a three-stage process:

1. What are our goals for student learning? What do we want students to understand?
2. How will we know when students have achieved the goals?
3. What learning experiences will best enable students to reach these goals?

While goals and objectives may already be stated in both library and content-area curricula, Wiggins and McTighe suggest that we frame learning goals in terms of the "big ideas" or essential understandings that we want students to develop. From these big ideas, we can develop—or guide students in developing—questions that will engage them and help them construct knowledge through the inquiry process. Examples of essential understandings are found in common instructional themes such as, What does it mean to be a friend? What makes someone a good citizen? Why do we have wars? What are the characteristics of a healthy person? In the library setting, our specific goal may be for students to learn how to use the library catalog or how to locate books on the library shelves. But the essential understanding we want students to gain is that information is organized in a variety of ways to enable people to locate resources for both personal and school-related needs. The library's literature curriculum is an excellent place for discussion of some of these essential understandings, as picture books often deal with "big ideas" in the guise of simple stories. The template shown in Figure 5.1 is used in planning unit goals in terms of both essential questions and curriculum goals.

After the essential understandings have been articulated, the second step of the backward design model requires that we decide how we will know if students have achieved the learning goals that have been established. This is the critical assessment piece and it is dealt with in detail in Chapter 6. Multiple forms of assessment should be used, including self-assessment by the student. It is critical that the question of how achievement will be demonstrated is considered early in planning because it impacts the learning activities that are developed in the third step of the Wiggins and McTighe model. Once we have clearly determined what students need to know and what they will be able to do as a result of this instruction, teaching and learning experiences are designed that enable students to achieve the desired understandings.

DIFFERENTIATION

Differentiated instruction is an imperative today as schools deal with learner differences of many kinds—learning styles, learning abilities, English language learners, gender or cultural differences, gifted learners, etc. Howard Gardner's work with multiple intelligences demonstrates the need for designing learning experiences in many different modes (Gardner, 2006). Libraries are all about differentiation. They provide resources to meet many learning levels and styles, facilities to accommodate learning in small and large groups and in different formats, and programming to address a wide variety of student interests. Visual resources such as picture books and videos contribute to an

Unit Plan Civil War Desired Results
Established Goal(s) • Social Studies Standard 2: The student will understand the ways human beings view themselves in and over time. • Library Standard 2: Uses inquiry and critical thinking skills to acquire, analyze and evaluate, use, and create information. • Library Standard 3: Seeks multiple perspectives, shares information and ideas with others, and uses information and resources ethically.

Understanding(s)	Essential Question(s)
• What caused the Civil War? • What were some of the significant battles of the Civil War? • Who were some of the important people involved in the Civil War? • How were the wounded treated? • What (if anything) changed because of the Civil War?	Why do we have war? How do civil wars differ from other kinds of war?

Figure 5.1. Unit Plan Reflecting Content Goals and Essential Understandings

understanding of race, ethnicity, and gender issues through their presentation of people from different races and cultures. One way Iowa City librarians support cultural diversity is through booktalks and displays on multicultural and gender-fair (MCGF) titles at the district's annual Martin Luther King day workshop. Bibliographies from these booktalks are available on the website.

bibliographies.htm

School librarians support differentiated instruction initiatives through their knowledge of a broad range of resources and technology. They can also model effective design for differentiated instruction in planning with teachers by suggesting the use of a variety of activities and technologies. All students will have the same learning goals, but how those goals are met will vary according to student needs and abilities. Differentiating the product a student may create to communicate his or her findings from an inquiry project is a common practice. Giving students options allows for creativity, and for accommodation of their learning styles and preferences as well as talents. The list of Create and Communicate Products shown in Figure 5.3 (see p. 40) includes different types of projects, presentations, and performances, and with the rapid growth, availability, and accessibility of technology tools, this list is expanding.

Often those who present workshops on differentiated instruction suggest giving students more input into planning their own learning and giving them choices about achieving goals. This method is at the heart of inquiry-based learning—the two fit well together.

GUIDE TO PLANNING

Employing a planning guide as teachers and librarians discuss the role each will play in integrated units has proven to be useful. Planning guides for elementary and high school, as well as the junior high/middle school planner shown in Figure 5.2 (pp. 38–39), are available on the website that accompanies this book. Each planner reflects tools and benchmarks appropriate to those grade levels.

curriculum/lessons.htm

As planning begins, it is essential that the teacher and librarian share a clear understanding of the unit's focus and goals as noted previously. Writing an overview statement with content objectives will ensure that the instructional goals are clearly understood. When the librarian and teacher share a clear focus and set of objectives, it is highly likely that students will understand expectations as well. This is the time to agree on the essential questions and essential understandings that students should gain from the project. The planner also includes a section on the "Assignment Level" as a reminder to press beyond the simple recall level to more complex thinking using Bloom's Taxonomy as a guide. These two areas of the planner help us "nudge" projects toward inquiry.

Determining the product of the inquiry unit will impact skills to be taught or reinforced. It is important to remember that the end product is not the goal of the assignment, but instead it is a way for students to demonstrate what they have learned. While the research paper remains a valuable way for students to present some kinds of information (and is still the most frequently assigned project in colleges), there are literally dozens of other products that can be considered to communicate the results of students' learning, and to develop their skill in using different media and technology tools. A list of products that may be used in the collaborative planning process to suggest projects for "creation and communication" is in Figure 5.3 (p. 40). Since Web 2.0 and other applications change so frequently, this list is simply a starting point intended to spur discussion of what project will best demonstrate the student's understanding of the inquiry in which they have been engaged.

In the assessment step, we decide how it will be determined if students have learned what they were intended to learn in the unit. The ability to clearly demonstrate that student learning has taken place is critical. Assessment is discussed in detail in Chapter 6, and numerous assessment tools—

Library Planner

Today's Date _____   Date of Unit _____

Department _____   Course _____

Teacher _____   Unit _____

Librarian _____   Grade(s) _____ Period(s) _____

Number of Students _____   Project Due Date _____

Unit Overview/Content Objectives _____

_____

_____

_____

_____

End Product *(consider differentiation options)* _____

_____

_____

_____

Assessment _____

_____

_____

_____

Preparation *(facility, schedule, resources, equipment, etc.)* _____

_____

_____

_____

Notes _____

_____

_____

_____

Things to consider next year... _____

_____

_____

_____

Level of Involvement					
❑ plan	❑ gather resources	❑ prepare materials	❑ teach lesson	❑ assist students	❑ assess

Figure 5.2. Junior High Planner

Assignment Level (Bloom's Taxonomy)					
❑ remembering	❑ understanding	❑ applying	❑ analyzing	❑ evaluating	❑ creating

Inquiry Model	Research Tools	Production Tools	ICCSD Standards

❑ 1 define info need
❑ 2 locate info
❑ 3 process info
❑ 4 create/communicate
❑ 5 assess
 	
❑ literature
	❑ Destiny
	❑ Almanac
	❑ Print Encyclopedia
	❑ Nonfiction Books
	❑ World Book Online
	❑ EBSCO
	❑ CultureGrams
	❑ AP Multimedia
	❑ Web Search Engines
	❑ Web—Selected Sites
		❑ Word
		❑ Desktop Pub
		❑ Excel
		❑ PowerPoint
		❑ Inspiration
		❑ Movie Maker
			❑ 1 Reads widely
			❑ 2 Uses inquiry
			 • accesses info
			 • evaluates &
			   extracts info
			 • uses info
			❑ 3 Seeks perspectives,
			   shares, ethics

Benchmarks		
❑ info need ❑ question/theses ❑ possible sources ❑ keywords ❑ search strategies/techniques ❑ operators ❑ navigation techniques	❑ catalog ❑ print/electronic reference ❑ electronic indexes ❑ Internet ❑ evaluates information ❑ note-taking techniques ❑ other extraction techniques	❑ bibliographic citation ❑ graphic organizer ❑ outlining ❑ creates product ❑ lit selection ❑ ethical use

Monday	Tuesday	Wednesday	Thursday	Friday

Figure 5.2. Junior High Planner *(Continued)*

Product List

The following list of possible student projects may be used in the collaborative planning process to suggest products for student work. The Tools list includes some of the production tools we have used in student projects.

Written Projects	Visual Projects	Oral Projects	Activity
• annotated bibliography	• advertisement	• audio recording	• archaeological excavation
• article	• animation	• campaign speech	• auction
• autobiography, biography	• art gallery	• commercial	• dance
• blog	• badge	• court trial	• demonstration
• book	• banner	• debate	• game
• book jacket	• blueprint	• interview	• Olympic games
• book review	• bulletin board display	• narrated slideshow	• pantomime
• brochure, pamphlet	• bumper sticker	• news broadcast	• play
• checklist	• cartoon, comic strip	• oral report	• puppet show
• code	• cd case liner	• panel discussion	• Readers' Theater
• cookbook	• coat of arms	• play	• scavenger hunt
• crossword puzzle	• collage	• podcast	• simulation
• diary	• costume	• protest	• wax museum
• essay	• dance demons	• puppet show	
• eulogy, obituary, epitaph	• diagram	• radio program	
• graffiti wall	• exhibition	• rap	
• interview transcript	• family tree	• Readers' Theater	
• I-search paper	• flag	• skit	
• jokes, riddles	• flip chart	• song	
• journal	• globe	• speech	
• lesson	• graph/table/chart	• storytelling	
• letter	• graphic, graphic organizer	• television show	
• letter to the editor	• greeting card	• video, movie	
• magazine	• machine	• website	
• newspaper	• map, map collection		
• poem (sonnet, limerick)	• mask		
• recipe	• mobile		
• research paper	• model		
• short story, fairy tale, fable	• mosaic		
• slogan or motto	• mural		
• song, lyrics, rap	• museum		
• story problems	• photo album		
• survey, questionnaire	• photo essay		
• wiki	• poster		
• word find	• scrapbook		
	• scroll		
	• sculpture		
	• shadow box		
	• suitcase of artifacts		
	• terrarium		
	• timeline		
	• totem pole		
	• travelogue		
	• T-shirt		
	• web		

Tools
- Word processing (Word)
- Google Apps
- Publisher
- InDesign
- Illustrator
- Photoshop
- Kidblog
- Blogger
- Excel
- Wall wisher
- Peach...
- SMART Notebook files
- PowerPoint
- Comic Life
- KidPix
- iMovie
- Windows Movie Maker
- PhotoStory
- Google Sites
- Dreamweaver
- Webspiration/Inspiration
- Prezi
- Animoto
- iPhoto
- iMovie
- Blabberize
- Audicity
- GarageBand
- Voice Thread
- Wordle

Figure 5.3. Create and Communicate Product List

both formative and summative—are included there, in specific lessons and on the website. It is important that students know from the beginning the criteria upon which they will be evaluated. This helps them considerably in understanding the assignment and its expectations. The old saying, "If you don't know where you are going, you are likely to end up somewhere else," applies to both the assignment definition and assessment portions of the teaching process.

The planning guide allows for discussion between the teacher and librarian of the inquiry model described earlier and how each of its components will be addressed in learning activities. It is also important to discuss prerequisite skills. Sometimes an assumption is made that students know how to use a particular resource or understand how to perform effective searches. Defining skills the student will need helps to open the door for teaching or review of skills and concepts in the use of the library. Recording these elements of the lesson also provides data for the librarian on which standards, tools, and elements of the curriculum have been addressed at what levels, and where gaps may exist.

This is also the time to decide who will teach what, and to develop a realistic calendar for the activity. A calendar is provided in the planner, so that days for library work and classroom work can be detailed. Providing adequate time for each step in the process is critical, and scheduling can be difficult because of the many demands on teachers' time. A thorough discussion of instructional goals and the importance of inquiry learning will help persuade teachers of the necessity of taking this time.

Once planning is completed and the schedule is set, the project begins to unfold. Students may come as a large group to the library for initial instruction on resources and strategies, or they may work in smaller groups with the teacher and the librarian, in the library or in the classroom. In a fixed-schedule situation, some of this initial work might be done during the librarian's scheduled time with the students. Frequent one-on-one consultation between the student and teacher or librarian to assess progress is essential as students search for and use information. This is the power of working collaboratively: the ability to divide instructional responsibilities and give more individual attention to students as they work through the process of solving complex problems.

A final—and too often neglected—step in the collaborative planning process is that of assessing the unit and the process itself at the conclusion of the project. If the teacher and librarian plan to teach the unit again, these questions should be discussed:

- What worked well in the unit? What did not work?
- What materials were most helpful? What materials were not available and should be purchased for next time?
- Was the instructional time adequate? Was the time given to students for research adequate?
- Was there adequate time for the completion of student projects?

Answers to these questions can be recorded on the "things to consider next year" portion of the planner. Asking students these same questions will provide useful information and also allow them to reflect upon the unit, as described in the Inquiry Learning Model in Chapter 3. Finally, saving these planners from year to year will save time if the unit is to be taught again.

A lesson design form based upon the Madeline Hunter (1993) model is used in the ICCSD to record and share teaching activities. This form is available on the website. It is a useful tool that guides librarians through the teaching process to ensure that needed materials are secured and that the lesson is well planned for students. It also facilitates the sharing of lessons, since there is a common understanding of what the elements of each lesson contain. Each of the lessons that appear later in the book and on the website is presented in this lesson design format.

curriculum/lessons.htm

A final note: Sometimes it is necessary to simply teach kids basic skills—how to complete an online search, how to format documents, how to locate a book on the library shelves, how to access the network, or how to prepare a bibliography. These are important skills for students to learn. And, while it is best to teach such skills as a part of a unit or activity where students have an immediate need to practice what they have learned, this may not always be possible. Relating these basic skills to larger understandings about the organization of information or why it is important to respect intellectual property rights will help students integrate the skills into a broader context.

REFERENCES AND ADDITIONAL RESOURCES

Covey, Stephen. 2004. *The Seven Habits of Highly Effective People*. New York: Simon and Schuster.

Donham, Jean. 2010. "Enduring Understandings—Where Are They in the Library's Curriculum?" *Teacher Librarian* 38, no. 1: 15–19.

Gardner, Howard. 2006. "Multiple Intelligences: New Horizons in Theory and Practice." New York: Basic Books.

Hunter, Madeline. 1993. "Planning for Effective Instruction: Lesson Design." In *Enhancing Teaching*. New York: Macmillan.

Wiggins, Grant, and Jay McTighe. 2005. *Understanding by Design*. 2nd ed. Upper Saddle River, NJ/Alexandria, VA: Pearson Education/Association for Supervision & Curriculum Development.

Zmuda, Allison, and Violet Harada. 2008. *Librarians as Learning Specialists: Meeting the Learning Imperative for the 21st Century*. Westport, CT: Libraries Unlimited.

6

Assessment to Support Learning

> *The worth of any school program is based upon its contribution to student achievement.*
>
> —Violet Harada

There can be no doubt that the school librarian's teaching responsibility includes that of assessing student learning. As noted in an earlier chapter, deciding how we will know when students have achieved the learning goals we set for them is a key part of the instructional planning process. Students need a clear understanding from the outset about goals and expectations, and assessment must be tied to these goals so that effective ways may be found to evaluate their work.

Since much of what we teach in the library involves the inquiry process, we place a strong emphasis on formative assessment to support and assure learning. When students are assessed, formally and informally, at significant points in the process, we gain a good sense of how they are doing from beginning to end. Breaking student work down into steps and assessing some piece of the work at each of these steps keeps students informed of their progress and helps ensure the integrity of their work. The librarian and teachers decide upon assessment checkpoints during planning, targeting key steps in the students' research process. This also helps students see a sometimes overwhelmingly large task as a series of smaller steps to be completed, one by one, until the project is done. It provides for assessment of the process while students are engaged in information searching.

An example might look like this: At the beginning of a research project, students are given a checklist. At each checkpoint, the librarian or teacher examines what the student has done to gauge completeness and understanding and then either gives the student permission to proceed, or suggests that he or she go back and spend a bit more time on the step, offering specific strategies for improving the work. Such checks might be done when students have decided upon a topic or focus for their work, when they have identified several sources of information, when they have completed a section of notes, and when they begin to turn notes into meaningful text. Students will often work harder if points are awarded at each of the checkpoints. If this is appropriate, the librarian and teacher set up a structure for incentives that can be incorporated into the teacher's grading scheme. Such assessment along the way also helps students to self-assess and to be more reflective about what they are doing—Have I done this correctly? Have I found good information? Are my notes understandable? Am I ready to have this checked? An example of such a checklist appears in Figure 6.1. This type of assessment can often be done "on the fly," while students are working independently in the library.

Requirements/Grading Criteria	
POINTS TO EARN DURING RESEARCH	—————————**Out of 105**
Keyword Worksheet	_____ out of 5
Book Checkout	_____ out of 5
Book Bib Card	_____ out of 5
2 Bib Cards-SIRS Articles	_____ out of 10
Note Cards (Minimum: 3 bib + 15 note)	_____ out of 15
2 Bib Cards-EBSCO Articles	_____ out of 10
Idea Organizer	_____ out of 5
Research Recap	_____ out of 5
Note Cards (Minimum: 5 bib + 50 note)	_____ out of 20
Outline	_____ out of 15
Bibliography	_____ out of 10

Figure 6.1. Score Sheet Showing Checkpoints at Significant Steps in Research

This is another advantage of collaborative teaching—both teacher and librarian, along with others who may be assisting with a class can assist with providing one-to-one feedback to students.

FORMATIVE ASSESSMENT IN THE LIBRARY

In her monograph, *Assessment of Information Processes and Products*, Jean Donham makes an interesting distinction between "assessment" and "evaluation." A former Latin teacher, Donham cites the origin of the word "assessment," noting that the root word "assidere" means "to sit down beside"—in other words to make a judgment from close observation of the student at work. This is contrasted with evaluation, which usually occurs at the end of a project and literally involves placing a value or grade on a project, usually at a distance and by some external standard (Donham, 1998).

http://cissl.rutgers.edu/ Another well-known school library researcher, Carol Kuhlthau, has written about the "zone of intervention," a point at which the student "can do with advice and assistance what he or she cannot do alone or can do only with great difficulty" (Kuhlthau et al., 2007: 23). As part of her information search process model, Kuhlthau suggests periodic "interventions" designed to help students at critical moments in the inquiry process.

Looked at together, the work of these two library leaders suggests a different way of thinking about assessment in the library. The idea of assessment as "sitting down beside" students while they are engaged in their work in order to monitor progress and "intervene" at appropriate times is a powerful model. At those times when students are struggling or seeming a little lost, a brief discussion of the problem along with advice from the librarian or teacher may be all that is needed for the student to make a connection that will set him or her on a course toward success. This method also involves students in their own assessment, requiring reflection upon their own work and learning.

Assessment embedded into the inquiry process, as a series of formal or informal checkpoints, is highly compatible with the way librarians work with student projects and has great potential to improve both student performance and instruction. It also helps us to deal with the problem of plagiarism in a positive way, by providing students with help when needed and monitoring student work throughout the inquiry process.

The librarian may or may not be involved in evaluating final projects, depending upon the nature of the project, the teacher's wishes, time constraints, and other factors. However, the librarian must be involved in formative assessment to ensure that students understand what they are doing in the inquiry process and receive assistance at key points. The overall goal in all of this is to foster student success. Many of the assessments or checkpoints included here, in the lessons that follow, and on the website are based upon this idea of structured interventions at key steps in the research process. This puts the emphasis on learning, rather than evaluation.

ASSESSMENT METHODS

Sample assessment tools for evaluating reading and inquiry learning activities are included in each lesson and other examples appear in the "Assess Product and Process" section on the website. There are many different ways of assessing student performance. While a pencil-and-paper test might occasionally be used to evaluate learning of terminology or other "knowledge-level" content, more authentic methods of performance assessment are very appropriate in the library, where a strong emphasis is placed on project work. Student self-assessment and peer review can be used very successfully in the library as well.

curriculum/lessons.htm

The following methods and examples of assessment are intended to provide models for teachers and librarians when they plan instruction.

Rubrics

A rubric is a set of criteria that clearly defines for the student the range of acceptable and unacceptable performance along a continuum. A rubric describes what a successful project looks like. Research shows that people perform better when they are given a clear model of what is expected before they begin a project (Donham, 1998: 9). This commonsense notion is too often overlooked.

Sample rubrics, which might be used to assess both the inquiry process and the product of such an activity, are found on the website. These will need to be refined and tailored to individual situations. The rubrics also illustrate different ways of formatting and different techniques for the use of rubrics. Some incorporate student self-assessment as well as teacher scoring (see Figure 6.2). Since

Note-Taking Rubrics			

S   Student   T   Teacher

Relevance of Notes

	S	T	
Expert			My notes relate directly to my questions.
Proficient			My notes include information that answers my questions, but there is also information in my notes that I don't need.
Apprentice			My notes don't answer all of my questions.
Novice			My notes relate to my topic but they don't answer my questions.

Figure 6.2. Sample Assessment Rubric

TRAILS

TRAILS (http://www.trails9.org) is a promising web-based tool that provides online testing of students' information literacy skills at several grade levels. The multiple-choice items are keyed to the Ohio Academic Content Standards for information use and to *Information Power* standards. TRAILS includes excellent reporting features that will provide librarians with feedback on areas of information search and usage in which students may need more instruction. It is flexible, easy to use, and best of all, free. Using this tool as a pretest would provide direction for which specific skills students need more instruction on in the activity or unit being planned.

standards and benchmarks include social goals such as "participates and collaborates as a member of a team of learners," rubrics may also be used to evaluate students' work in groups and other behavioral dimensions of their research.

Score Sheets

Sometimes using a simple "scoring" approach for the elements of a project will fit better with a teacher's evaluation system. Each of the steps in the process is assigned an appropriate number of points. The checklist shown in Figure 6.3 also functions as a score sheet. Once again, if students are given such a score sheet at the beginning of their work, they will have a far better understanding of expectations and their learning will be assessed throughout the inquiry process.

Checklists

If a skill or concept is either mastered or not mastered, a checklist may serve as the best means of assessment. The checklist in Figure 6.4 serves to document completion of specific steps required to learn a skill such as use of the library catalog. This checklist is also a self-assessment, engaging students in determining their own skill level. Simple checklists might be used for students to record information sources consulted, to indicate completion of steps in a process, or to assess their own or a peer's project.

Research Interviews or Conferences

As noted earlier, discussions with individual students during the inquiry process provide the student with critical assistance and feedback as he or she works through the process. They can also provide information to both the teacher and librarian on ways that instruction could be improved. These interventions can be formal, structured interviews at critical times in the students' work, or informal

Evaluation for Natural Disaster Project		
REQUIREMENTS:	**Possible Points**	**Points Earned**
Use of Information/Organization of Information • Identified information relevant to the topic and assignment • Took notes in own words; avoided plagiarism • Recorded appropriate information on note-taking guide • Used notes to create well-organized and cohesive article	_____	_____
List of Sources • Listed sources of information • Accurately followed instructions on page 8	_____	_____
Work Habits • Came to class prepared • Was on task; used time efficiently; did not disrupt others • Was respectful of LMC and computer lab resources	_____	_____
TOTAL:	_____	_____

Figure 6.3. Sample Score Sheet

Library Catalog Self-Check			
	Always	Sometimes	Never
I feel comfortable using the library catalog to look up authors, titles, and keywords.			
I know how to tell whether or not any copies of a book are in.			
I know what a call number is and how to find the call number of a book I want on the computer.			
By looking at the call number, I can tell whether I have selected a book or another type of material.			
I know how to browse for an author, title, or keyword.			
I know how to erase mistakes when I type search words in the library catalog.			
I know how to go to the next screen to find out more information about a book.			
I can tell the difference between fact and storybooks by looking at the call number.			
I take good care of materials and equipment.			

Figure 6.4. Library Catalog Self-Assessment Checklist

check-ins with the student to assess progress and identify and solve problems. Structured conferences (as opposed to simply asking, "How are you doing?") built into the unit are most valuable because they provide a consistent means to assess whether all students are on track and to help them if they are not. Because the librarian and the teacher work as a team, there is time for such individual assistance.

Depending upon where the student is in the inquiry process, a structured interview might include questions such as the following:

- What is the focus of your research? What are your significant questions?
- Did you need to adapt or change your questions?
- What resources have you used and which were the most valuable?
- Are you frustrated with any aspect of this research?
- Are you satisfied with the information that you have? What further information do you need?
- Will you share your notes with me? Are you satisfied with the way the note-taking process is going?
- What are two or three major "Ahas" so far in your research?

A sample organizer for a conference with students is shown in Figure 6.5.

Learning Logs or Journals

Learning logs and journals have been used to record progress through an information problem-solving project. Another version of this technique is the exit card (see Figure 6.6). These can be turned in at the end of each day to reflect what the student has accomplished. Learning logs or exit cards may include the same sort of content as the sample interview questions listed previously. Sometimes just a simple, "What did you learn today in your research?" will cause the student to reflect upon the day's work.

Research Recap (5 points)

Topic: _____

Complete your **Idea Organizer** and this form **prior** to your meeting with the librarian. **Bring both with you.**

Research Tool	# of Useful Resources Found	Type of Resource (e.g., book, magazine or newspaper article, pamphlet, webpage)	Where accessed (school or home)
West Lib Catalog			
SIRS			
EBSCO			
Other databases			
Websites			

Be prepared to discuss the following:

1. In two minutes, explain what you know about your topic. Address each of the subtopics briefly.

2. Do you have thought-provoking ideas for your introduction and conclusion?

3. Which resource has been the most valuable to you so far in helping you understand your topic? Why?

4. What has been the most difficult step in this research process?

Figure 6.5. Assessment Interview

Online Research Exit Card

Name _____ class period _____

Today, I chose to use this website: _____

Navigation tools I used include _____
_____
_____

Will you use this website again tomorrow?   Yes   No   Why or why not? _____
_____
_____
_____

Figure 6.6. Sample Exit Card

The teacher and/or librarian should examine these before the next class to document progress and identify students who may be struggling as well as areas where further instruction might be of value.

Peer Assessment and Self-Assessment

These types of assessments help students recognize their accomplishments and pinpoint areas for improvement (see Figure 6.7). They engage students in metacognition—thinking about their own and others' work in a constructive way.

Portfolios of Student Work

Student portfolios are used to provide an authentic picture of the student's capabilities and accomplishments and show progress over time. Student projects, written, oral, and in multimedia formats, may be stored electronically for easy access and portability. Local area networks, where students and teachers have individual folders, are a convenient place to create portfolios.

FORMAL EVALUATION

In the elementary grades, the Iowa City Community School District utilizes a formal evaluation process wherein the librarian prepares an evaluation of each student's mastery of selected skills, using data collected from assessments throughout the school year. These evaluations are provided to parents at the end of the school year. In schools of several hundred students, this is a huge undertaking during the busy end-of-the-year time. Nevertheless, accountability demands some method of reporting on the significant time students spend in the library during scheduled classes.

> While some schools may not require such reporting (and some librarians may be understandably reluctant to take it on), the skills identified could easily be incorporated into a less formalized reporting system for parents. It is important that parents are aware of the important work students are doing with the librarian in developing reading, inquiry, and technology skills, and some system of informing them should be in place.

Specific skills to be reported upon at the end of the year have been identified for each elementary grade level. A complete list of these "graded" skills appears in Chapter 9. On the website, these skills are indicated in bold-faced *curriculum/objectives.htm* type in the Objectives section. Figure 6.8 is an example of an evaluation completed for a fourth-grade student by a librarian at the end of each year. This is done via PowerSchool, a web-based reporting system that allows individualized comments on each student as well. Library evaluations

---

Peer Review of Project

Name of Designer _____

Name of Reviewer _____

What I really like about your project:

Suggestions I would offer for improvement of your project:

Figure 6.7. Sample Peer Review

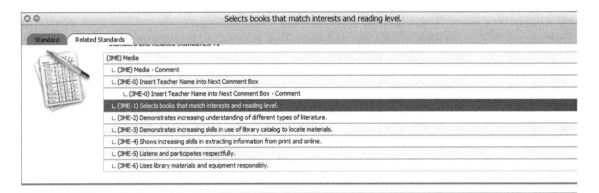

Figure 6.8. Sample Formal Evaluation Stems

are compiled with those of teachers in other special areas and the classroom teacher's comprehensive evaluation of the student.

OTHER COMMUNICATION WITH PARENTS/GUARDIANS

Public libraries do an excellent job of communicating with their patrons, and the public in general, about services and programs. This communication wins them support in the community. People understand and advocate for public libraries because they are well informed about their programs and goals. We need to work to be certain that parents and the community understand the role and mission of school libraries as well.

While this may not traditionally be considered as a means of assessment, communication with parents about the goals and activities of the library program serves three purposes:

1. It provides specific information about what students are learning in the library at a given point in the school year.
2. It provides an overview of the library program.
3. It serves as a method to advocate and win support for library media programs.

By varying the methods and places in which we communicate, we will reach a larger number of parents, and parents will see the many facets of our programs. The following are suggestions for maintaining communication with parents.

Letters to Parents
Letters and notes—whether printed or electronic—can be used to highlight projects being done in the library throughout the year. A letter at the beginning of the year explaining library activities and procedures, especially for younger students, is also of value. A sample set of web-based summaries of library activities is found on the web at the link shown to the left.

http://www.iccsd.k12.ia.us/schools/ Penn/library/parentlinks.htm

Opportunities to Visit
Parents can be invited to come to the library during a special event to view projects. Student projects should be displayed during open houses, family literacy nights, PTO meetings, family technology nights, or on conference days.

Parent-Teacher Conferences
Communication with parents during conference time can present an overview of the library program and curriculum presented to students during the time covered by the conference. A student

self-assessment of inquiry skills currently being taught or reading activities done in the library could be shared by the teacher at conference time. This is also a good time for some marketing—displaying student projects, providing bookmarks on various themes, and giving parents the opportunity to try out Animoto or other tools students have been using for projects. If parents are waiting to meet with teachers, suggest that the library is an ideal place to do that.

School Newsletters

The school or classroom newsletter—again, in print or e-formats—should include specific news from the library. Include a few reviews of good new books, or a list of books you would suggest that parents buy as gifts for children. For younger students, articles on the importance of reading to children and techniques for reading to children would be of value. Sharing of good, new websites for children would be welcomed by parents. Statistics or interesting facts about your library might be included, e.g., "Did you know that our library circulated 3,000 books last month, or nearly 10 books per student?" or "The library added 100 new materials this month, including 40 fiction titles, 28 nonfiction books, 34 e-books, and a SMART Board." An article on new technologies and how they are being used would also be of interest to parents and guardians. Statistics presented in brief bulleted lists are easy to read, and consequently, more likely to be read.

Library Webpages and Blogs

Almost all schools maintain websites, and the library makes an important contribution to the site. High schools have done a particularly good job of making the library webpage a portal to information useful to students, as well as a place where assignments involving the library and online information tools may be accessed (see Chapter 8). Library webpages can also include reading lists, research and technology tips, notes about special programs, and information about staff, hours, and policies. All of this can be helpful to parents as they assist students with homework and monitor progress. Some librarians have chosen to establish blogs, post information to Flickr, or use other online tools to provide information about the library and its programs.

THE LIBRARY ADVISORY GROUP

A library advisory group consisting of parents, teachers, and perhaps students can provide significant support for your library. This group should be well informed about the mission, curriculum, and goals of the library and should be involved in major initiatives such as program evaluation and technology planning. This model is similar to the "Friends of the Library" groups in the public libraries. The library advisory group could also form the core of volunteers organizing book fairs and other fundraising activities, family library nights, author visits, and other library programming. Having such a group of volunteers can be very helpful, but the most important role for this group will be to communicate about your program with other parents, to report what they see going on in your library to the community, and to serve as a ready group of advocates for your program.

In these days of data-driven decision making, we have a professional responsibility to provide evidence of student learning in the library. There are many ways to accomplish this, made somewhat easier by all of the technology at our disposal. Sharing our assessments of student information and technology skills, along with frequent communication with parents about library activities, keeps the library program visible so that it is seen as an indispensable part of the learning community.

REFERENCES AND ADDITIONAL RESOURCES

Copeland, Cynthia L. 2005. *Really Important Stuff My Kids Have Taught Me*. New York: Workman Publishing.

Donham, Jean. 1998. *Assessment of Information Processes and Products*. McHenry, IL: Follett Software Company.

Harada, Violet H. 2005. "Working Smarter: Being Strategic about Assessment and Accountability." *Teacher Librarian* 33, no. 1: 8–15.

Harada, Violet, and Joan M. Yoshina. 2005. *Assessing Learning: Librarians and Teachers as Partners*. Westport, CT: Libraries Unlimited.

Kuhlthau, Carol C., Leslie K. Manoites, and Ann K. Caspari. 2007. *Guided Inquiry: Learning in the 21st Century*. Westport, CT: Libraries Unlimited.

7

Technology as a Tool for Teaching and Learning: The School Librarian's Role

Throughout this book, you will find sidebars featuring the small link icon shown here with either a full or abbreviated URL. The full URLs lead to items referenced in the text; the shorter ones are for the ICCSD website that contains actual lessons and other information. The webpages for the short URLs begin with http://www.iccsd.k12.ia.us/library/. Once you have bookmarked the main site, you will have no difficulty finding the specific tool you wish to access.

If we teach today as we taught yesterday, we rob our children of tomorrow.
—John Dewey

Marc Prensky has described today's students as digital natives who were born into a technology-rich world and come to us knowing how to use a wide variety of electronic tools for their personal needs (Prensky, 2008). Our 21st century learners are constantly connected to their friends across the country and even around the world via computers, smartphones, and a host of other digital devices, monitoring a variety of social media including blogs, wikis, lists, and networking sites. It is difficult to even imagine the digital tools and resources that will be available to the current generation of students during their lives. Our challenge as educators is to take this affinity for technology and use it to help students become not only continuous consumers and creators of information, but efficient, critical, and ethical ones as well. This is the central goal of 21st century literacy.

Competence in the use of technology is essential for teachers and librarians as well as for students. Many of us may not possess "native" abilities with technology, and require assistance and support in developing personal proficiency in technology use. Even when educators are skilled with technology, it is often difficult to identify the most effective applications to improve student learning from among the dozens of new tools that present themselves. Librarians are adept at the management of information and information tools, and can assist students and teachers in using technology more productively. The librarian has three roles in the successful integration of technology into learning, serving as a technology leader, teacher/trainer, and manager.

LEADER/ADVOCATE

The school librarian serves as an advocate for up-to-date technology tools, robust infrastructure, effective training for teachers, and using technology in ways that have the greatest impact on student learning and achievement. Along with other tech-savvy teachers, technology staff, parents, and sometimes students, librarians are members of the building technology team and work closely with building and district IT staff to ensure the smooth functioning of technology systems. As part of the technology team, they are involved in planning for technology acquisition and replacement and for the development of policies that clarify and enhance access for both teachers and students.

The school librarian keeps his or her own tech skills up-to-date and serves as a "crows-nester," one who is constantly looking ahead to spot the best of new technology tools and resources. Through continued professional development, attendance at conferences and workshops, and reading of journals, blogs, and other media, librarians develop a sense of what is on the horizon that will be useful in the school program, while maintaining a healthy skepticism about the claims made by vendors. This is a vital role, as technology funds are always limited, and care must be taken that they be spent on those things that best serve school goals. This is, once again, the critical resources specialist role of the school librarian.

In the Iowa City Community School District, librarians and the information technology department are partners in ensuring that students and teachers have access to technology with a minimum of barriers. They share a common goal of using technology wisely to enhance the educational program. Because of the Children's Internet Protection Act (CIPA), many districts use filtering software and block access to Facebook, YouTube, and other Web 2.0 sites. It often falls to the school librarian to champion the use of such sites because of their potential to contribute to the learning process. Librarians have long been advocates for intellectual freedom in the print realm, and this commitment carries over to the digital world. Clear policies for acceptable use, including the use of social media, help in navigating the issues surrounding the filtering and blocking of sites. By developing a good working relationship with technology staff and communicating frequently with administrators, librarians can facilitate the use of certain tools or sites when they have the potential to enhance teaching and learning. Cultivating a good relationship with IT will assure that they understand the central role of the library in achieving school goals. This is yet another area where the librarian's collaborative skills are essential.

TEACHER/TRAINER

Working with Teachers

While the jury is still out on whether technology has positively impacted student achievement, it is clear that technology of many types increases student engagement in their learning while addressing multiple learning styles and needs. Differentiated instruction requires that we present information in multiple formats and use varied activities to promote better learning by all students. Various technologies support differentiation in numerous ways. This is another area where the school librarian can positively impact learning, as he or she is often the person, or one of the people, in the school most skilled in using technology tools and knowledgeable about applications and web-based tools. Sharing this knowledge with both students and teachers is a natural part of the school librarian's job.

Research does support the fact that effective technology use is dependent upon teachers receiving relevant and in-depth training as new tools are adopted. Building-level school librarians offer workshops for teachers to help them develop their technology skills and become aware of new tools. Such training should have two goals:

1. To ensure that teachers feel competent and comfortable with technology tools
2. To discuss where these tools and resources would interface with curricula—what content would best be taught, reinforced, or practiced through the use of this particular technology

Rather than designing technology training time solely to learn applications and explore all of the "bells and whistles" of certain tools, some time should be used to deliberately plan how the technology can best impact student learning. Technology should never be the first step in instructional planning

("I want my students to create a PowerPoint presentation") but should follow consideration of instructional goals and which teaching techniques best address those goals. Good instructional planning, as outlined in Chapter 5, will consider content goals and instructional needs first, and then determine whether and how technology can enhance the instruction. Care must also be taken not to overwhelm teachers (or librarians) with the continuous barrage of new sites and applications that are promoted as the "latest and greatest" tools for teaching. Focusing on a few applications, learning them well, and integrating them thoughtfully into instruction will result in more and better use of technology by teachers.

> "Play the role of a doctor. One does not begin with the various drugs or machines. Rather, one begins with a diagnosis of a learning challenge or problem and then prescribes a treatment that will cure, improve, or, at least, do no harm to the patient." (Loertscher, 2009: 48)

There are many good online training sites available for teachers and school staff to learn the features of a variety of tools at their convenience. Atomic Learning, one example of a subscription database that provides tutorials on a wide range of applications, is available in many areas, and YouTube and other sites host a variety of brief training programs. The school librarian can facilitate the use of these sites. Students might also be used to help with tech training and

http://www.atomiclearning.com/

support, especially on some of the social networking applications with which they are so adept. This sort of collaboration empowers students and contributes to building communities of learners, where the information flow is not just one way.

Working with Students

Today's students are very competent users of technology for a variety of personal needs. Most students have cell phones or other digital devices and use them to stay in constant communication with friends and even parents through texting, Facebook, and other means. Various devices enable students to be on the web at any time, day or night. We need to respect and build upon the technology skills that students bring with them. There is a need for good policies regarding the use of personal technology, but those policies should be cognizant of the important roles such technologies play in students' lives.

The school librarian provides instruction for students in the use of a variety of specialized technology applications, especially those that are used to locate and communicate the results of inquiry projects. Clearly, technology has dramatically changed the way we do research and has provided a vast menu of ways to communicate the results of an inquiry project. The librarian designs instruction to enable students to use information tools effectively, modeling techniques and strategies that save time and increase the relevance of what is found. Since applications change frequently, such instruction extends beyond teaching specific tools to helping students understand underlying concepts relative to the use of information: advanced searching options, extracting information appropriately, and proper citation to name just a few.

For example, most of us use Google regularly and feel that we understand how that tool works. But librarians can teach students advanced search features like phrase searching (using quotation marks), author searching, truncation, and wildcards that can greatly increase the effectiveness of a search. These strategies transfer to other tools as well, both on the free web and in subscription databases. Students also need an understanding of the difference between a commercial or individual website, and professional sites and publications that have a higher degree of authority. These are sometimes more difficult to access than the commercial and individual postings found quickly through a search engine. Increasingly, federated searching is blurring the lines concerning the origin of many types of information, and students must develop critical thinking and evaluation skills in order to filter reliable, researched information from postings that are biased in favor of a particular viewpoint or product. The lesson "Evaluating Sources of Information," found in Chapter 11 and on the website, is one example of a strategy that guides students in understanding the conventions of websites and the information they contain.

curriculum/lessons.htm

The librarian can also facilitate independent use of the web and various applications through effective signage, how-to guides, and a well-organized library website (see Chapter 8). A good goal for the librarian in working with students is to be seen as a person who, like the students themselves, is interested in and adept with technology, and who is available to assist them with using and producing information.

One of the ICCSD library standards states that, "The learner uses information accurately, creatively, and ethically." This goal is especially applicable as students use technology in inquiry learning projects. In an earlier chapter, we discussed developing assignments that discourage plagiarism by engaging students in questions that take them beyond copy and paste to construction of their own knowledge. It is also important that students understand the idea of intellectual property and why it is important for authors, musicians, artists, and others to receive suitable acknowledgment for their work. Having this understanding—and relating it to their own lives and pastimes—takes students beyond simply being told that it is "wrong" to plagiarize. Other ethical issues including respecting and preserving privacy, online bullying, and prudent use of resources should also be addressed. These topics provide a valuable area for collaboration with a civics or government teacher.

Teacher-Librarian's Role in Technology and Learning

The teacher-librarian and classroom teachers collaborate to enhance learning and teaching through technology.

- The teacher-librarian has expertise in technology and plays a leadership role in building-level technology planning and use.
- The teacher-librarian models and facilitates the use of instructional technology to support teaching and learning goals.
- The teacher-librarian promotes or provides professional development on new technology.
- Technology is used to expand curriculum goals and support students in developing critical thinking and evaluation skills.
- The teacher-librarian participates in district-level technology planning. (Iowa Department of Education and State Library of Iowa, 2007)

MANAGER

The third area of the school librarian's responsibility for technology is the management of resources, both hardware and software. He or she is responsible for the technology hardware—computers, printers, e-readers, scanners, and cameras—housed in and circulated from the library. The librarian also maintains a resources collection including audio, video, online subscriptions, and software applications. In our district, librarians are responsible for managing technology throughout the school building. This role includes scheduling of computer labs, scheduling and deployment of technology tools to classrooms, coordinating tech support, and maintaining inventories. The librarian makes decisions about the purchase of technology hardware and software, including library tools such as the online catalog and subscription databases. Fortunately, there are useful technology tools available to assist the librarian in this role,

http://www.schooldude.com/

including the library management system, databases, spreadsheets, and online IT inventory and tech support systems such as SchoolDude.

Because librarians are experienced in the use of technology hardware and software, they are often called upon to provide tech support in the building. While being helpful in this area may win friends for the librarian, it can also divert time from the librarian's day that is better used working with students and teachers instructionally. Several strategies may be useful in minimizing the amount of time librarians spend doing tech support:

- Train library support staff in the use of software and in dealing with tech issues such as loose cables and lost files.
- Create "how-to" guides for using applications or troubleshooting problems; make them available on the library website. These can be done as documents, but also as brief videos—see second link (Jing) in the sidebar.

https://sites.google.com/site/ icwestlibrary/home/how-to-guides

http://www.techsmith.com/jing/free/

- Develop and communicate procedures for reporting tech problems and securing support.

Again this is an area where a collaborative relationship with IT staff and the development of sound technology policies is essential.

It is difficult to imagine a school or library today without technology. Computers and other tech tools enhance instruction and motivate and involve students. As we move forward in the 21st century, new technologies will continue to excite and engage students, and our challenge as educators will be to identify and implement those that make learning better.

REFERENCES AND ADDITIONAL RESOURCES

Cunningham, Jeremy, and Lisa Gonzalez. 2009. "Collaboration: The Library Media Center and Educational Technology." *Teacher Librarian* 36, no. 5: 33–35.

Harris, Judi, and Mark Hofer. 2009. "Grounded Tech Integration." *Learning and Leading with Technology* 37, no. 2: 22–25.

Hawkins, Brian L. 2007. "Charting the Course for IT in the Twenty-First Century." *Educase* 42, no. 6: 56–70.

Iowa Department of Education and State Library of Iowa. 2007. *Iowa School Library Program Guidelines: Libraries, Literacy and Learning for the 21st Century*. Des Moines: Iowa Department of Education and State Library of Iowa. http://www.iowa.gov/educate/index.php?option=com_content&view=article &id=959&Itemid=2524#guidelines.

Loertscher, David. 2009. "Does Technology Really Make a Difference?" *Teacher Librarian* 37, no. 2: 48–49.

Prensky, Marc. 2008. "Turning On the Lights." *Educational Leadership* 65, no. 6: 40–45.

Weigel, Margaret, and Howard Gardner. 2009. "The Best of Both Literacies." *Educational Leadership* 66, no. 6: 38–41.

8

The School Library Website

Throughout this book, you will find sidebars featuring the small link icon shown here with either a full or abbreviated URL. The full URLs lead to items referenced in the text; the shorter ones are for the ICCSD website that contains actual lessons and other information. The webpages for the short URLs begin with http://www.iccsd.k12.ia.us/library/. Once you have bookmarked the main site, you will have no difficulty finding the specific tool you wish to access.

The Virtual Library is always open!
—Joyce Valenza

A school library website gives a presence to the library program that is not constrained by the physical walls of the school building, the day of the week, or the time of day or night. It is, as Joyce Valenza has described it, a library's second front door, accessible to students where and when they need the library's resources and services (Valenza, 2007). This chapter will outline features of good library website design by using examples from the Iowa City Community School District. All of the sites described in this chapter may be accessed from the District website. *schools.htm*

PLANNING YOUR WEBSITE

Planning and constructing a virtual library is just as challenging for most librarians as planning for, developing, and opening a physical library—in fact, perhaps even more so. Whereas architects and various contractors are behind the design and construction of a school and library, most school librarians are not able to hire professional web designers to create and maintain their virtual libraries. But a strong web presence is an essential component of today's school library program—to provide a portal to a wide range of resources, to support and enhance the instruction we offer during the school day, and to guide, motivate, and challenge learners. It also serves as an effective communication tool to inform students and the school community about the library program and its resources, services, events, and mission. A well-designed, content-rich library website can be an effective instrument for library advocacy.

> **When developing a school library website, consider:**
> - Audience: Who will visit? What do they need to know?
> - Content Elements
> - About the Library
> - Link to Library Catalog
> - Databases
> - Class Links
> - Reading and Literature
> - Parent and Staff Information

The first consideration when planning a website is the primary audience and their needs: Who will visit the site, and what do they need to know and do? Clearly, students are the main focus, and their needs include resources to support their academic studies, particularly related to inquiry activities involving research and production; resources and guidance to support and motivate them as readers; and information about opportunities and events in the library, the school, and beyond.

Most library websites include information about the library. For example, the Longfellow Elementary School Library website includes the library program mission statement, and a translation

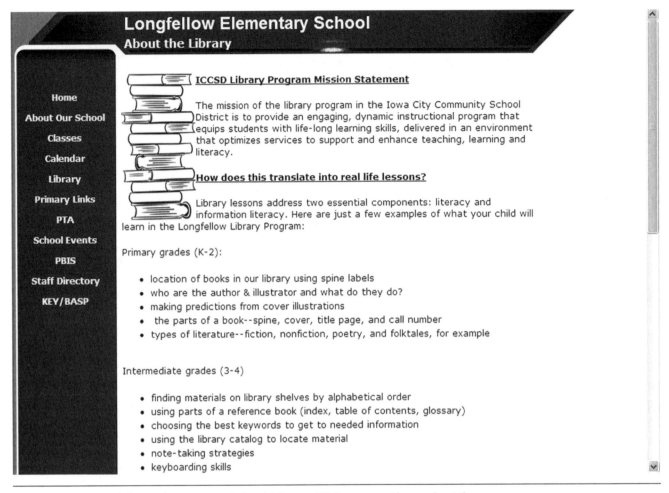

Figure 8.1. Longfellow Elementary School Library Webpage—About the Library

of how this mission translates into real-life lessons (Figure 8.1). The West High School Library website briefly states the goals and philosophy of the library program and includes information about the librarians and library staff, as well as when the physical library is open. A description of the library's "Late Night" event during finals week each trimester is offered (Figure 8.2).

The school library website should include a link to the library's online catalog. This is usually found in a prominent location so that it is readily accessible to users. Tips for searching the catalog and details about the types of resources available through the catalog are common. The North Central Junior High School Library website has a prominent link to the Destiny catalog system, as do most of the library websites in our district (Figure 8.3).

Also common to most school library websites is a listing of available databases. This list is similarly located in a central position so that the links may be easily accessed. There are several decisions to make concerning this listing, particularly if there are numerous available resources: arrange by alphabetical order or by subject; annotate or not; and keep the subscription databases separate from resources on the free web or integrate them. While librarians might prefer to keep these resources separate, perhaps even elevated, most users will find it helpful to have these resources listed along with other high-quality, reputable websites of similar content. The Weber Elementary School Library website, which is a blog, has a message from the librarian with a link to databases (Figure 8.4). The Elizabeth Tate High School Library website also displays their online databases clearly (Figure 8.5).

About the Library

Goals and philosophy

The purpose of the WHS library program is to enable all students to be effective users of information and to appreciate and enjoy literature and other creative expressions.

We believe that independent, life-long learning is the ultimate goal of schools in our society, and that the library program is vital to creating independent learners.

We are also striving to bring our library and its users into the 21st century by increasing our online resources, providing more digital tools for student use and integrating new technologies into our instruction.

For more information about the information literacy program in the Iowa City schools, please visit our district library site.

Meet the librarians

Beth Belding has taught elementary school and is also certified in special education. She has been a teacher-librarian for 20 years.

Jill Hofmockel originally taught U.S. history and American government. This is her 13th year as a teacher-librarian.

Our doors are open!

Before/During/After
The library is open daily at 7:30 and remains open until 4:30, even on early out Thursdays.

Evenings
On Wednesday evenings, the library is available and staffed by a teacher-librarian until 5:30 pm.

Late Nights
The library is open late each trimester during finals, serving coffee, juice, snacks, and pizza to help students succeed each trimester.

WHS library staff

Becky Peterson, Library Secretary, North Circulation Desk

Kathryn Nock, Library Secretary, North Circulation Desk

Lynda Miller, Library Textbook Secretary, South Circulation Desk

Sandy Fleming, Library Audio/Visual Secretary, 2nd Floor

Figure 8.2. West High School Library Webpage—About the Library

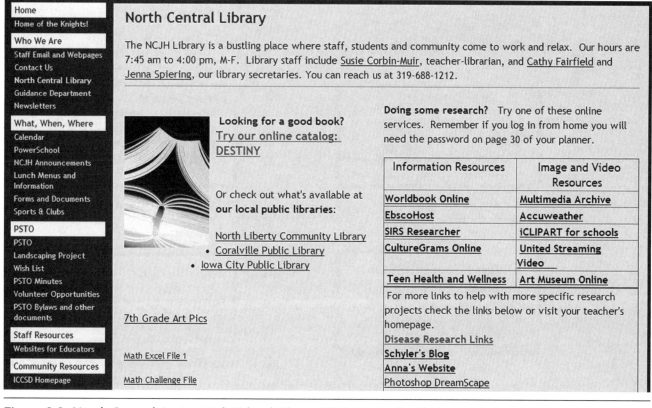

Figure 8.3. North Central Junior High School Library Webpage—Catalog

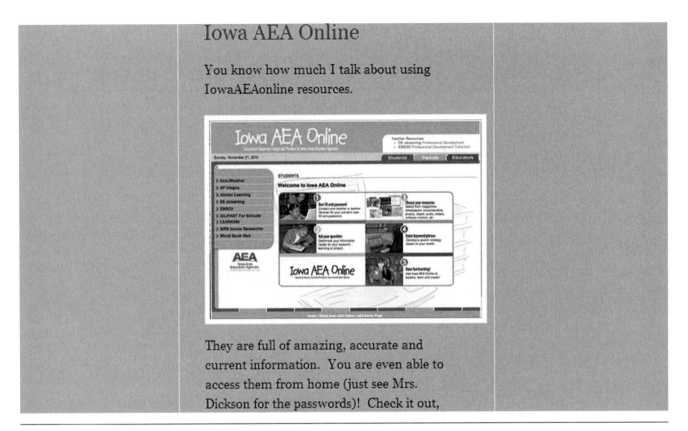

Figure 8.4. Weber Elementary School Library Webpage—Databases

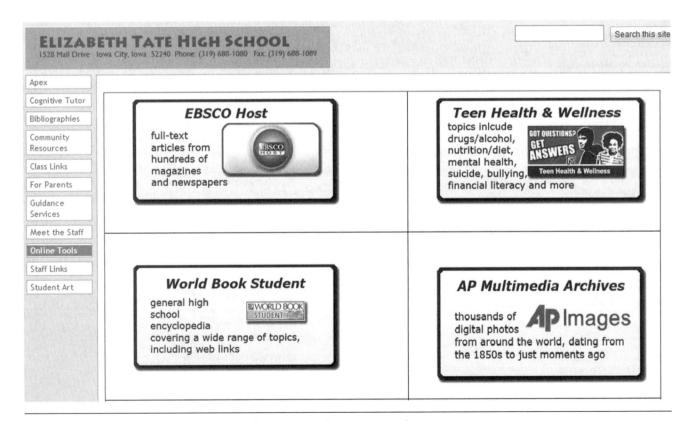

Figure 8.5. Elizabeth Tate High School Library Webpage—Databases

CLASS LINKS

Many librarians develop "Class Links" pages where they compile a variety of deliberately chosen resources to be used by students for particular units, selecting varied, appropriate, and relevant web resources to link and make accessible. The pages often include bibliographies of available print resources as well, or tips for effectively searching the library catalog to locate relevant resources. This webpage is the result of collaboration with a classroom teacher, usually to support an integrated unit. In many schools, before teachers had their own webpages, librarians would create these pages for their collaborative projects. This is how many teachers were first introduced to databases and web resources.

These class links pages often include components other than topic-specific informational links. Inquiry units generally involve research, but also include some type of project where a product is created to communicate what the student has learned. Details, suggestions, instructions, advice about planning and creating various products, including the various productivity tools, or links to online production resources are also incorporated into the page. This type of webpage, where all of the information and tools that the student needs to initiate and undertake an inquiry project are unified in one place, is an effective instrument for both the librarian and the teacher, as well as the student. The class links page for "The Twenties" unit at West High School includes links to relevant databases for research, links to other selected websites, and downloadable templates for the newsletters the students will produce (Figure 8.6).

The Twenties

Mrs. Strief
American Studies
October, 2010

Mrs. Strief's classes: select one of the following newsletter templates and save it to your WHS folder.

Newsletter Template in   Newsletter Template in
Microsoft Publisher   Microsoft Word

Then, try several of these subscription databases. All of these are available from home as well as school, but you'll need to enter a login/password at home. See page 42 of your planner.

- **WorldBook Online** provides basic overview articles on a wide range of topics.
- **Britannica Online** provides more in-depth coverage.

Finally, the following are links to a few selected websites covering various aspects of **The Twenties**:

- **The Roaring 1920s** This ThinkQuest covers such topics as World News, Finance, Science and Technology, Sports, Arts and Literature, and Life.
- **Henry Ford and His Model T** From the Learner.org website. Covers mass production, assembly line, rise of the automobile, labor conditions, etc.
- **Sacco-Vanzetti Case** Information on the Sacco-Vanzetti case. Maintained by English Professor, University of Penn.
- **A Look At Gertrude Ederle** Photographs, links and biographical information about Ederle. Maintained by Michigan State University.

Figure 8.6. West High School Library Webpage—The Twenties

Web-Based Science Inquiry Unit

Freshmen students at West High School are guided through a collaborative research unit by a webpage developed by the librarians working with the science teachers. The calendar for the week-long unit, project requirements, topic ideas, worksheets and templates, writing expectations, and even writing models are all on the website (see Figures 8.7, 8.8, and 8.9).

This brief inquiry unit includes lessons introducing two databases—SIRS Researcher and EBSCO Science Reference Center—and a review of evaluating information. Students select research questions based on topics and issues that relate to recent science units, locate relevant articles that address the research question, and prepare annotated bibliographies as the end product. This is a brief unit—only a week long—but incorporates the introduction and review of several key research tools and skills, and guides and models for students the formal writing style that is expected in other, future research and writing projects. This inquiry unit and all of its components are available on the website.

READING PROMOTION

Another important role of the library webpage is to encourage and promote reading. Library websites include lists of new books and bibliographies of books on various topics, either curricula-related or for personal, leisure reading. The Hills Elementary Library website has a page called the Reading Corner and includes suggestions and recommendations of books, plus links to many sites and bibliographies. The Coralville Central Elementary Library website is a blog. The librarian there has a weekly literature-related contest that encourages her students to read and comment on the blog.

http://sites.google.com/site/hillslibrary/
http://coralvillecentrallibrary.blogspot.com/

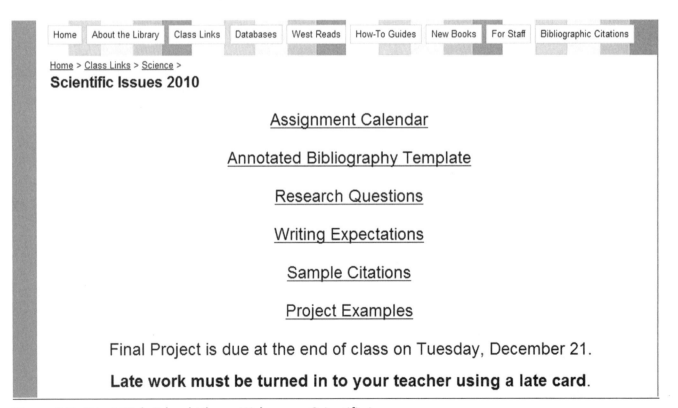

Figure 8.7. West High School Library Webpage—Scientific Issues

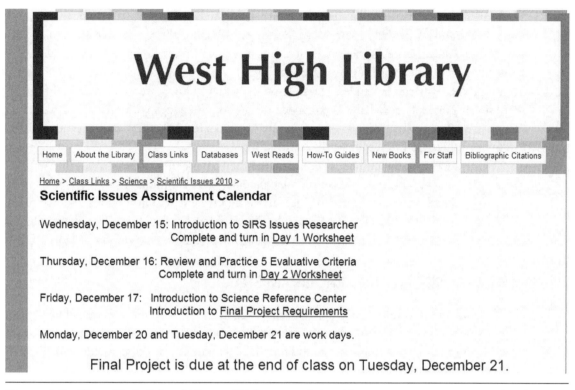

Figure 8.8. West High School Library Webpage—Scientific Issues—Assignment Calendar

Home > Class Links > Science > Scientific Issues 2010 > Scientific Issues Assignment Calendar >

Scientific Issues Final Project Requirements

Scientific Issues Annotated Bibliography

Project Requirements:

1. Save a copy of the Annotated Bibliography Template found on our class links page to your WHS folder. This will be what you print to hand in when it is complete.

2. Choose a research question from the 5 on the class links page. Copy and paste your question in the box provided on the template.

3. Carefully choose two (2) articles that answer your research question. One should be an article accessed through Science Reference Center and one should be an article accessed through SIRS Issues.

4. Print and read each article. Highlight or underline 2-5 sentences in each article that are most relevant to your research question.

5. On your downloaded template, write a paragraph that answers the research question, using information from your two articles. This should be a detailed, complete paragraph of 5-6 sentences.

6. On your downloaded template, write bibliographic citations for each article in the boxes provided. We will expect these citations to follow MLA style and you may use the sample citations on our class links page.

7. Under your bibliographic citation for each article, write a detailed paragraph that describes how well the article exemplifies the 5 evaluative criteria. We will look at a sample paragraph in class and you can use this list of the 5 evaluative criteria to help you write.

8. Print your completed template, staple it to your two highlighted/underlined articles, and turn them in.

This project is due before the end of class on Tuesday, December 21.

Figure 8.9. West High School Library Webpage—Scientific Issues—Final Project Requirements

Many school libraries provide space for displaying students' work: artwork, projects, presentations, etc. The libraries provide a larger venue for showcasing the work than most classrooms, and also offer a larger, more varied audience. Likewise, the library website can also be a place where students' work is displayed. Artwork (either digital or digitized), blogs, podcasts, and videos—all of these productions can be made accessible on the school library website, or linked from there. The Roosevelt Elementary website is enhanced throughout its pages with original artwork by students (Figure 8.10). The City High Library website has links to booktalk podcasts produced by students in their sophomore English class (Figure 8.11).

While students and their needs should be the focus, many librarians also use the web to communicate with and provide resources to staff and parents. The Parent Links page on the Penn Elementary Library website includes a report of the various library curriculum lessons and activities that the students in each grade level are undertaking (Figure 8.12). On the Hills Elementary Library website there is a parent page with links and resources of interest to parents (Figure 8.13).

THE DISTRICT LIBRARY PROGRAM SITE

index.htm

In addition to individual school library websites, a district library website can also provide valuable support for library curricula and programming. The ICCSD site provides a wealth of information for librarians, including all of the curriculum documents and lessons that are printed in this book. This information is stored for easy access and is updated regularly by the district coordinator, so that new lessons, units, and assessments, as well as other materials, are readily

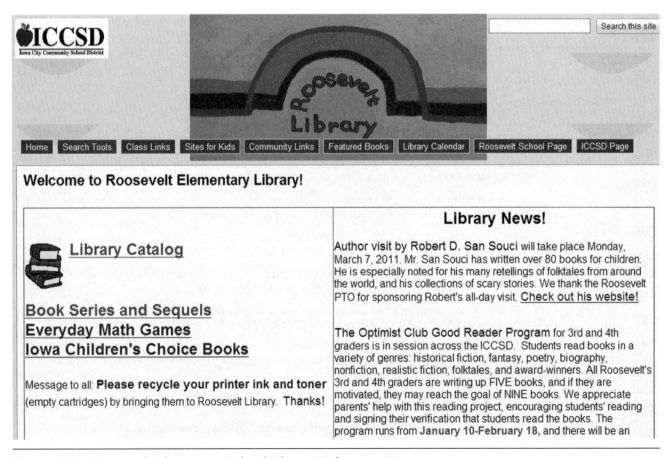

Figure 8.10. Roosevelt Elementary School Library Webpage—Home

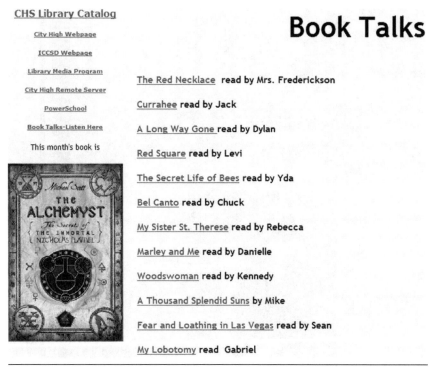

Figure 8.11. City High School Library Webpage—Booktalk Podcasts

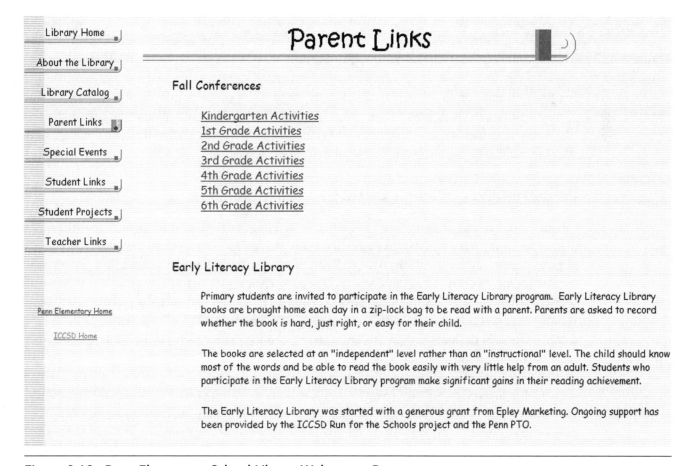

Figure 8.12. Penn Elementary School Library Webpage—Parents

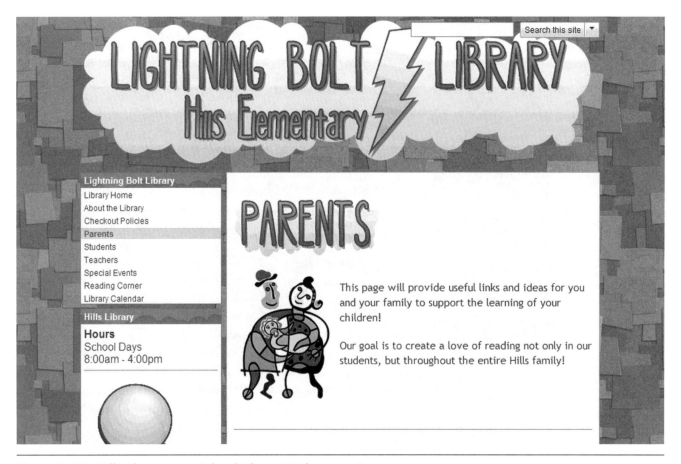

Figure 8.13. Hills Elementary School Library Webpage—Parents

available. In addition to the curriculum documents, the site contains information on policies and procedures; frequently needed forms; meeting calendars, agendas, and minutes; access to the district's union catalog, and links to other sites useful to the library staff. All of the school library websites highlighted in this chapter are accessible from the district site.

WEBSITE DEVELOPMENT OPTIONS

Librarians devote a great deal of time and effort to selecting resources and arranging and maintaining their order on the shelves. They give attention to helpful appropriate signage, and most design their library space to accommodate the needs of their users. Similarly, librarians create and select useful content for their websites, and this content is the most critical element. However, unless the content is organized in a logical way to enable users to find what they need, and unless appropriate navigation is built into the structure of the site, users will quickly abandon it. The library website should have a cohesive visual design, clear, consistent signage, and logical pathways to facilitate users as they maneuver throughout.

There are a number of options for staking some space for the library on the web. Certainly a website developed with HTML is viable, and is still the most frequently used method. The website may be designed by writing the code or using an authoring program, then uploading the site and its pages and resources to the web. Many librarians have learned and use authoring programs to create and maintain the pages on their websites. Some also maintain their web presence through blogs, an easy-to-update option. Google Apps for Education is becoming widely accepted and provides another vehicle for library websites, using Google Sites templates which may be adapted to local needs. In some school districts a content management system (CMS) is used, which brings consistent design and navigation elements to every level of the website, from the district level to the school and department level. Finally, there are library websites created with and hosted by a site such as LibGuides, where the local content and elements are designed

http://www.springshare.com/libguides/

within a structure which is then hosted by a provider. LibGuides can be used to accompany a library website, or may be used as the website itself. The options for developing a web presence are numerous and evolving.

The school library website is "the second front door" to the library, the one that is open and accessible not only during school hours, but 24/7. It is a reflection of the library program, and a valuable tool in supporting teaching, learning, inquiry, and literacy.

REFERENCES AND ADDITIONAL RESOURCES

Valenza, Joyce. 2007. "A Webquest about School Library Websites." School Library Websites: Examples of Effective Practice. Revised July 11. http://schoollibrarywebsites.wikispaces.com/WebQuest+on+School+Library+Websites.

Valenza, Joyce Kasman, and Doug Johnson. 2009. "Things That Keep Us Up at Night." *School Library Journal* 55, no. 10: 28–32.

Walbert, David. 2006. "Best Practices in School Library Website Design." Learn NC. http://www.learnnc.org/lp/pages/969.

PART II

Curriculum Blueprint and Sample Lessons and Units

9

The Iowa City Library Curriculum: An Overview

> Throughout this book, you will find sidebars featuring the small link icon shown here with either a full or abbreviated URL. The full URLs lead to items referenced in the text; the shorter ones are for the ICCSD website that contains actual lessons and other information. The webpages for the short URLs begin with http://www.iccsd.k12.ia.us/library/. Once you have bookmarked the main site, you will have no difficulty finding the specific tool you wish to access.

> *...all students will become responsible, independent learners capable of making informed decisions.*
>   —Iowa City Community School District Mission Statement

The library curriculum is the centerpiece of a library program. A commitment to teaching and learning has long been the focal point of the Iowa City library program's mission. In the recently completed formal curriculum review, the various elements and components that define and shape the library curriculum—the mission, standards, benchmarks, and objectives—were systematically examined, analyzed, and refined. As an ongoing process, new lessons and assessments are being continually developed that provide opportunities for students to learn the content, and to learn and practice the skills and strategies articulated within the curriculum.

MISSION

curriculum/mission.htm

The Iowa City Community School District mission statement makes a commitment to ensuring that "...all students will become responsible, independent learners capable of making informed decisions...." It further states that this is accomplished by "challenging each student with a rigorous and creative curriculum...." To that end, the ICCSD library program has as its mission,

> to provide an engaging, dynamic instructional program that equips students with life-long learning skills, delivered in an environment that optimizes services to support and enhance teaching, learning, and literacy.

As this mission statement was discussed and prepared, a series of belief statements were also articulated. These detail program convictions as follows: (1) the purpose of the library program in enhancing student learning and development; (2) the role of the librarian in a school's instructional program, as it relates to resources, technology, literature, inquiry, and leadership; (3) collaboration with teachers, administrators, staff, and parents to further student achievement; (4) fostering and supporting literacy, literature, and reading; (5) promoting inquiry learning and critical thinking skills; (6) promoting the responsible use of technology;

and (7) providing a rich, abundant, diverse collection of resources in a variety of formats to reflect and address the varied interests, needs, and learning styles of our students.

The mission statement and the accompanying belief statements guide and inform the work of district librarians and serve as the foundation of the library program. The library program standards and benchmarks comprise the scaffolding that frames teaching and learning endeavors. As part of the curriculum review, local library program standards and benchmarks were examined by comparing local guidelines with those articulated in the American Association of School Librarians (AASL) standards and National Educational Technology Standards (NETS), searching for commonalities and gaps. This resulted in a modification of the document to reflect current thinking and to align with national standards and state guidelines. Standards, benchmarks, and learner objectives have also been examined in light of the Common Core standards (see Figure 9.1).

STANDARDS

curriculum/standards.htm

Standards describe what students are expected to know and be able to do.
Standard 1 of the ICCSD curriculum framework states that, "Student reads widely both for information and in pursuit of personal interests." This standard reflects a commitment to literacy, reading, and literature. Each student must have the opportunity to become a competent and self-motivated reader, knowing how to select fiction and nonfiction

---

Mission and Belief Statements

The mission of the library program in the Iowa City Community School District is to provide an engaging, dynamic instructional program that equips students with lifelong learning skills, delivered in an environment that optimizes services to support and enhance teaching, learning, and literacy.

We believe that

- lifelong learning is the ultimate goal of schools in our society, and that the library program is vital to creating independent, informed, responsible learners.
- the teacher-librarian is an instructional leader in the school with expertise in resources, technology, and literature.
- the teacher-librarian works in collaboration with teachers, administrators, support staff, and parents to provide learning experiences that promote student achievement.
- the library program promotes critical thinking, engagement with information in all its forms, and the responsible use of technology to enhance teaching and learning.
- the library program fosters and supports the development of literacy and reading for enjoyment and for information.
- the library curriculum promotes inquiry learning through information literacy instruction that enhances and reinforces classroom content and instruction.
- the library program cultivates connections with the larger learning community by providing students access to learning resources and activities beyond classroom and school walls.
- all children have the right to equal access to literature, information, and information technologies.
- the diverse needs and learning styles of students require differentiation in learning resources and instruction.
- a rich and abundant collection of resources in many formats is essential to meet the teaching and learning needs of the school curriculum, and to reflect diversity and intellectual freedom principles.

Adopted: Spring 2009

Figure 9.1. ICCSD Library Mission and Belief Statements

at an appropriate level for fluent reading. School librarians teach, model, and reinforce a variety of reading comprehension strategies to understand literature and informational text, complementing and extending the reading instruction that goes on in the classroom. We want each student to develop a background in types of literature/genres and literary elements. We provide opportunities to help students connect ideas to personal interests and previous knowledge and experience. We teach and help students apply critical thinking skills when reading, viewing, and listening. And finally, we teach students to respond to literature and other creative expressions of information in varied formats.

Standard 2 states that a student uses inquiry and critical thinking skills to acquire, analyze and evaluate, use, and create information. Librarians teach and model inquiry and information literacy skills and strategies, following an information problem-solving model, wherein the learner (1) accesses information efficiently and effectively; (2) evaluates and extracts information critically and competently; and (3) uses information accurately, creatively, and ethically. Throughout this inquiry process, we teach students to develop questions, follow strategies, and use technology to facilitate information access, retrieval, and production.

Standard 3 establishes that a student seeks multiple perspectives, shares information and ideas with others, and uses information and resources ethically. To address this standard, school librarians teach and offer opportunities and resources for students to broaden viewpoints. We teach about plagiarism and intellectual property rights, and how and why to document sources. We teach students how, when, and why to use technology and resources responsibly and ethically. We create opportunities for students to work collaboratively (see Figure 9.2).

BENCHMARKS

Benchmarks align with the standards and articulate the concepts, skills, and strategies that students at a given grade level will achieve. The benchmarks are spiraling: skills introduced at one level are reviewed and reinforced at higher levels. An additional understanding regarding benchmarks is that students are assumed to have a reasonable understanding of the benchmark so that instruction after the level of the benchmark can build upon it.

curriculum/benchmarks.htm

OBJECTIVES

Specific learner objectives describe the detailed tasks students will be able to do to demonstrate that they have achieved the benchmarks. As with the benchmarks, objectives are sometimes repeated across levels, with some learner objectives introduced at one level, then addressed again at higher grade levels. Additionally, at the elementary level, some of the objectives have been tagged for special consideration. As described in Chapter 6, elementary librarians in the ICCSD are required to assess and describe students' progress in end-of-year reports. Collaboratively, they have identified from three to seven critical objectives for each grade level. (These are listed in Figure 9.3, bolded in Figure 9.5, and included on the website.) These objectives are uploaded into the district's student information system (PowerSchool) and each librarian provides an assessment indicating the students' attainment of their grade level objectives. The report includes an evaluation as to whether the student is able to perform the skill described in the objective (1) consistently, (2) some of the time, or (3) with support. In addition, the librarian provides a brief general comment about each student. It is critical that the librarians do assessments and document results throughout the school year (see Figure 9.3).

curriculum/objectives.htm

The librarians in the secondary schools do not provide this type of formal evaluation for each student. However, many are involved in formative assessments when working with students during

Library Program Standards

Standard 1: Reads widely both for information and in pursuit of personal interests.
- Is a competent and self-motivated reader
- Selects fiction and nonfiction at an appropriate level for fluent reading
- Uses a variety of reading comprehension strategies to understand literature and informational text
- Develops a background in types of literature/genres and literary elements
- Connects ideas to personal interests and previous knowledge and experience
- Applies critical thinking skills when reading, viewing, and listening
- Responds to literature and other creative expressions of information in varied formats

Standard 2: Uses inquiry and critical thinking skills to acquire, analyze and evaluate, use, and create information.

A. The learner accesses information efficiently and effectively.
- Recognizes the need for information
- Formulates essential questions based on information needs
- Identifies a variety of potential sources of information
- Develops and uses successful strategies for locating information
- Uses technology effectively to locate information
- Uses a variety of print and electronic tools to find information

B. The learner evaluates and extracts information critically and competently.
- Determines relevancy, suitability, authority, objectivity, and currency
- Distinguishes among fact, point of view, and opinion
- Selects and records information relevant to the problem or question at hand
- Derives meaning from information presented in a variety of formats

C. The learner uses information accurately, creatively, and ethically.
- Organizes information for practical application
- Integrates new information into current knowledge
- Creates and communicates information and ideas in appropriate formats
- Uses technology effectively to organize, present, and document research findings
- Designs and develops information products and solutions both for school assignments and personal interests
- Evaluates process and product based on information need and essential questions
- Revises and improves process and product
- Practices ethical behavior with regard to information and information technology

Standard 3: Seeks multiple perspectives, shares information and ideas with others, and uses information and resources ethically.
- Seeks information from diverse sources, contexts, disciplines, and cultures
- Respects the differing interests and experiences of others and seeks a variety of viewpoints
- Respects intellectual property rights and understands the need for documenting sources
- Uses technology and resources responsibly and ethically
- Works independently and in groups to pursue information to solve problems
- Participates and collaborates as a member of a team of learners

Adopted: Spring 2009

Figure 9.2. ICCSD Library Standards

Assessed Skills in End-of-Year Reports

Kindergarten
- Identifies and locates fiction and nonfiction in the library
- Listens and participates respectfully
- Uses library materials and equipment responsibly

Grade 1
- Selects books that match interests and reading level
- Demonstrates increasing understanding of library organization
- Identifies parts of a book: cover, spine, title page, title, and call number
- Listens and participates respectfully
- Uses library materials and equipment responsibly

Grade 2
- Selects books that match interests and reading level
- Demonstrates increasing understanding of different types of literature
- Demonstrates increasing understanding of library organization
- Identifies parts of a book: author and illustrator
- Listens and participates respectfully
- Uses library materials and equipment responsibly

Grade 3
- Selects books that match interests and reading level
- Demonstrates increasing understanding of different types of literature
- Demonstrates increasing skills in use of library catalog to locate materials
- Shows increasing skills in extracting information from print and online
- Listens and participates respectfully
- Uses library materials and equipment responsibly

Grade 4
- Selects books that match interests and reading level
- Demonstrates increasing understanding of different types of literature
- Locates materials in library catalog and on the shelves by call number
- Shows increasing skills in extracting information from print and online
- Demonstrates increasing computer skills
- Listens and participates respectfully
- Uses library materials and equipment responsibly

Grade 5
- Selects books that match interests and reading level
- Shows increasing skills in finding and using information from print and online
- Demonstrates increasing skills in creating a bibliography
- Demonstrates increasing computer skills
- Listens and participates respectfully
- Uses library materials and equipment responsibly

Grade 6
- Selects books that match interests and reading level
- Shows increasing skills in finding and using information from print and online
- Demonstrates increasing skills in creating a bibliography
- Demonstrates increasing computer skills
- Listens and participates respectfully
- Uses library materials and equipment responsibly

Adopted: Spring 2010

Figure 9.3. ICCSD Assessed Skills in End-of-Year Reports (K–6)

research and production activities. In order to ascertain whether students are achieving the objectives of the curriculum, assessment and evaluation must be ongoing.

A chart indicating the standards and the corresponding benchmarks and objectives is shown in Figure 9.5 at the end of this chapter.

LESSONS

With the content of the curriculum identified, the next step is to create lessons and assessments, clearly an ongoing process. Lessons to teach and reinforce the various learner objectives have been developed and are accessible from the website. Sample lessons and units are included in the chapters that follow. Any given lesson may incorporate and *curriculum/lessons.htm*   address a number of objectives, and may be adapted to use with students at a different grade level, or to better integrate with a particular content area. The lessons are outlined using a common lesson design template, closely modeled on the Madeline Hunter lesson design structure (see Further Reading sidebar). Many of the lessons, in addition to the lesson plan, include other resources: student handouts, activity manipulatives, charts or graphics, PowerPoint slides, SMART Board files. These supplemental resources are also accessible from the website.

Differentiated Instruction

When developing lessons, an important consideration is to address the varied learning needs and styles of students by differentiating instruction. Differentiation in instruction is defined by Tomlinson and Allan as "a teacher's reacting responsively to a learner's needs" (see Further Reading sidebar) and the differentiation can be applied to the content, the process, and/or the product, according to students' readiness, interests, and learning profiles. Librarians have an edge when it comes to differentiation, equipped with a wide range of resources and tools to be used with and by students for their learning experiences.

Assessments

Along with the lessons, assessments to measure students' achievement of benchmarks and objectives have been developed. Generally, the assessments are incorporated into instruction so that students receive feedback and support throughout the inquiry process, not just at the end. As described in Chapter 6, the curriculum includes a number of different formative assessment tools and instruments that help inform the librarian and teacher about a student's progress, as well as guide, redirect, and encourage students in their work.

> **Further Reading**
>
> Hunter, Madeline. 1994. "Planning for Effective Instruction: Lesson Design." In *Enhancing Teaching*. New York: Macmillan.
> Tomlinson, Carol Ann, and Susan Demirsky Allan. 2000. *Leadership for Differentiating Schools and Classrooms*. Alexandria: ASCD.

CURRICULUM MODELS

Educators, including librarians, typically view curricula in the language of standards, benchmarks, and objectives, and these elements provide the framework of the ICCSD curriculum. But we have also adopted models that provide an alternate view of the curriculum—a graphical representation that is clearer for our students to comprehend. The content of the library curriculum can be viewed as comprised of two major elements: the reading and literature element and the inquiry element. Each of these elements is represented by a model (see Figure 9.4).

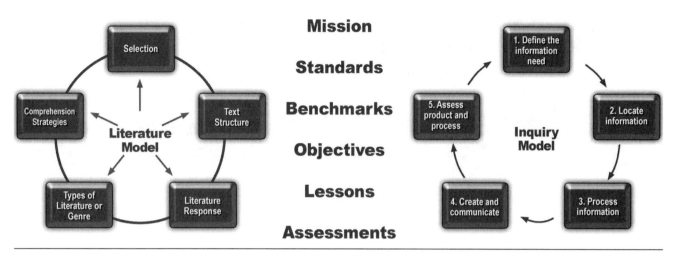

Figure 9.4. ICCSD Curriculum Model

The reading and literature model is comprised of five components, described in Chapter 2. These components are not sequential. Most of the descriptors of this model reside within Standard 1, for the literature model first and foremost focuses on reading and literature. However, some descriptors of this model are evidenced in Standard 2 with its emphasis on inquiry and critical thinking. In the course of teaching and learning about literature, learners address some of the benchmarks inherent in Standard 3.

The other model that overlays the library curriculum is the inquiry model. As described in Chapter 3, the inquiry model is based on and has evolved from several information literacy or information problem-solving models developed by school library leaders over the last fifteen years. Unlike the literature model, the components of the inquiry model are sequential, although not absolutely linear, for there is some recursive movement inherent in the inquiry process. Although most of the literature model resides in Standard 1, with smaller portions of the model seeping into Standards 2 and 3, the inquiry model resides soundly in Standards 2 and 3, with some elements of inquiry emerging in Standard 1.

On the website, the library curriculum may be approached through the models—the reading and literature model and the inquiry model. Lessons and assessments are *curriculum.htm* accessible by clicking the various components of each of the models. Additionally, the lessons and assessments are also linked to and accessible from the Standards—Benchmarks—Objectives framework, with lessons and assessments linked to this structure.

ICCSD Library Program
Standards—Benchmarks—Objectives

Standard 1: **Reads widely both for information and in pursuit of personal interests.**

Note: Objectives in **BOLD** and marked (**EOY**) are addressed in the end-of-year assessment/report for each student.

Kindergarten	
Benchmarks	**Objectives**
• Selects books based on personal interests	• Selects an "Everybody" book to share at home
• Uses illustrations and other visual elements to understand text	• Tells a story based on illustrations in the text
• Makes connections to background knowledge (Text to Self)	• Participates in discussion by sharing personal experiences related to text • Responds to stories by participating in a variety of activities such as drama, puppetry, songs, and visual arts
• Distinguishes between fiction and nonfiction	• Identifies fiction as "made-up" story and nonfiction as "real" • **Identifies a book as fiction or nonfiction (EOY)**
• Begins to recognize story structure	• Identifies the beginning, middle, and end of a story
• Identifies roles of author and illustrator	• Defines author as the person who writes the words • Defines illustrator as the person who makes the pictures
Grade 1	
Benchmarks	**Objectives**
• Selects a "Just Right" book independently for personal reading	• **Applies guidelines for choosing a "Just Right" book during library checkout (EOY)**
• Uses illustrations and other visual elements to understand text	• Points to picture book design elements
• Makes connections to background knowledge (Text to Self)	• Participates in discussion by sharing personal experiences related to text
• Uses predictions to understand text	• Uses picture book design elements to make predictions about the text • Predicts what could happen next in the story
• Recognizes basic story structure	• Identifies the story's problem and solution
• Begins to recognize different types of literature	• Distinguishes between a fantasy story and a realistic story • Identifies nonfiction books as informational text
Grade 2	
Benchmarks	**Objectives**
• Selects a "Just Right Book" independently for personal reading	• **Applies guidelines for choosing a "Just Right" book during library checkout (EOY)**
• Begins to recognize different types of literature	• **Distinguishes between several types of literature such as biography, poetry, and folktales (EOY)**
• Makes connections to background knowledge (Text to Text, Text to World)	• Participates in discussion by sharing personal knowledge of other texts and the world
• Uses mental images to understand text	• Creates mental pictures from text and shares them through telling, drawing, or writing
• Begins to identify literary elements of character, plot, and setting	• Identifies elements of character, plot, and setting with support through participation in discussion or use of graphic organizers

Figure 9.5. ICCSD Standards, Benchmarks, and Objectives   *(Continues)*

ICCSD Library Program Standards—Benchmarks—Objectives *(Continued)*	
Grade 3	
Benchmarks	**Objectives**
• Uses retelling and paraphrasing to understand text	• Restates meaning of text verbally or in writing through oral literature or note-taking process
• Recognizes different types of literature/genres	• **Identifies types of literature/genre through activities such as oral literature, reading promotion programs, booktalks, or reading logs (EOY)** • Reads different types of literature/genres through reading activities collaboratively planned by the teacher-librarian and the classroom teacher
• Identifies literary elements of character, plot, and setting	• Identifies elements of character, plot, and setting independently through graphic organizers or other reading activities
• Begins to use text features to understand informational text	• Identifies text features (such as headings, fonts, captions, and graphics) with support
• Selects a variety of "Just Right" fiction and nonfiction for independent reading	• **Checks out a variety of "Just Right" fiction and nonfiction from the library (EOY)**
Grade 4	
Benchmarks	**Objectives**
• Recognizes different types of literature/genres	• Reads different types of literature/genres through reading activities collaboratively planned by the teacher-librarian and the classroom teacher • **Identifies types of literature/genres through activities such as oral literature, reading promotion programs, booktalks, or reading logs (EOY)**
• Identifies literary element of point of view	• Identifies point of view independently through reading activities
• Uses text features to understand informational text	• Identifies text features (such as headings, fonts, captions, and graphics) independently
• Selects a variety of "Just Right" fiction and nonfiction for independent reading	• **Checks out a variety of "Just Right" fiction and nonfiction from the library (EOY)**
• Uses summarizing to understand text	• Briefly identifies the main points or gist of text through oral literature or note-taking process
Grade 5	
Benchmarks	**Objectives**
• Uses questions to understand text	• Asks questions with support before, during, and after reading literature or informational text
• Selects a variety of "Just Right" fiction and nonfiction for independent reading	• **Creates a reading list of books for independent reading based on personal interests (EOY)**
Grade 6	
Benchmarks	**Objectives**
• Uses questions to understand text	• Asks questions with support before, during, and after reading literature or informational text
• Selects a variety of "Just Right" fiction and nonfiction for independent reading	• **Creates a reading list of books for independent reading based on personal interests (EOY)**

Figure 9.5. ICCSD Standards, Benchmarks, and Objectives   *(Continues)*

ICCSD Library Program Standards—Benchmarks—Objectives *(Continued)*	
Grades 7–12	
Benchmarks	**Objectives**
• Is a competent and self-motivated reader	• Reads for pleasure to learn and to solve information needs • Uses library catalogs to generate a list of books on a topic of choice
• Selects fiction and nonfiction based on interest, need, and reading level	• Uses knowledge of types of literature/genres to select appropriate titles
• Develops a background in types of literature and literary elements	• Reads across genres and formats
• Connects ideas to personal interests and previous knowledge and experience	• Explores topics of interest
• Applies critical thinking skills when reading, viewing, and listening	• Reads widely and fluently to make connections with self, the world, and previous reading
• Responds to literature and other creative expressions of information in varied formats	• Shares response to literature with others

Standard 2: Uses inquiry and critical thinking skills to acquire, analyze and evaluate, use, and create information.

    A. The learner accesses information efficiently and effectively.

    B. The learner evaluates and extracts information critically and competently.

    C. The learner uses information accurately, creatively, and ethically.

Kindergarten	
Benchmarks	**Objectives**
• Understands basic organizational pattern of library	• **Locates everybody and nonfiction sections of the library (EOY)**
• Recognizes parts of a book	• Identifies cover, spine, and title page
Grade 1	
Benchmarks	**Objectives**
• Understands basic organizational pattern of library	• Locates relevant sections of the library based on personal interests or needs • **Applies alphabetical order skills to everybody section (EOY)**
• Recognizes parts of a book	• **Identifies cover, spine, title page, title, and call number (EOY)**
• Understands a fact as a true statement	• Distinguishes between fact and make-believe
• Recognizes nonfiction as a source of information	• Identifies information after reading or listening to a nonfiction text
Grade 2	
Benchmarks	**Objectives**
• Understands organizational pattern of library	• Applies alphabetical order skills to all fiction sections of the library

Figure 9.5. ICCSD Standards, Benchmarks, and Objectives

(Continues)

ICCSD Library Program	
Standards—Benchmarks—Objectives *(Continued)*	

Grade 2 *(Continued)*	
Benchmarks	**Objectives**
• Understands how call numbers are used to locate books	• **Matches call number prefix with section of library (EOY)**
• Recognizes parts of a book	• **Identifies author and illustrator (EOY)**
• Begins to use nonfiction as a source of information	• Identifies facts in nonfiction text with support

Grade 3	
Benchmarks	**Objectives**
• Understands how call numbers are used to locate books	• Uses call number to locate fiction and nonfiction books on library shelves with support • **Uses library catalog to identify and locate materials with support (EOY)**
• Uses technology to locate information	• Uses selected online resources to locate information with support
• Uses nonfiction as a source of information	• Uses table of contents and glossary to locate information in text with support • Identifies appropriate reference source (dictionary, atlas, encyclopedia) based on information need with support
• Begins to identify information need	• Identifies keywords to guide information search with support
• Begins to use keywords to initiate an information search	• Uses keywords to search library catalog or table of contents with support
• Begins to extract information from text based on need	• **Uses note-taking strategies to record information with support (EOY)**

Grade 4	
Benchmarks	**Objectives**
• Understands how call numbers are used to locate books	• **Locates fiction and nonfiction books on library shelves by call number (EOY)** • **Uses library catalog to identify and locate materials (EOY)**
• Uses technology to locate information	• Uses selected online resources to locate information with support
• Uses nonfiction as a source of information	• Uses table of contents and glossary to locate information in text • Identifies appropriate reference source (dictionary, atlas, encyclopedia) based on information need with support
• Begins to identify information need	• Identifies keywords to guide information search with support
• Uses keywords to initiate an information search	• Uses keywords to search library catalog or table of contents
• Begins to extract information from text based on need	• **Uses note-taking strategies to record information with support (EOY)**
• Uses technology appropriately to create and share information	• **Demonstrates appropriate technology skills such as keyboarding and word processing (EOY)**
• Begins to cite information sources	• Records sources of information with support • Locates bibliographic information in a source with support

Figure 9.5. ICCSD Standards, Benchmarks, and Objectives   *(Continues)*

ICCSD Library Program Standards—Benchmarks—Objectives *(Continued)*	
Grade 5	
Benchmarks	**Objectives**
• Uses technology to locate information	• Uses selected online resources to locate information • Selects appropriate resources from a results list obtained from an electronic search
• Uses nonfiction as a source of information	• Uses index to locate information in text • Identifies appropriate reference source (dictionary, atlas, encyclopedia, almanac) based on information need
• Identifies information need	• Identifies keywords to guide information search
• Uses keywords to initiate an information search	• Uses keywords to search library catalog or index
• Extracts information from text based on need	• **Uses note-taking strategies to record information (EOY)**
• Uses technology appropriately to create and share information	• **Demonstrates appropriate technology skills such as keyboarding and word processing (EOY)**
• Cites information sources	• Locates bibliographic information in a source with support • **Creates bibliography with support (EOY)**
Grade 6	
Benchmarks	**Objectives**
• Uses technology to locate information	• Uses selected online resources to locate information • Selects appropriate resources from a results list obtained from an electronic search
• Uses nonfiction as a source of information	• Uses index to locate information in text • Identifies appropriate reference source (dictionary, atlas, encyclopedia, almanac) based on information need
• Identifies information need	• Identifies keywords to guide information search
• Uses keywords to initiate an information search	• Uses keywords to search library catalog or index
• Extracts information from text based on need	• **Uses note-taking strategies to record information (EOY)**
• Uses technology appropriately to create and share information	• **Demonstrates appropriate technology skills such as keyboarding and word processing (EOY)**
• Begins to evaluate information sources	• Determines relevancy, suitability, and authority of information sources with support
• Cites information sources	• Locates bibliographic information in a source • **Creates bibliography with support (EOY)**

A. **The learner accesses information efficiently and effectively.**

Grades 7–8	
Benchmarks	**Objectives**
• Recognizes and refines the need for information	• Articulates an information need
• Identifies potential sources of information	• Uses a variety of appropriate sources of information
• Develops and uses successful strategies for locating information	• Generates appropriate keywords to use as access points in a search and refines searches as necessary • Uses technology effectively to locate information

Figure 9.5. ICCSD Standards, Benchmarks, and Objectives

(Continues)

ICCSD Library Program Standards—Benchmarks—Objectives *(Continued)*	
Grades 7–8 *(Continued)*	
Benchmarks	**Objectives**
• Uses technology effectively to locate information.	• Conducts effective searches using identified online resources such as databases, online encyclopedias, online catalogs, Internet
• Uses a variety of print and electronic tools to find information	• Uses resource-specific navigational features such as table of contents and index to locate and access information
Grades 9–12	
Benchmarks	**Objectives**
• Recognizes and refines the need for information	• Formulates essential questions to refine an information need • Develops purpose or thesis statement
• Identifies a variety of potential sources of information	• Identifies multiple sources of appropriate scope and depth
• Develops and uses successful strategies for locating information	• Identifies and uses various strategies and techniques to execute and refine successful searches, including multiple keywords, Boolean searches, truncation, etc.
• Uses technology effectively to locate information	• Applies advanced functions of electronic catalogs and online databases
• Uses a variety of print and electronic tools to find information	• Navigates within print and online resources effectively and independently

B. The learner evaluates and extracts information critically and competently.

Grades 7–8	
Benchmarks	**Objectives**
• Determines usefulness of information	• Applies evaluative criteria to determine the appropriateness of the information with respect to: relevancy, suitability, authority, objectivity, and currency of the information
• Selects and records information relevant to the problem or question at hand	• Identifies information relevant and essential to the information need • Uses appropriate techniques such as highlighting or paraphrasing to extract and record information from resources
Grades 9-12	
Benchmarks	**Objectives**
• Determines accuracy, relevance, authority, and suitability	• Applies evaluative criteria to determine the relative value of the information: relevancy, suitability, authority, objectivity, currency
• Distinguishes among fact, point of view, and opinion	• Successfully recognizes and purposefully integrates others' points of view and opinion as well as factual information into research process
• Selects and records information relevant to the problem or question at hand	• Uses appropriate extraction techniques or strategies to identify and record pertinent information

Figure 9.5. ICCSD Standards, Benchmarks, and Objectives   *(Continues)*

ICCSD Library Program
Standards—Benchmarks—Objectives *(Continued)*

C. The learner uses information accurately, creatively, and ethically.

Grades 7–8

Benchmarks	Objectives
• Organizes information for practical application	• Uses graphic organizers, outlines, storyboards, rough drafts, or other tools to synthesize information
• Creates and communicates information and ideas in appropriate formats	• Selects an appropriate format for communicating ideas • Presents, performs, or shares information and ideas successfully
• Evaluates process and product based on information need and essential questions	• Uses a checklist or rubric to reflect on research process
• Practices ethical behavior with regard to information and information technology	• Avoids plagiarism • Observes copyright guidelines by recording sources using a standard format • Creates a properly formatted bibliography

Grades 9–12

Benchmarks	Objectives
• Organizes information for practical application	• Employs a systematic method of organizing extracted information
• Creates and communicates information and ideas in appropriate formats	• Analyzes information and identifies topics, subtopics, and relationships • Selects suitable format for clearly expressing ideas and information
• Uses technology effectively to organize, present, and document research findings	• Uses appropriate technology to develop a formal outline or storyboard
• Designs and develops information products and solutions both for school assignments and personal interests	• Creates a product that clearly expresses ideas
• Evaluates process and product based on information need and essential questions	• Evaluates product or presentation
• Revises and improves process and product	• Revises and refines as necessary
• Practices ethical behavior with regard to information and information technology	• Respects others' intellectual property by avoiding plagiarism and observing copyright guidelines • Cites sources in a properly formatted bibliography

Standard 3: Seeks multiple perspectives, shares information and ideas with others, and uses information and resources ethically.

Kindergarten

Benchmarks	Objectives
• Uses library materials responsibly	• **Demonstrates proper care of library materials (EOY)** • Follows proper checkout procedures • **Returns library materials on time (EOY)** • Demonstrates proper use of computers and other equipment
• Understands expected classroom behaviors	• **Listens and participates respectfully (EOY)**

Figure 9.5. ICCSD Standards, Benchmarks, and Objectives　　　　　*(Continues)*

ICCSD Library Program Standards—Benchmarks—Objectives *(Continued)*	
Grade 1	
Benchmarks	**Objectives**
• Uses library materials responsibly	• **Demonstrates proper care of library materials (EOY)** • Follows proper checkout procedures • **Returns library materials on time (EOY)** • Demonstrates proper use of computers and other equipment
• Understands expected classroom behaviors	• **Listens and participates respectfully (EOY)**
Grade 2	
Benchmarks	**Objectives**
• Uses library materials responsibly	• **Demonstrates proper care of library materials (EOY)** • **Returns library materials on time (EOY)** • Demonstrates proper use of computers and other equipment
• Understands expected classroom behaviors	• **Listens and participates respectfully (EOY)**
Grade 3	
Benchmarks	**Objectives**
• Uses library materials responsibly	• **Demonstrates proper care of library materials (EOY)** • **Returns library materials on time (EOY)** • Demonstrates proper use of computers and other equipment
• Understands expected classroom behaviors	• **Listens and participates respectfully (EOY)**
• Begins to understand the ICCSD technology resources policies	• Uses Internet as instructed for educational purposes
• Begins to work appropriately in groups	• Works actively and productively in groups with support
Grade 4	
Benchmarks	**Objectives**
• Uses library materials responsibly	• **Demonstrates proper care of library materials (EOY)** • **Returns library materials on time (EOY)** • **Demonstrates proper use of computers and other equipment (EOY)**
• Understands expected classroom behaviors	• **Listens and participates respectfully (EOY)**
• Begins to understand the ICCSD technology resources policies	• **Uses Internet as instructed for educational purposes (EOY)**
• Works appropriately in groups	• Works actively and productively in groups
• Begins to understand intellectual property rights	• Identifies plagiarism as copying the work of others • Recognizes need to cite information sources
Grade 5	
Benchmarks	**Objectives**
• Uses library materials responsibly	• **Demonstrates proper care of library material (EOY)** • **Returns library materials on time (EOY)** • **Demonstrates proper use of computers and other equipment (EOY)**
• Understands expected classroom behaviors	• **Listens and participates respectfully (EOY)**

Figure 9.5. ICCSD Standards, Benchmarks, and Objectives   *(Continues)*

ICCSD Library Program Standards—Benchmarks—Objectives *(Continued)*	
Grade 5 *(Continued)*	
Benchmarks	**Objectives**
• Understands the ICCSD technology resources policies	• **Uses Internet as instructed for educational purposes (EOY)** • **Uses student network accounts responsibly and ethically (EOY)**
• Works appropriately in groups	• Works actively and productively in groups
• Understands intellectual property rights	• Identifies plagiarism as copying the work of others • Recognizes need to cite information sources
Grade 6	
Benchmarks	**Objectives**
• Uses library materials responsibly	• **Demonstrates proper care of library materials (EOY)** • **Returns library materials on time (EOY)** • **Demonstrates proper use of computers and other equipment (EOY)**
• Understands expected classroom behaviors	• **Listens and participates respectfully (EOY)**
• Understands the ICCSD technology resources policies	• **Uses Internet as instructed for educational purposes (EOY)** • **Uses student network accounts responsibly and ethically (EOY)**
• Works appropriately in groups	• Works actively and productively in groups
• Understands intellectual property rights	• Identifies plagiarism as copying the work of others • Recognizes need to cite information sources
Grades 7–12	
Benchmarks	**Objectives**
• Seeks information from diverse sources, contexts, disciplines, and cultures	• Maintains openness to new ideas by considering divergent opinions or conclusions
• Respects the differing interests and experiences of others and seeks a variety of viewpoints	• Understands intellectual freedom and recognizes various viewpoints
• Respects intellectual property rights and understands the need for documenting sources	• Establishes and maintains a working bibliography throughout the research process
• Uses technology and resources responsibly and ethically	• Understands and follows the ICCSD technology resources use policies • Complies with library patron policies
• Works independently and in groups to pursue information to solve problems	• Assesses own ability to work with others in a group setting by evaluating varied roles, leadership, and demonstrations of respect for other viewpoints
• Participates and collaborates as a member of a team of learners	• Contributes to the exchange of ideas within and beyond the learning community

Adopted: Spring 2009
Revised: 2010

Figure 9.5. ICCSD Standards, Benchmarks, and Objectives

10

Sample Lessons: Literature Model

 Throughout this book, you will find sidebars featuring the small link icon shown here with either a full or abbreviated URL. The full URLs lead to items referenced in the text; the shorter ones are for the ICCSD website that contains actual lessons and other information. The webpages for the short URLs begin with http://www.iccsd.k12.ia.us/library/. Once you have bookmarked the main site, you will have no difficulty finding the specific tool you wish to access.

OVERVIEW

In this chapter, we present a sampling of lessons that are a part of the literature portion of our curriculum. These also include basic library orientation lessons that lay the foundation for work the students do in the library in the later grades. The lessons are presented in a standardized lesson design format. These lessons, and a variety of other lessons, may also be found on the website.   *curriculum/lessons.htm*

They are arranged according to the elements of the literature model presented in Chapter 9. Handouts, activity sheets, visuals, and/or assessments accompany most lessons. **Boldfaced** type indicates that an item is printed with the lesson; page numbers are included too for ease in locating the materials.

Lessons in Chapter 10

LIBRARY ORIENTATION

 Lesson
Alphabetical Order
Grades 1–2
(Lesson developed by Jenahlee Chamberlain and Sarah Latcham)

Standard	Benchmark	Objective	EOY Skill
Standard 2: Uses inquiry and critical thinking skills to acquire, analyze and evaluate, use, and create information.	Understands basic organizational pattern of library.	Locates relevant sections of the library based on personal interests or needs. Applies alphabetical order skills to Everybody section. Identifies title and call number. Applies alphabetical order to Fiction sections of the library. Matches call number prefix with section of the library (Everybody).	Demonstrates increasing understanding of library organization.

Tools and Resources
- Oversized book spines
- **Book Spine Worksheet/Assessment** (p. 91)
- **Blank Call Number Form** (p. 92)
- ABC books
- Books for examples of call numbers

Anticipatory Set
Introduce the alphabet and how the Everybody section is arranged in alphabetical order. Read an ABC book to reinforce alphabetical order. Use oversized book spines to show what a call number looks like. As the students grasp the concepts of alphabetical order, continue the lesson by talking about the arrangement of the library and how alphabetical order is used. Discuss how a call number is created and what the letters mean. Finally, use oversized book spines as examples.

Objectives
Students will:

- Learn how to alphabetize Everybody books using the first three letters of the author's last name (call number).
- Learn about arrangement of the Everybody book section.
- Be able to alphabetize books by call number.
- Learn about arrangement of the Fiction sections of the library.

Input/Modeling/Checking for Understanding

Use oversized book spines to demonstrate alphabetical order based on first letter only. As a class, have students help arrange them in alphabetical order. Show them how the E stands for Everybody and ask if they know where they are located. Explain how call numbers are created from the first three letters of the author's last name. Using familiar authors, have the students tell you what the call numbers would be for those books.

Guided Practice/Independent Practice

Each student can create their own call number using the first three letters of their last name. If you laminate the **Blank Call Number Forms** (p. 92), you can reuse them for multiple classes. Small groups can alphabetize their call numbers or you can have the whole class line up to alphabetize themselves. The students then try to find a book that is the closest to their call number on the shelf. If the students are first graders, you may want to adapt this to finding only the same initial letter. If the students are more mature, you may want them to get more specific. You can also have the students try to locate books in the fiction or biography sections of the library as well.

Assessment

- You can assess the students as they locate the books on the shelves.
- For additional alphabetical order assessment use the **Book Spine Worksheet/Assessment** (below).

Help! The library books are out of order!

Cut out each book spine and glue them to a piece of construction paper in **Alphabetical** order

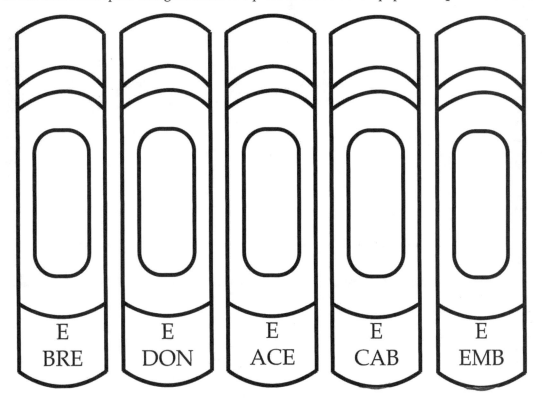

Figure 10.1. Book Spine Worksheet/Assessment

Blank Call Number

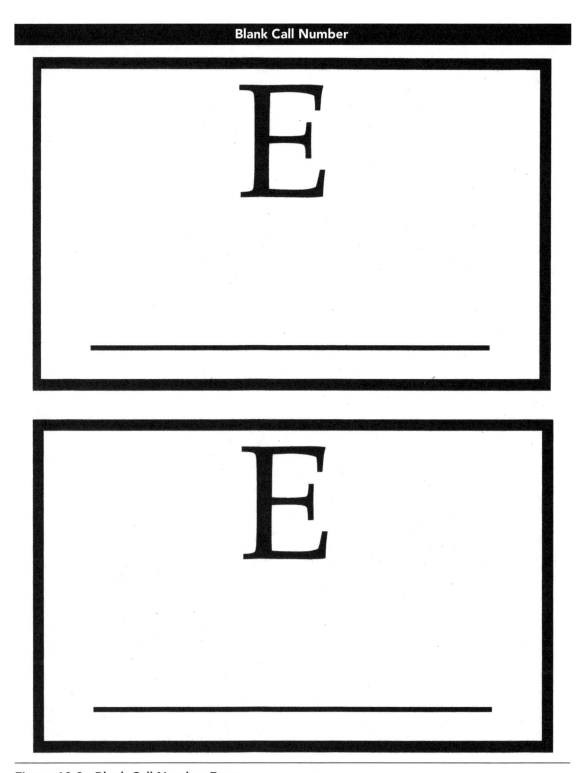

Figure 10.2. Blank Call Number Form

Lesson
Sections of the Library
Grades 3–4 (adaptable for Grades 2–5)
(Lesson developed by Anne Marie Kraus, Sarah Lacham, and Michael Schlitz)

Standard	*Benchmark*	*Objective*	*EOY Skill*
Standard 2: Uses inquiry and critical thinking skills to acquire, analyze and evaluate, use, and create information.	Understands how call numbers are used to locate books.	Grade 3: Uses call number to locate fiction and nonfiction books on library shelves with support. Grade 4: Locates fiction and nonfiction books on library shelves by call number.	Grade 3: No specific EOY skill, but relates to book selection (3ME1) and library catalog (3ME3). Grade 4: Locates material in library catalog and on the shelves by call number

Tools and Resources

- SMART Board equipment with brief matching activity and SMART **Call Number Prefix Form** (p. 94)
- If a SMART Board is not available, prepare a **Sections of the Library Chart** (p. 94) with the call number prefixes for the sections of the library, and another with a brief explanation of the contents of each section. This may be done on an easel, overhead transparency, or with Power-Point or another presentation tool.
- Envelopes with a set of call number prefixes, one set per student: **Call Number Prefix Form** (p. 94)
- Pile of books from each section (E, F, ER, B, R, and non-fiction)
- Computer lab ready with link to Photopeach slide show and quiz: http://photopeach.com/album/7u9fkp
- **Orientation Assessment** (p. 96)
- **Learning Style Feedback** (p. 96)

> *Note*: This is a lesson with activities for use at the start of the school year. Focusing on the "Sections of the Library," this lesson is a precursor to call number order. Its purpose is to review the sections of the library, articulate the basic description of the books in each section, and have the students visit each section. The activities may be used as a menu of choices to be done either sequentially or as a "circuit" of simultaneous activities that students may independently route through, sampling different learning styles and experiences.

Anticipatory Set

At the start of the school year, it is a good idea to get reacquainted with all the sections of the library. Lead a brief discussion of E, F, ER, B, R, and nonfiction. Write each call number prefix on an easel or transparency, or use a SMART Board. Have students point to the sections. Look at the chart on the SMART Board. (Slide 3 of the "Call Number Prefix Orientation" activity) to facilitate the discussion of the description of each kind of book. Use the window-shade feature to reveal and discuss one at a time.

Play the *Library 6 Sections Game*: Remind the class of the six main sections of the library, as shown in the **Sections of the Library Chart** (p. 94). Select one student to be the "caller." The caller will sit (usually off in a corner) with his or her eyes closed so he or she cannot see the rest of the class. The rest of the class will then have five seconds to pick one of the sections of the library and stand in that section. The librarian will count down from five to let everyone know how much time

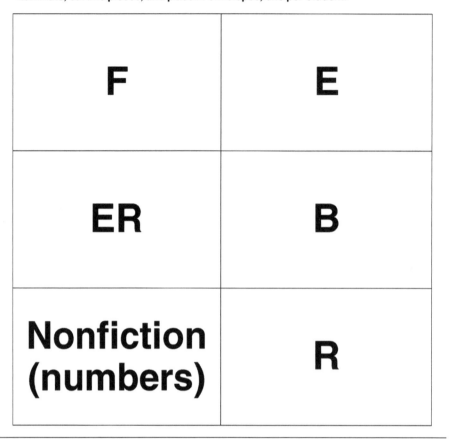

Call Number Prefixes

Laminate, cut into pieces, and place in envelopes, one per student.

F	E
ER	B
Nonfiction (numbers)	R

Figure 10.3. Call Number Prefix Form

Sections of the Library

Call Number	Section of the Library
E	Everybody Books
ER	Easy Readers
F	Fiction
numbers	Nonfiction
B	Biography
R	Reference

Figure 10.4. Sections of the Library Chart

they have. Once the librarian reaches zero, he or she will announce "freeze" (the class must remain in the section they are in) and this time the caller will call out one section. The students who are in that section must sit down at their tables. Then the librarian will restart the countdown and repeat the cycle until there is one student left. The last student wins, and can either be the next caller or pick someone to be the next caller.

Objectives

Students will:

- Match call number prefix to the sections of the library.
- Briefly describe the kind of book in each section.
- Visit all the sections of the library.

Input/Modeling/Checking for Understanding

The following list of activities will provide students with varied experiences. This offers differentiation for different learner profiles/styles. Use sequentially or as an independent student circuit:

- Match call number prefix ("top line of call number") to the section of the library (SMART Board activity).
- Match the type of book (fiction, everybody, etc.) to its description (SMART Board activity).
- Using a pile of books on a table, pairs of students explain/define the different kinds of books (what is nonfiction/Dewey, fiction, everybody, biography, reference, easy reader).
- Complete the online (Photopeach-created) slide show/quiz on "Sections of the Library."
- Pull a call number prefix from the envelope; walk to that section of the library.

Guided Practice/Independent Practice

Students move through the above activities with increasing independence.

Assessment

- Use a brief half-sheet **Orientation Assessment** (p. 96) as either a formative or summative assessment. The librarian tapes a colored sheet to a shelf in each section with a number on it. Students take the half-sheet assessment to each section, and write the name of the section next to the number.
- **Learning Style Feedback** (p. 96): Prepare a 12" × 18" paper mat as shown in Figure 10.6. Invite students to place two tokens on "learned best" and "hard." This will provide the librarian with information on how students prefer to practice skills.

Orientation Assessment

Name: _____

Homeroom: _____

Go to each section of the library. There is a colored paper taped to the shelf with a number in each section.

Next to each number on this sheet, write the section of the library you visited (Everybody, Fiction, Nonfiction, Biography, Easy Reader, Reference).

Section number	Write the section of the library:
1	
2	
3	
4	
5	
6	

Figure 10.5. Orientation Assessment

Learning Style Feedback

	I learned best with	This was hard
SMART Board matching		
Explain the pile of books to a partner		
Computer slide show and quiz		
Call number in the envelope		
Six sections game		

Figure 10.6. Learning Style Feedback

Lesson
Book Care
Grades K–1
(Lesson developed by Cindy Kunde)

Standard	Benchmark	Objective	EOY Skill
Standard 3: Seeks multiple perspectives, shares information and ideas with others, and uses information and resources ethically.	Uses library materials responsibly.	Demonstrates proper care of library materials. Returns library materials on time.	Uses library materials and equipment responsibly.

Tools and Resources

- Craig, Paula M. *Mr. Wiggle's Book*. Grand Rapids, MI: Instructional Fair, 2000.
- Perry, John. *The Book That Eats People*. Berkeley: Tricycle Press, 2009.
- Schoenherr, Ian. *Read It, Don't Eat It!* New York: Greenwillow Books, 2009.
- Several damaged library books
- Two paper sacks—one labeled "Yes, Yes, Always" and one labeled "No, No, Never"
- One backpack filled with these objects—baby bottle, package of Kleenex, water bottle, box of crayons or pencils, bookmark, candy bar, soap, stuffed animal dog, umbrella

> Note: The above titles and other books about book care and library use can be found in the **Book Care and Library Use Bibliography**—see p. 98.

Anticipatory Set

Display several damaged library books for students to see as they come in to class. Ask them what's wrong with these books and what do they think happened to them. Ask students what they know about how to take care of books, especially books from a library. Make a list of their suggestions on the whiteboard.

Objectives

Students will:

- Demonstrate proper care of library materials.

Input/Modeling/Checking for Understanding

Read a picture book about book care. (Three suggestions are listed in the Tools and Resources section of this lesson plan.) Ask students to share new book care suggestions from this book; add them to the list on the whiteboard.

Check for understanding by doing the "Yes, Yes, Always/No, No, Never" activity. Set the two paper sacks on chairs, one on each side of the group. (Make sure that students can easily get to them.) Take the objects out of the backpack one by one, in each case asking students if this is something that should be used with or around books. (Some of the objects like the baby bottle and the stuffed dog may need to be explained; they represent a real baby and a real dog.) Students answer by nodding their heads and saying "Yes, yes, always" or shaking their heads and saying "No, no, never." For each object, ask a student who is signaling appropriately to put the object in the correct sack and explain why he or she chose that sack. Finish the activity by asking the students in which bag the empty backpack should be placed.

Assessment

- Assess student understanding of book care at subsequent classes by showing or naming the objects from the backpack, asking students to agree (thumbs up) or disagree (thumbs down) that those objects should be used with books. The list of book care suggestions made at the beginning of the lesson (with some suggestions changed to false statements) can also be used as an assessment in the same way.
- Students' proper care of library materials can also be assessed by reviewing students' checkout records—number and frequency of overdue materials, lost and/or damaged books, etc.

Book Care and Library Use Bibliography
Kindergarten and First Grade

Bertram, Debbie, and Susan Bloom. *The Best Book to Read.* New York: Random House, 2008.

Bottner, Barbara. *Miss Brooks Loves Books! (and I Don't).* New York: Alfred A. Knopf, 2010.

Bruss, Deborah. *Book! Book! Book!* New York: Arthur A. Levine Books, 2001.

Child, Lauren. *But Excuse Me That Is My Book.* New York: Dial Books for Young Readers, 2005.

Child, Lauren. *Who's Afraid of the Big Bad Book?* New York: Hyperion Books for Children, 2002.

Cousins, Lucy. *Maisy Goes to the Library.* Cambridge, MA: Candlewick Press, 2005.

Craig, Paula M. *Mr. Wiggle's Book.* Grand Rapids, MI: Instructional Fair, 2000.

Ernst, Lisa Campbell. *Stella Louella's Runaway Book.* New York: Simon & Schuster Books for Young Readers, 1998.

Faulkner, Keith. *The Monster Who Loved Books.* New York: Orchard Books, 2002. (pop-up pages)

Gorman, Jacqueline Laks. *The Library.* Milwaukee, WI: Weekly Reader Early Learning Library, 2005.

Harris, Robie. *Maybe a Bear Ate It!* New York: Scholastic, 2008.

Jeffers, Oliver. *The Incredible Book Eating Boy.* New York: Philomel Books, 2006.

Klein, Adria K. *Max Goes to the Library.* Minneapolis, MN: Picture Window Books, 2006.

Knudsen, Michelle. *Library Lion.* Cambridge, MA: Candlewick Press, 2006.

Lies, Brian. *Bats at the Library.* Boston: Houghton Mifflin, 2008.

Lock, Deborah. *A Trip to the Library.* New York: DK, 2004.

Miller, Pat. *We're Going on a Book Hunt.* Fort Atkinson, WI: Upstart Books, 2008.

Perry, John. *The Book That Eats People.* Berkeley: Tricycle Press, 2009.

Rey, Margret and H. A. *Curious George Visits the Library.* Boston: Houghton Mifflin, 2003.

Ruurs, Margriet. *My Librarian Is a Camel: How Books Are Brought to Children Around the World.* Honesdale, PA: Boyds Mills, 2005.

Schoenherr, Ian. *Read It, Don't Eat It!* New York: Greenwillow Books, 2009.

Sierra, Judy. *Wild About Books.* New York: Knopf, 2004.

Stadler, Alexander. *Beverly Billingsley Borrows a Book.* Orlando, FL: Harcourt, 2002.

Lesson
Book Parts
Grades 1–2
(Lesson developed by Sarah Latcham)

Standard	Benchmark	Objective	EOY Skill
Standard 2: Uses inquiry and critical thinking skills to acquire, analyze and evaluate, use, and create information.	Recognizes parts of a book.	Identifies title and call number. Identifies author and illustrator.	Identifies parts of a book: cover, spine, title pages, title, and call number. Locates author and illustrator on title page.

Tools and Resources
- Arnold, Tedd. *Parts*. New York: Dial Books for Young Readers, 1997.
- PowerPoint of book parts; go to http://reading.pppst.com/partsofabook.html (third one down on the list)
- **Cover and Spine Worksheet** (p. 100)
- **Book Parts Assessment** (p. 101)

Anticipatory Set
Read *Parts* by Tedd Arnold. (Make the connection from body parts to book parts by relating to the boy who thinks that all of his parts are falling apart.)

Objectives
Students will:

- Be able to identify/define and locate parts of a book.

Input/Modeling/Checking for Understanding
Identify the parts of a book using the book just read or another book as a model. The PowerPoint of book parts could also be used here or as a review of the material. Giving the students a clue or action helps them remember the parts.

- *Cover*—Knock on the cover: "The hard outside part of the book is called…"
- *Spine*—Touch your spine: "We have one, too! The skinny back of the book is called…"
- *Title page*—Put up three fingers: "The title page needs three pieces of information: the title, author/illustrator, and publisher."
- *Call number*—Put your hand over your eyes like you are searching for something: "The address of the book is the…"
- *Book Jacket*—Pretend to put on a jacket: "We wear these when we go outside in the fall and spring."
- *Flaps*—Flap your arms like wings: "The front flap tells us about the book; the back flap tells us about the author and illustrator."
- *Verso*—Squint because the print is so small: "This is the librarian information you may need to use when you are older."
- *Title*—Make a "T" with your fingers: "The name of the book is…"

- *Author*—Pretend to write with your fingers: "The person who writes the words is . . ."
- *Illustrator*—Pretend to draw with your fingers: "The person who draws the pictures is . . ."

Guided Practice/Independent Practice

Review parts of a book at any storytime. Use the PowerPoint of book parts (see p. 101) on a SMART Board for small groups of students to review independently or as a whole class presentation. Students can also create their own "book" by writing the title, call number, and author/illustrator on the **Cover and Spine Worksheet** (below). This could be their own title, name, and call number based on their name or it could be created based on the author or books used during the lesson.

> *Note:* A follow-up lesson providing practice in labeling parts of the book is available on the website.

Assessment

- To assess students, use the **Book Parts Assessment** (p. 101) or provide each student with a book and removable labels of the book parts to stick on.

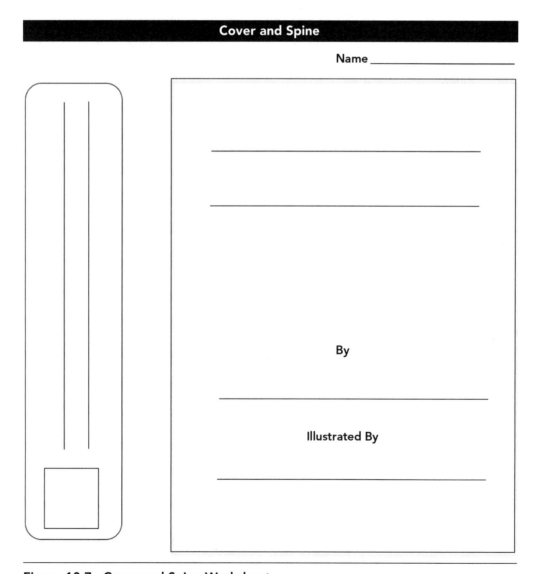

Figure 10.7. Cover and Spine Worksheet

Book Parts Assessment

Name _____

1. The person who writes the book is called the:
   - Illustrator
   - Banker
   - Author
   - Teacher

2. The person who draws the pictures for the book is called the:
   - Banker
   - Illustrator
   - Author
   - Teacher

3. The name of the book or story is called the:
   - Call Number
   - Barcode
   - Title
   - Author

4. The page inside the book that lists the title, author, illustrator, and publisher of the book is the:
   - End pages
   - Barcode
   - Call Number
   - Title Page

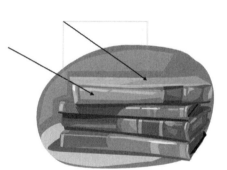

5. Label a **spine** on this picture of books:

6. Label a **cover** on this picture of books:

7. Using the picture below, circle the author's name.

8. Using the picture below, underline the illustrator's name.

9. Using the picture below, draw a star by the title.

Goodnight Moon
By Margaret Wise Brown
Illustrated by Clement Hurd
HarperCollinsPublishers

Figure 10.8. Book Parts Assessment

BOOK SELECTION

Lesson
Selecting a Just Right Book
Grades 1–2
(Lesson developed by Ann Holton, Lynn Myers, and Cindy Kunde)

Standard	*Benchmark*	*Objective*	*EOY Skill*
Standard 1. Reads, views, and listens widely both for information and in pursuit of personal interests.	Selects a Just Right book independently for personal reading.	Applies guidelines for choosing a Just Right book during library checkout.	Selects books that match interests and reading level.

Tools and Resources
- Miller, Pat. *We're Going on a Book Hunt*. Fort Atkinson, WI: Upstart Books, 2008.
- "Choosing a Just Right Book" poster and **Choosing a Just Right Book Bookmark** (p. 106) (one bookmark for each student)
- Four books—two easy reader, one fiction, one nonfiction
- Easy reader and fiction books for students to select—20 titles for each, various levels of difficulty

curriculum/lessons/BookSelection/
Posters/JustRightBookPoster.pdf
- **Choosing a Just Right Book Bookmark** (p. 106) and **Choosing a Book That I Pick Chart** (p. 106)
- **Book Selection Rubrics** (p. 104)

Anticipatory Set
Read *We're Going on a Book Hunt* using the hand motions suggested in the book.

Ask students what it means if something is "just right" or a "good fit." What does it mean if a *book* is "just right" or a "good fit"? How do you find a Just Right book?

Tell students that ideas about books come from many sources—friends, teachers, librarians, and the library catalog. All are good ways to get ideas for books. No matter how you get suggestions for reading, the key is for each of you to learn to choose the right book for you.

For younger students, you may also want to use *We're Going on a Book Hunt* to review the three ways to "read" a book described in the Book Selection lesson for Kindergarten and First Grade—reading the pictures, reading the words, and retelling a book you read before. Remind students that the "Choosing a Just Right Book" process is used for when you are reading the words.

Objectives
Students will:

- Be able to apply the guidelines for choosing a Just Right book to select a book for personal reading.

Input/Modeling/Checking for Understanding
Using the "I Pick Chart" (p. 106) and the "Just Right Book Bookmark" (p. 106) read the four steps, adding explanatory comments. Explain to students that there are two categories of decisions to make when you are choosing a book:

1. Does the book interest you? You can tell by examining the external features of the book such as the cover, blurb, illustrations, and number of pages.
2. Can you read the book? You can tell this by reading a bit of the book, performing the five-finger test, and asking questions about the language and the story.

Demonstrate the four steps shown on the bookmark and poster using two books of different reading levels. Take students through the entire process of deciding about a book by thinking out loud through the process while they observe. Model the five-finger test with each book. Also explain to students that it is okay to turn down a suggestion of a book. You might say, "I don't really like mysteries," or "I prefer books with lots of conversations," or "I like more illustrations."

If students are learning about "good fit" books in their classroom, show and explain the Just Right/Good Fit chart to demonstrate how these two methods can be used at the same time.

Check for understanding with the following true/false questions by asking students to signal thumbs up or down.

1. The first thing I think about is, "Does this book seem like something that I'd like to read?"
2. If I miss half the words on the first page, it doesn't matter. I still can check the book out.
3. Books that are "just right" are books my friend wants me to read.
4. In choosing a book, I should be interested enough to want to read the whole book.
5. Just Right books are those I can read that interest me and ones I want to read the whole way through.
6. It's okay to turn down somebody's suggestion of a book for me to read.

Another way to check for understanding would be to ask students how they would decide if a book is "just right" and list their ideas on the whiteboard.

Guided Practice/Independent Practice

Hand out the "Just Right Book Bookmarks" (p. 106); read through the one-word name of each step. Divide the students in pairs. (Try to pair beginning readers with stronger readers.) Each student selects a book from those laid out on the tables (easy readers on one table, fiction on another table). Show sample books from each table and guide students to the appropriate table for selection. Each student in the pair will go through the four steps of the process to decide if the book is "just right" with the other student assisting (listening to his or her partner read aloud, counting the words he or she doesn't know, etc.). If necessary, students should go back to the tables and select another book if their initial selection is not "just right." When the students in each pair have completed the process and each has a Just Right book, they should quietly read these books until the end of class.

The above guided practice in pairs can be followed with this independent practice activity:

- Students will select a Just Right book from the Easy Reader or Fiction section of the shelves. They will find a spot alone to go through the four steps. The students will go back to the shelves to select another book if needed. The process is completed when they find a Just Right book. The librarian will check with students while they are going through the process to monitor their understanding and provide assistance. When finished with the process, the students will read their selected books until the end of class.

Assessment

- Observe students choosing books on several occasions and record observations based upon the **Book Selection Rubrics** (p. 104). This is an ongoing process, so a student may be a novice early in the year but should proceed to proficiency with ongoing guidance and reteaching.

Book Selection Rubrics

1st–3rd Grades

Consistently	Most of the time	With support
Chooses books that are "just right" using four–step guide	Likes to have help to choose a book	Does not like to choose books or needs help
Recognizes when books are challenging	Chooses easy or familiar books	Chooses books that are too easy or too difficult

4th–6th Grades

Consistently	Most of the time	With support
Chooses books that are "just right" using four–step guide	Likes to have help to choose a book	Does not like to choose books or needs help
Recognizes when books are challenging	Chooses easy or familiar books	Chooses books that are too easy or too difficult
Reads a wide variety of authors and types of literature	Reads a somewhat varied selection of authors and types of literature	Chooses easy or familiar books

Figure 10.9. Book Selection Rubrics

Other Book Selection Assessment Options
- Use one of the options below to get an idea of a student's current reading level:
  1. Get the student's most recent DRA level from his or her classroom teacher.
  2. Ask the classroom teacher to quickly assess the student's reading abilities as Above Grade Level, At Grade Level, or Below Grade Level.
- Then use one of the activities listed below to determine if students are selecting books that are close to their reading levels:
  1. Review students' checkout history in Destiny (must be logged in at administrative level).
  2. Make a box of approximately 15 books of various reading levels for each table group. (Use the **Book Reading Levels Chart**, p. 105, to assist in selecting books of a variety of reading levels.) Students select books from the box at their table to use in completing the **Choosing a Just Right Book Activity Chart** (p. 107).
  3. Meet individually with students identified as reading below grade level and follow this process:
     - Observe the students as they go through the process of selecting a Just Right book.
     - Conference with the students, asking them to talk about the process and to read the book to see if it is actually "just right."
     - Complete a rubric from the **Book Selection Rubrics** (above) using today's observations and observations at checkout times throughout the school year.
  4. During a library class period, ask each student to select a book from the shelves that is a Just Right book at the current time. Ask each student to label the selected book with his or her name. Use Destiny and/or Follett's Titlewave to identify the reading grade level of each selected book. Compare this level to the student's identified reading level.

Grade	Grade Equivalent	Basal	Reading Recovery	Fountas & Pinnell	Rigby Literacy	DRA	Lexile
K	K	Readiness	— 1 2	— A B	K: 1 K: 2 K: 3,4	A — 2	
		PP1	3–4	C	Gr.1: 5	3	
1	1.0	PP2	5–6	D	Gr.1: 6	4	
	1.1	PP3	7–8	E	Gr.1: 7	6–8	
	1.2	Primer	9–10	F	Gr.1: 8	10	
	1.3		11–12	G	Gr.1: 9	12	
	1.4	1	13–14	H	Gr.1:10	14	
	1.5–1.9		15–16	I	Gr.1: 11	16	200–299
2	2.0–2.2	2	17–18	J	Gr. 2: 12	18	300–349
	2.3–2.4		19	K	Gr. 2: 13	20	350–399
	2.5–2.7			L	Gr.2: 14–15	24	400–449
	2.8–2.9		20	M	Gr.2: 16–17	28	450–499
3	3.0–3.3	3	22	N	Gr.3: 18	30	500–574
	3.4–3.6			O	Gr.3: 19	34	575–649
	3.7–3.9		24	P	Gr.3: 20	38	650–699
4	4.0–4.4	4	26	Q		40.1	700–749
	4.5–4.9			R		40.2	750–799
5	5.0–5.4	4/5	28	S		44.1	800–849
	5.5–5.9			T		44.2	850–899
6	6.0–6.4	5/6	30	U		50	900–949
	6.5–6.9			V		60.1	950–999
7	7.0–7.4	6/7	32	W		60.2	1000–1041
	7.5–7.9			X		60.3	1050–1099
8	8.0–8.4	8	34	Y		60.4	1100–1149
	8.5–8.9			Z		60.5	1150–1199
9							
10							
11							
12							

Table title: **Book Reading Levels**

Figure 10.10. Book Reading Levels Chart

Choosing a Just Right Book

Choosing a
**Just Right
Book**

Find

Read

5 Finger Rule

Ask

Choose

If **YES**...
Read it
If **No**...
Start over
or get help

Figure 10.11. Choosing a Just
Right Book Bookmark

Choosing a Book That I Pick

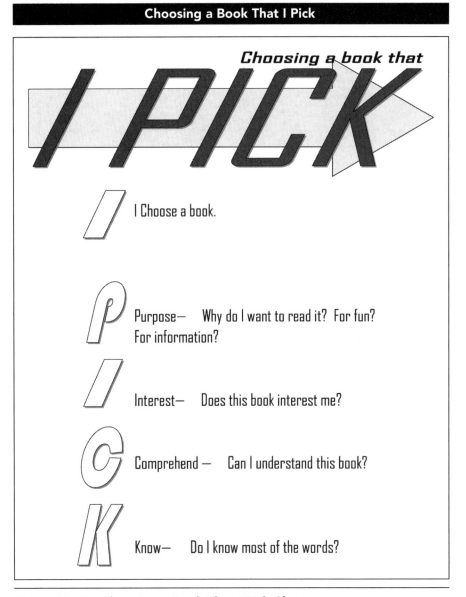

Choosing a book that

I PICK

I — I Choose a book.

P — Purpose— Why do I want to read it? For fun?
For information?

I — Interest— Does this book interest me?

C — Comprehend — Can I understand this book?

K — Know— Do I know most of the words?

Figure 10.12. Choosing a Book That I Pick Chart

Choosing a Just Right Book Activity

Name _____   Class _____

Title of Book	Look at the size of print, space, # of pages. MY BEST GUESS	Read the summary on the jacket or back cover.	5 Finger Rule (Read one full page—more than five unknown words?)	What kind of book is this for me?
1.	Too hard ___ Just right ___ Too easy ___	I'd like it ___ Maybe ___ Not for me ___	How many fingers? 0 ___ 1 ___ 2 ___ 3 ___ 4 ___ 5 ___ Too hard ___	___ Too easy/ vacation book ___ Just right ___ Right level, not interesting ___ Too hard
2.	Too hard ___ Just right ___ Too easy ___	I'd like it ___ Maybe ___ Not for me ___	How many fingers? 0 ___ 1 ___ 2 ___ 3 ___ 4 ___ 5 ___ Too hard ___	___ Too easy/ vacation book ___ Just right ___ Right level, not interesting ___ Too hard
3.	Too hard ___ Just right ___ Too easy ___	I'd like it ___ Maybe ___ Not for me ___	How many fingers? 0 ___ 1 ___ 2 ___ 3 ___ 4 ___ 5 ___ Too hard ___	___ Too easy/ vacation book ___ Just right ___ Right level, not interesting ___ Too hard
4.	Too hard ___ Just right ___ Too easy ___	I'd like it ___ Maybe ___ Not for me ___	How many fingers? 0 ___ 1 ___ 2 ___ 3 ___ 4 ___ 5 ___ Too hard ___	___ Too easy/ vacation book ___ Just right ___ Right level, not interesting ___ Too hard
5.	Too hard ___ Just right ___ Too easy ___	I'd like it ___ Maybe ___ Not for me ___	How many fingers? 0 ___ 1 ___ 2 ___ 3 ___ 4 ___ 5 ___ Too hard ___	___ Too easy/ vacation book ___ Just right ___ Right level, not interesting ___ Too hard

Figure 10.13. Choosing a Just Right Book Activity Chart

TEXT STRUCTURE/LITERARY ELEMENTS

Lesson
Using the Table of Contents in a Nonfiction Book to Locate Information
Grades 3–4
(Lesson developed by Anne Marie Kraus)

Standard	*Benchmark*	*Objective*	*EOY Skill*
Standard 2: Uses inquiry and critical thinking skills to acquire, analyze and evaluate, use, and create information.	Uses nonfiction as a source of information.	Uses table of contents and glossary to locate information in text with support.	No specific EOY skill.

Tools and Resources
- Document camera and photocopy or transparency of a table of contents from a selected nonfiction book.
- Multiple copies of nonfiction books (from a series with similar uniform layout).

Anticipatory Set
Ask the students, "What kind of book is this?" (Hold up *Bobcats*, by Caroline Arnold, or another animal book with good text features.) "How can you tell?" (Do not look just at the cover; check the call number.) "Lots of students check out books about animals—why would you want to read a book like this? You might read this book just for fun, or you might read it because you need to know something specific, like, how can you tell if the animal is a bobcat, or some other kind of cat? Do you know how you can zero in on the information you want, without reading the entire book? What would help you find the right place in the book?" (Show the table of contents in the book. Discuss *front* of book.)

Objectives
Students will:

- Identify the table of contents in a nonfiction book, and will use it to locate specific information.

Input/Modeling/Checking for Understanding
Say to the students, "Look at this transparency on the screen. This is the table of contents from this book. Let's look at the chapters (read aloud). What are the numbers on the right side for?

"Now, let's practice using this table of contents. We'll start with really easy questions. What part of the book would you go to, to find out about: Bobcats' tails? What do they hunt? What are the dangers to a bobcat? What PAGE would you turn to...? What CHAPTER would you read?

"Okay, that was too easy. Now we will notch it up."

Guided Practice
Instruct the students to pass around the papers on the tables; note that this is the same table of contents. Say, "This time I want you to be more thoughtful, read your table of contents, listen to the question, and then raise hands to give the answer. With your other hand, point to the chapter you choose for your answer."

- "What chapter would you read to find out what a bobcat eats?" (Discuss inference: Does it say "eat" anywhere? No, you have to read and infer.) Rephrase: "What PAGE...?"
- "What page would you read to find a description of a bobcat's appearance? What chapter?" (Discuss inference.)
- "What chapter would you read to find the habitat of a bobcat? Page?"
- "What chapter would tell you if the bobcat has any predators? Page?"
- "What page would you turn to, to find out how bobcats have their babies? Chapter?"

Independent Practice

Say to the students, "Now, please put your papers on a pile in the middle of the table. In a moment, you will be looking at these books about different countries of the world. We will be passing them around; you don't get to pick your favorite country at the moment, but you may do so during your next book checkout. The first thing you will do is flip through for about ten seconds, and then locate the table of contents. Then wait for instructions."

- "Now, do you see a chapter that tells about schools in that country? Turn to that part of the book."
- "Okay, back to the table of contents. Now you may pick any chapter, and make up a question that you would have to answer. Now turn to that chapter in the book. What question did you make up?"
- Repeat as time allows.

Assessment

- Ask, "What did you learn today? Where is the table of contents? Why would you use it?"
- Assessment today is informal. Walking around to tables, to see the chapter students are pointing to, tells if they are correctly using the table of contents (and reading and inferring).

Lesson
Using Nonfiction Book Elements to Locate Information
Grades 3–4
(Lesson developed by Michelle Morey)

Standard	*Benchmark*	*Objective*	*EOY Skill*
Standard 2. Uses inquiry and critical thinking skills to acquire, analyze and evaluate, use, and create information.	Uses nonfiction as a source of information. Begins to extract information from text based on need.	Uses table of contents and glossary to locate information in text with support (ITBS). Identifies appropriate reference source (dictionary, atlas, encyclopedia) based on information need with support (ITBS).	Demonstrates increasing skills in extracting information from print resources.

Tools and Resources
- SMART Notebook file on nonfiction book parts and reference sources; on the website.

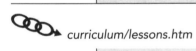

curriculum/lessons.htm

Note: This file is available on the website, but a PowerPoint or similar presentation could easily be created by using scanned images of a table of contents, index, and glossary.

- Enough nonfiction animal books containing table of contents, glossary, and index for students to work in pairs with one book per pair
- Pencils
- A large, thick, nonfiction book to hold up as an example
- **Nonfiction Elements Assessment** (p. 111)

Anticipatory Set
Remind the students that they will be taking the Iowa Tests of Basic Skills (ITBS) exam this fall and there will be a section covering reference sources. Nonfiction books generally all have certain elements that help us to find information in the book. Show them the thick nonfiction book and ask them how they would feel if they knew they had to read the entire book to find one piece of information. The tools inside a nonfiction book save us a lot of work because they can help us get right to the information we need the most.

Objectives
Students will:

- Identify the purpose of a table of contents, index, and glossary.
- Locate these elements in a nonfiction book.
- Use them to answer basic questions about the contents.

Input/Modeling/Checking for Understanding
Go through the SMART Notebook lesson on nonfiction elements. Call on students randomly to choose the correct answer and drag it into the question box. Use the answer slides to look at the nonfiction elements and ask further questions, such as:

- In what chapter could we learn something about where a rabbit lives?
- What order is the table of contents in? Alphabetical? Subject? Page?
- On what pages in the index can you find information about the rhinoceros iguana?
- Use the glossary to define the term "genus."

Be sure to point out the answer choices that say "none of the above" and "all of the above." This is a good time to review what these mean since they appear on the ITBS test.

Guided Practice/Independent Practice

Send partners to the tables with a worksheet and nonfiction book. The rest of the time the students will work together to answer the questions using their books. Students who finish early can use the back of their sheets to write down interesting facts about their animals.

Assessment

- Use the sheets to assess how well students are doing finding the information within a nonfiction book.
- Reteach concepts that the students are weak on and report your findings to the classroom teacher.
- This lesson would also be good done in conjunction with classroom animal reports.

Nonfiction Elements Assessment

Names_____

Use your nonfiction book to find the following information:

1. **One of the chapters in my book is called:**

_____

_____

2. **Write one word from the glossary and its meaning:**

_____

_____

3. **Write down three topics in the index and the page numbers we can find them on:**

   1.

   2.

   3.

Bonus: Tell me an interesting fact you found in your book:

Figure 10.14. Nonfiction Elements Assessment

Lesson
Identifying Elements of Setting
Grades 3–6
(Lesson developed by **Kristi Harper and Connie McCain**)

Standard	Benchmark	Objective	EOY Skill
Standard 1. Reads, views, and listens widely both for information and in pursuit of personal interests.	Identifies literary elements of character, plot, and setting.	Identifies elements of character, plot, and setting independently through graphic organizers or other reading activities.	N/A

Note: For each Literary Element and Type of Literature, a description of the area and a bibliography of relevant titles are presented at the end of the lesson to assist in planning instruction. A selection of books in addition to those in the printed lists is also located on the website, as is an Excel spreadsheet that can be sorted by literary type, element, grade level, author, and a number of other ways.

curriculum/lit/LComponent1.htm
curriculum/lit/LComponent2.htm
bibliographies.htm

Tools and Resources
- Wiviott, Meg. *Benno and the Night of Broken Glass.* Minneapolis: Kar-Ben Publishing, 2010.
- **Literary Element—Setting** (p. 113)
- **Books with a Strong Element of Setting** (p. 114)

Anticipatory Set
Show students two photos of the same place with obvious differences (for example, search Google images for a picture of the White House covered with snow and a similar picture of the White House on a summer day). Ask the students how these pictures are the same or different. Remind students that these two images are different because they are shown in different seasons. Ask what other things they can think of that would make a place change over time (storm damage, aging buildings, war, etc.).

Objectives
Students will:
- Identify and compare changes in the setting of an amicable multicultural neighborhood at the beginning of *Benno and the Night of Broken Glass* to the harsh, socially isolated setting after the Nazi influence begins.

Input/Modeling/Checking for Understanding
1. Say to the students, "The setting helps the reader understand the time and place of the story. There are several things the setting can do for a story.
   - The setting may help determine the mood for the story.
   - The setting may be an antagonist (barrier) to the character, as in stories where the environment is harsh and the character has to fight to survive.
   - The setting may give the reader background about a time in history.

Literary Element—Setting

The setting of a story—its location in time and place—helps readers share what the characters see, smell, hear, and touch, as well as makes the characters' values, actions, and conflicts more understandable. Whether a story takes place in the past, present, or future, its overall credibility may depend on how well the plot, characterizations, and setting support one another. (Norton, Donna E. 1995. *Through the Eyes of a Child: An Introduction to Children's Literature*. New York: Prentice Hall.)

Different types of literature have their own requirements as far as setting is concerned. When a story is set in an identifiable historical period or geographical location, details should be accurate. Plot and characters also should be consistent with what actually occurred or could have occurred at that time and place. Some settings are so well-known that just a few words place readers immediately in the expected location, e.g., "Once upon a time." In some books, setting is such an important part of the story that the characters and plot cannot be developed without understanding the time and place. In other stories the setting only serves as a backdrop.

The setting helps the reader understand the time and place of the story. There are several things the setting can do for a story:

- The setting may help determine the mood for the story. In *Benno and the Night of Broken Glass* by Meg Wiviott (2010), Benno the cat observes his World War II–era neighborhood as it shifts from an amicable, multicultural community to a hateful, violent atmosphere due to the Nazi presence. Other strong examples of setting as mood include *Cloud Tea Monkeys* by Mal Peet and Elspeth Graham (2010) and *Steel Town* by Jonah Winter (2008).
- The setting may be an antagonist (barrier) to the character, as in stories where the environment is harsh and the character has to fight to survive. In *The City of Ember* by Jeanne DuPrau (2003), a community living underground must fight time and the possibility of living in a pitch-black environment when their sole source of electrical power threatens to die out. Other strong examples of setting as antagonist include *Diamond Willow* by Helen Frost (2008) and *Kami and the Yaks* by Andrea Stenn Stryer (2007).
- The setting may give the reader background about a time in history or provide a social context. In *Weedflower* by Cynthia Kadohata (2006), the reader learns of the injustices toward certain American citizens during World War II. The movement of a Japanese-American family and most of their neighbors to an internment camp provides the historical and social context for the story's plot. Other strong examples of setting as historical background include *A Song for Harlem* by Patricia C. McKissack (2007) and the other books in McKissack's Scraps of Time series.
- The setting may be a symbol that represents the author's message to the reader (the story's theme). The setting of *The Curious Garden* by Peter Brown (2009), an abandoned railway that becomes a lush garden, represents the ideal that one person's actions can change the world.

- The setting may be a symbol that represents the author's message to the reader (the story's theme)."

2. Read *Benno and the Night of Broken Glass*, instructing the students to observe the neighborhood at the beginning of the story and watch for changes as the story progresses.

3. Read up to the page where Benno is lying next to the furnace in the basement. Ask the students to describe the neighborhood where Benno lives. (How do people treat each other? How do they treat Benno?)

4. Continue reading the book. Ask students how the neighborhood has changed and why it changed. Ask students for specific examples of how the text and illustrations of the neighborhood changed from the beginning of the book.

Books with a Strong Element of Setting

K–2

Cunnane, Kelly. *For You Are a Kenyan Child*. New York: Atheneum Books for Young Readers, 2006.

Hucke, Johannes, and Muller, Danie. *Pip in the Grand Hotel*. New York: North South, 2009.

Levine, Ellen. *Henry's Freedom Box*. New York: Scholastic Press, 2007.

Manushkin, Fran. *The Shivers in the Fridge*. New York: Dutton Children's Books, 2006.

Stryer, Andrea Stenn. *Kami and the Yaks*. Palo Alto: Bay Otter Press, 2007.

3–4

Bunting, Eve. *Pop's Bridge*. Orlando: Harcourt, 2006.

DiCamillo, Kate. *The Miraculous Journey of Edward Tulane*. Cambridge, MA: Candlewick Press, 2006.

McKissack, Patricia C. *A Song for Harlem*. New York: Viking, 2007.

Winter, Jonah. *Steel Town*. New York: Atheneum Books for Young Readers, 2008.

Wiviott, Meg. *Benno and the Night of Broken Glass*. Minneapolis: Kar-Ben Publishing, 2010.

5–6

Avi. *The Seer of Shadows*. New York: HarperCollins, 2008.

Frost, Helen. *Diamond Willow*. New York: Farrar, Straus and Giroux, 2008.

Kahohata, Cynthia. *Weedflower*. New York: Atheneum Books for Young Readers, 2006.

Park, Linda Sue. *A Long Walk to Water*. New York: Clarion Books, 2010.

Roy, Jennifer. *Yellow Star*. Tarrytown, New York: Marshall Cavendish, 2006.

---

5. This book demonstrates many of the functions that setting can play in a book. As a class, or after dividing the students into small groups, discuss how *Benno and the Night of Broken Glass* demonstrates setting as mood, setting as an antagonist, setting as a source of information about a time in history, and setting as a symbol.

Guided Practice/Independent Practice

Choose another book(s) that has a distinct setting and/or exhibits changes in setting during the story and allow students to do an in-depth study of the setting and how it affects the story.

Allow students to brainstorm what a playground environment is like on a normal school day. Give students (in large or small groups) examples of events that may affect the setting in some way and have them describe what changes might occur. Examples would be a fight breaking out on the playground, a sudden storm sweeping in, a change in the setting from modern day to 100 years ago, etc.

Ask individuals or small groups of students to write an opening paragraph for a story that carefully describes the setting for that story. It may be helpful to read a few examples aloud ahead of time or to give students brief story scenarios if they are unable to generate ideas on their own. Read the students' paragraphs aloud and have the class discuss whether the description was intended to set the mood, provide background information, or if it was intended to be an antagonist or symbol.

Assessment

- Observe student participation in these activities and future discussions of setting.

Lesson
Identifying Elements of Character
Grades K–3
(Lesson developed by Joan DePrenger, Devin Redmond, and Michael Schlitz)

Standard	Benchmark	Objective	EOY Skill
Standard 1. Reads, views, and listens widely both for information and in pursuit of personal interests.	Begins to identify literary elements of character, plot, and setting (Grade 2). Identifies literary elements of character, plot, and setting (Grade 3).	Identifies elements of character, plot, and setting with support through participation in discussion or use of graphic organizers (Grade 2). Identifies elements of character, plot, and setting independently through graphic organizers or other reading activities (Grade 3).	Demonstrates increasing understanding of different types of literature (Grades 2–4).

Note: For each Literary Element and Type of Literature, a description of the area and a bibliography of relevant titles are presented at the end of the lesson to assist in planning instruction. A selection of books in addition to those in the printed lists is also located on the website, as is an Excel spreadsheet that can be sorted by literary type, element, grade level, author, and a number of other ways.

curriculum/lit/LComponent1.htm
curriculum/lit/LComponent2.htm
bibliographies.htm

Tools and Resources
- Picture books with strong character elements
- **Character Graphic Organizer** (p. 118)
- **Literary Element—Character** (p. 116)
- Suggested books; see **Books with a Strong Element of Character** (p. 117)

Anticipatory Set
Say to the students, "Think of the last time you saw a movie, TV show, or book that you really liked. Who were your favorite characters? How can you describe them?"

Objectives
Students will:

- Identify elements of character, plot, and setting with support through participation in discussion or use of graphic organizers.

Input/Modeling/Checking for Understanding
Say to the students, "Today we're going to really think about the characters as I read the story. We're going to think about their appearance, what they say, and how they act. We'll also think about how they respond to other characters in the story."

Read aloud one of the K–3 books and focus on the following:

- Appearance
- Thoughts and conversation
- Actions

Guided Practice/Independent Practice

Complete a **Character Graphic Organizer** (p. 118) using Kidspiration, the SMART Board, or the **Literary Element—Character** handout (below). In small groups students select a book and share their ideas of character focusing on appearance, what they say, and how they act and react.

Assessment

- Completed product or verbal demonstration of character traits.

Literary Element—Character

Character refers to a person, animal, or object in a story. Characters are well developed, believable, and consistent. At the beginning of a story a conflict is presented for the main character to resolve. By the end of a story, a character should change or grow somehow. This could be by learning something new or by growing in understanding of self.

Ways to Know a Character

Appearance
- how the character looks
- how the character dresses

Thoughts and Conversation
- what the character says, thinks, or feels
- what others in the story say or think about the character

Actions
- what the character does
- what the character chooses *not* to do
- what others in the story do to the main character

Good characters are . . .
- believable
- consistent
- multidimensional, that is, not stereotyped
- memorable
- grow or change over time

Readers who want to understand character can ask:
- Are the characters believable? Have you ever felt like this character, or have you known anyone who felt like this character? What about the character seemed real and true?
- Is each character's behavior consistent with what we know about him or her? Does the behavior remain consistent throughout the book? Is the change that occurs in the character reasonable?
- Does the character's behavior show that the character is a unique individual (or is the behavior stereotypical)?
- Do you identify with the character? How would you have reacted if you were the character?
- Does the character change or learn as the story progresses? Does the character reach a new understanding about the situation or about life?
- Is the character memorable? Will you remember this character in a month?

Books with a Strong Element of Character

K–3

Becker, Bonny. *A Visitor for Bear*. Cambridge: Candlewick Press, 2008. Bear's efforts to keep out visitors to his house are undermined by a very persistent mouse.

DiCamillo, Kate. *Bink & Gollie*. Cambridge: Candlewick Press, 2010. Two roller-skating best friends—one tiny, one tall—share three comical adventures involving outrageously bright socks, an impromptu trek to the Andes, and a most unlikely marvelous companion.

Gay, Marie-Louis. *Roslyn Rutabaga and the Biggest Hole on Earth*. Berkeley: Groundwood Books/House of Anansi Press, 2010. Roslyn Rutabaga, a little rabbit with a wild imagination, sets out one day determined to dig the biggest hole on Earth, and meets all sorts of irritating obstacles along the way.

Helakoski, Leslie. *Woolbur*. New York: Harper Collins Publishers, 2008. Woolbur, a young sheep who thinks differently than the others, worries his mother and father with his free-spiritedness, but his grandfather thinks he will be fine.

Long, Loren. *Otis*. New York: Philomel Books, 2009. When a big new yellow tractor arrives, Otis the friendly little tractor is cast away behind the barn, but when trouble occurs, Otis is the only one who can help.

4–6

Kelly, Jacqueline. *The Evolution of Calpurnia Tate*. New York: Henry Holt, 2009. In central Texas in 1899, eleven-year-old Callie Vee Tate is instructed to be a lady by her mother, learns about love from the older three of her six brothers, and studies the natural world with her grandfather, the latter of which leads to an important discovery.

Look, Lenore. *Alvin Ho: Allergic to Girls, School, and Other Scary Things*. New York: Yearling, 2008. A young boy in Concord, Massachusetts, who loves superheroes and comes from a long line of brave Chinese farmer-warriors, wants to make friends, but first he must overcome his fear of everything.

O'Connor, Barbara. *The Small Adventures of Popeye and Elvis*. New York: Farrar, Straus and Giroux, 2009. In Fayette, South Carolina, the highlight of Popeye's summer is learning vocabulary words with his grandmother until a motor home gets stuck nearby and Elvis, the oldest boy living inside, joins Popeye in finding the source of strange boats floating down the creek.

Philbrick, W.R. *The Mostly True Adventures of Homer P. Figg*. New York: Blue Sky Press, 2009. Homer P. Figg escapes from his wretched foster home in Pine Swamp, Maine, and sets out to find his beloved older brother, Harold, who has been illegally sold into the Union Army.

Wiles, Deborah. *Countdown*. New York: Scholastic Press, 2010. As eleven-year-old Franny Chapman deals with drama at home and with her best friend in 1962, she tries to understand the larger problems in the world after President Kennedy announces that Russia is sending nuclear missiles to Cuba.

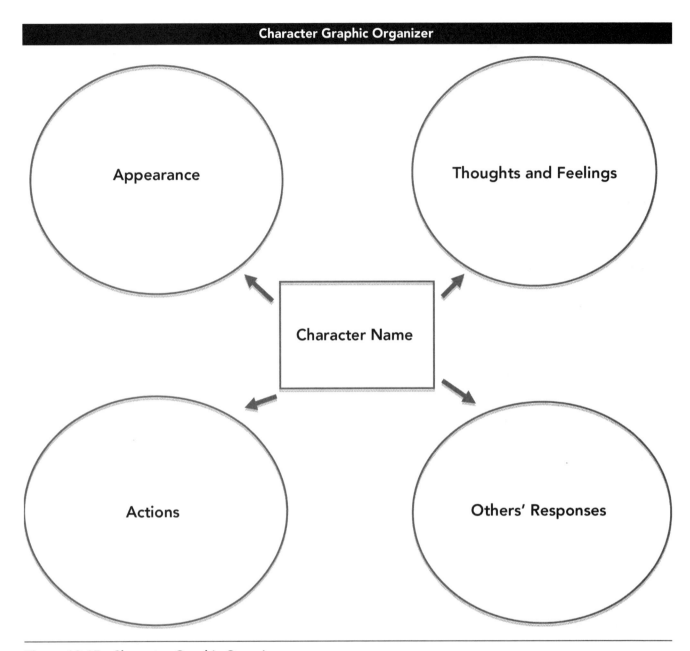

Figure 10.15. Character Graphic Organizer

TYPES OF LITERATURE

Lesson
Poetry
Grade 2
(Lesson developed by Cindy Kunde)

Standard	Benchmark	Objective	EOY Skill
Standard 1: Reads, views, and listens widely both for information and in pursuit of personal interests.	Begins to recognize different types of literature.	Distinguishes between several types of literature such as biography, poetry, and folktales.	Demonstrates increasing understanding of different types of literature.

Note: For each Literary Element and Type of Literature, a description of the area and a bibliography of relevant titles are presented at the end of the lesson to assist in planning instruction. A selection of books in addition to those in the printed lists is also located on the website, as is an Excel spreadsheet that can be sorted by literary type, element, grade level, author, and a number of other ways.

curriculum/lit/LComponent1.htm
curriculum/lit/LComponent2.htm
bibliographies.htm

Tools and Resources

- George, Kristine O'Connell. *Little Dog and Duncan: Poems.* New York: Clarion Books, 2002. (or another collection of poems)
- Greenfield, Eloise. *Honey, I Love.* New York: HarperCollins, 2003. (or another book that contains a single narrative poem)
- Hoberman, Mary Ann. *You Read to Me, I'll Read to You: Very Short Stories to Read Together.* Boston: Little, Brown, 2001. (multiple copies)
- Hoberman, Mary Ann. *You Read to Me, I'll Read to You: Very Short Fairy Tales to Read Together.* New York: Little, Brown, 2004. (multiple copies)
- **Poetry Anchor Chart** (p. 120) (Enlarge or reproduce to post or project.)
- **Types of Literature—Poetry** (p. 121)
- **Terms Associated with Poetry** (p. 121)
- **Types of Poetry** (p. 121)

Anticipatory Set

Read *Honey, I Love* (or another poem). Ask students to share what they noticed about the words. Then ask them what poetry is. Make a list of their responses on the whiteboard. Then read the **Poetry Anchor Chart** (p. 120), adding items as needed. Emphasize rhyme, rhythm, use of descriptive words, especially about the senses, and use of ideas or experiences instead of stories. Show students where poetry books are located on the library shelves.

Objectives

Students will:

- Be able to recognize poetry as writing that describes an idea or experience, often rhymes and has rhythm, uses words that refer to the five senses, has a theme, and is found in the 800s in the Nonfiction section.

Input/Modeling/Checking for Understanding

Show students three different types of poetry books: (1) a single narrative poem, (2) a collection of poems on a common theme, and (3) choral reading poems. Read an example of each of the first two types, asking students to identify any of the characteristics written on the whiteboard that they noticed and identifying those that they missed.

Read the introduction to *You Read to Me, I'll Read to You: Very Short Stories to Read Together*; explain to students how the book works. Also explain what choral reading is—a group reading together with the goal of listening to each other and blending their voices, like when singing a song. Divide students into pairs (stronger reader with weaker reader if possible) and hand a copy of the book to each pair. Read the introduction again with you reading one part and all students reading the other.

Guided Practice/Independent Practice

Read several poems from the book together with students reading both parts. Divide the class into two groups several different ways (by location, by sex, etc.). If necessary, read the poem first with you reading one of the parts so the words are familiar to the students.

This activity may be repeated with multiple copies of *You Read to Me, I'll Read to You: Very Short Fairy Tales to Read Together*.

A more independent practice activity would be to divide students into groups of four—two read one part and two read the other. Each group of four can choose on its own which poems to read from the two books.

Assessment

- Assess students' understanding of the characteristics of poetry by doing an "Agree (thumbs up)/Disagree (thumbs down)" activity at the end of class using true and false statements based on the **Poetry Anchor Chart** (below) and other information from the lesson. The following sentences are sample statements that could be used:
    1. Poems often rhyme.
    2. All poems tell a story.
    3. Descriptions using the five senses are often found in poems.
    4. Poetry books have a number as part of their call number.

After each statement, ask a student who signaled correctly to explain why the statement is true or false.

Poetry Anchor Chart

Poetry

Carefully selected language

Describes an idea
or experience

Often rhymed or rhythmic

Stimulates the senses

Promotes love of language

Theme easily identified

800s

Figure 10.16. Poetry Anchor Chart

- For assessing individual students' understanding of this type of literature, two other versions of the above assessment are:
  1. Read the statements and have students circle T for true or F for false on a previously prepared answer sheet (numbers 1–4 listed with the letters T and F after each number).
  2. Read the statements to a small group of students, marking on a checklist whether students correctly or incorrectly signal for each statement.

Types of Literature—Poetry

(Focus on Theme)

Poetry captures the essence of an idea or experience through carefully selected, distilled language. Poetry creates a rich sensory experience for the ear, mind, and emotions. Poetry is often rhythmic and rhymed. Sometimes the shape of a poem reinforces the idea. A love of poetry is fostered through repeated experiences of listening to, reading, writing, and discussing poetry.

The carefully selected, distilled language of poetry can:

- create a sensory experience
- express emotions
- promote love of language

Terms Associated with Poetry

alliteration: Repetition of initial consonant sounds of words at close intervals; e.g., Peter Piper picked . . . .

figurative language: Comparing two objects or ideas to provide added meaning; e.g., poem comparing cars at a distance moving slowly to tiny, crawling beetles.

imagery: Language that awakens our senses, helping us hear, smell, taste, see, or touch.

onomatopoeia: Words created from natural sounds associated with their actions; e.g., hiss, bang, snap, crack.

rhyme: Refers to words whose ending sounds are alike.

rhythm: Recurrence of specific sounds or stressed and unstressed syllables; rhythm of poetry is often metrical (ordered).

Types of Poetry

ballad: Narrative poem adapted for singing or written to provide the effect of singing when read; action in a ballad is usually heroic or tragic; developed in Europe during the Middle Ages when minstrels and bards (poets) sang legends.

concrete poetry: Shape of poem presents idea of language.

free verse: Doesn't rhyme and has a prose-like rhythm similar to regular speech.

haiku: Ancient Japanese verse form with seventeen syllables; first and third lines contain five syllables, the second line contains seven syllables; haiku first presents a description referring to the natural world followed by a mood or feeling.

limerick: Nonsense, five-line verse; first, second, and fifth lines rhyme and have three distinct beats each; third and fourth lines rhyme and have two distinct beats each; fifth line often presents surprise or humor; Edward Lear popularized the limerick in the 19th century.

lyric poetry: Language provides a musical quality emphasizing sound and imagery; began in ancient Greece.

narrative verse: Relates a specific event or tells a story, typically with chronological, fast action.

Lesson
Fantasy Characters
Grade 2
(Lesson developed by Michelle Morey)

Standard	Benchmark	Objective	EOY Skill
Standard 1: Reads, views, and listens widely both for information and in pursuit of personal interests.	Begins to recognize different types of literature.	Distinguishes between several types of literature such as biography, poetry, and folktales. Identifies elements of character with support through participation in discussion or use of graphic organizers.	Demonstrates increasing understanding of different types of literature.

Note: For each Literary Element and Type of Literature, a description of the area and a bibliography of relevant titles are presented at the end of the lesson to assist in planning instruction. A selection of books in addition to those in the printed lists is also located on the website, as is an Excel spreadsheet that can be sorted by literary type, element, grade level, author, and a number of other ways.

curriculum/lit/LComponent1.htm
curriculum/lit/LComponent2.htm
bibliographies.htm

Tools and Resources

- Ahlberg, Allan. *The Pencil*. Cambridge, MA: Candlewick Press, 2008.
- A variety of well-known fantasy books with animal characters such as *Curious George, Clifford the Big Red Dog*, Mo Willems' Pigeon or Elephant and Piggie series, Falconer's Olivia series, or Dr. Seuss books
- **Fantasy Anchor Chart** (p. 124) (Enlarge or reproduce to post or project.)
- **Types of Literature—Fantasy** (p. 123)
- **Suggested Books for Fantasy Study** (p. 124)

Anticipatory Set

Say to the students, "Today we are going to share a special kind of story called a fantasy. Show them the **Fantasy Anchor Chart** (p. 124) and explain that fantasy is a kind of Everybody or fiction story that could never happen in the real world. Use the example that in fantasy stories the characters don't have to be people. Real animals don't walk, talk, or wear clothes, but many fantasy stories feature animals that do just that. Show students the selection of well-known animal fantasy books one by one and ask them if the characters are like animals they have seen in real life.

Tell the students that characters in fantasy do not even have to be people or animals; they can be anything! Explain that today you will share a story in which the main character is an everyday object—a pencil!

Objectives

Students will:

- Identify fantasy as stories that could never happen in real life and understand that observing characters is one way to recognize fantasy.

Input/Modeling/Checking for Understanding

Read *The Pencil*. As you are reading check for understanding by asking questions such as:

- The pencil drew a boy. Is he like a real boy like some of you? Why or why not?
- Is the brush a character? Is the eraser a character? Have you ever seen a real pencil or eraser do things by itself?
- Do you think the story is funnier because we aren't used to thinking of objects as having personalities?

Guided Practice/Independent Practice

After sharing the book, ask the students to come up with an idea for their own fantasy character. The students could draw their character on paper or using a software program such as Kid Pix. Remind the students that when an author invents characters for fantasy, he or she can really use imagination.

Assessment

- In your next lesson, share another fantasy with an animal or object protagonist. Have each student write on an index card one or two reasons that they know this book is a fantasy.

Types of Literature—Fantasy

Fantasy contains elements not found in the real world and thus helps readers develop imagination and flexible thinking while providing new insights into reality. Fantasy suspends scientific explanation and natural laws.

Some fantasy is pure lighthearted fun. Magic, wit, wordplay, and/or humor are used to reveal the absurdity or comedy in the human condition. Other fantasies consider deeper truths, probing inner journeys and following the path of a hero or heroine. Important themes are explored: the struggle between good and evil, the confrontation of fear, belief in oneself, and faithfulness to others.

The roots of fantasy grow directly from folklore. Modern fantasy builds on and derives strength from traditions established in folktales, fables, ancient myths, and legends from the oral tradition.

Good fantasy tells an interesting story, and has well-developed characters, an engaging plot, and an identifiable theme. Authors manipulate story elements—particularly setting, character, and time—to create an imaginary world. If successful, readers willingly suspend their disbelief.

Common characteristics:
- The author creates a new world or invents extraordinary experiences in the real world.
- The reader enters imaginary realms of possibility.
- It requires suspension of disbelief, relying on internal consistencies of plot, character, and setting.

When evaluating fantasy ask yourself or your students these questions:

- Is the fantasy world believable within the context of the story?
- Is there an original and imaginative concept?
- Can you visualize the story while reading?

Suggested Books for Fantasy Study

K–2

Bergman, Mara. *Yum Yum!: What Fun!* New York: Greenwillow Books, 2009.

Burningham, John. *It's a Secret!* Somerville, MA: Candlewick Press, 2009.

O'Malley, Kevin. *Captain Raptor and the Space Pirates.* New York: Walker, 2007.

Rosoff, Meg. *Jumpy Jack and Googily.* New York: Holt, 2008.

Weisner, David. *Art and Max.* Boston: Clarion Books/Houghton Mifflin Harcourt, 2010.

3–4

Barnett, Mac. *Oh No! Or How My Science Project Destroyed the World.* New York: Hyperion, 2010.

DiCamillo, Kate. *Louise, the Adventures of a Chicken.* New York: Joanna Cotler Books, 2008.

Gerstein, Mordecai. *A Book.* New York: Roaring Brook Press, 2009.

Graham, Bob. *April and Esme, Tooth Fairies.* Somerville, MA: Candlewick Press, 2010.

Manushkin, Fran. *The Shivers in the Fridge.* New York: Dutton Children's Books, 2006.

5–6

Browne, Anthony. *Into the Forest.* Cambridge, MA: Candlewick Press, 2004.

Gaiman, Neil. *The Wolves in the Walls.* New York: HarperCollins, 2003.

Juster, Norton. *The Odious Ogre.* New York: Michael Di Capua Books/Scholastic, 2010.

San Souci, Robert. *The Faithful Friend.* New York: Simon & Schuster Books for Young Readers, 1995.

Tan, Shaun. *The Arrival.* New York: A. A. Levine, 2006.

Fantasy Anchor Chart

Fantasy

**Story that
could NOT happen
in the real world**

**Well-constructed
characters, setting, & plot**

**Creates believable
fantasy world**

**Everybody = E
Fiction = F**

Figure 10.17. Fantasy Anchor Chart

Lesson
Exploring Historical Fiction, Biography, and Nonfiction through Baseball
Grades 3–4
(Lesson developed by Cindy Kunde)

Standard	Benchmark	Objective	EOY Skill
Standard 1: Reads, views, and listens widely both for information and in pursuit of personal interests.	Recognizes different types of literature/genres.	Identifies types of literature/genres through activities such as oral literature, reading promotion programs, booktalks, or reading logs.	Demonstrates increasing understanding of different types of literature.

Note: For each Literary Element and Type of Literature, a description of the area and a bibliography of relevant titles are presented at the end of the lesson to assist in planning instruction. A selection of books in addition to those in the printed lists is also located on the website, as is an Excel spreadsheet that can be sorted by literary type, element, grade level, author, and a number of other ways.

curriculum/lit/LComponent1.htm
curriculum/lit/LComponent2.htm
bibliographies.htm

Tools and Resources

- Dann, Sarah. *Baseball in Action.* New York: Crabtree Publishing Co., 2000.
- Uhlberg, Myron. *Dad, Jackie, and Me.* Atlanta: Peachtree, 2005.
- Winter, Jonah. *Roberto Clemente: Pride of the Pittsburgh Pirates.* New York: Atheneum Books for Young Readers, 2005.
- **Types of Literature—Historical Fiction** (p. 126), **Biography** (p. 127), and **Nonfiction** (p. 129)
- **Historical Fiction** (p. 126), **Biography** (p. 127), and **Nonfiction** (p. 128) **Anchor Charts** (Enlarge or reproduce to post or project.)

Anticipatory Set

Say to the students, "Are any of you following the World Series? Who is your favorite team? Did you know that we have many books about baseball in our library? In fact, there are different kinds of baseball books."

Objectives

Students will:

- Learn the following characteristics of biographies, historical fiction books, and nonfiction books:
  - Biographies—true story about the life of a real person
  - Historical fiction—story that is based on real events from the past but didn't really happen
  - Nonfiction—book that contains facts and information about a topic

Input/Modeling/Checking for Understanding

Class 1

The first type of baseball book is historical fiction. Read the **Historical Fiction Anchor Chart** (p. 126). Ask students if any of them have heard of Jackie Robinson. If yes, ask what they know

Historical Fiction Anchor Chart

Historical Fiction

**Story that is based on real
events from the past but didn't
really happen**

Setting is important

Everybody = E
Fiction = F

Figure 10.18. Historical Fiction Anchor Chart

about him. Explain that Jackie Robinson is famous today because he "broke the color barrier" in professional baseball. Read and explain the book's call number. Identify the setting—time and place. Explain that this historical fiction book describes what *could* have happened at that time from the point of view of a boy and his father.

1. Read *Dad, Jackie, and Me*.
2. Check for understanding with the following questions:
   - Give an example of one event/detail from the story that is based on an actual event from the past. Ask students to identify other examples of this.
   - How do the boy and his father feel about the Los Angeles Dodgers?
   - The boy's father is deaf. How is that important in the story?
   - What do we learn about the year 1947 from this story? About Jackie Robinson? About baseball? Historical fiction books are a great way to learn about the past.
3. Explain that historical fiction books are shelved alphabetically by author in the Everybody and Fiction sections of the library.

Types of Literature—Historical Fiction

Historical fiction tells a story of the past with a strong focus on setting and character. Historical fiction helps readers develop a sense of history and an awareness of people living in the past. Through historical fiction readers can vicariously experience history. Even though times change, the universal needs of people remain relatively unchanged. For students' understanding and enjoyment, it is particularly important to build background when reading historical fiction.

Historical fiction includes:
- Historical accuracy
- Setting that is vivid and accurate
- Characters who reflect the values of the time period
- Universal human themes

Class 2

Say to the students, "Our library also has biography baseball books. Read the **Biography Anchor Chart** (p. 127). Raise your hand if you have heard of the Pittsburgh Pirates baseball team. Have you heard of Roberto Clemente? Today we'll learn about another baseball player from the past, only

Biography Anchor Chart

Biography
Information about a Person's Life

B	B = Biography
Was (Spine Label)	Was = last name of person biography is about

Figure 10.19. Biography Anchor Chart

this time we will learn about his life. Biographies are true stories; they tell us what actually happened in the lives of real people." Read and explain the book's call number. Identify the setting—time and place.

1. Read *Roberto Clemente: Pride of the Pittsburgh Pirates*.
2. Check for understanding with the following questions:
   - Give an example of one event/detail in the story from Roberto's life. Ask students to identify other examples of this.
   - What can we learn from Roberto's life?
   - What do we learn about our world 40–50 years ago from this story? About baseball? Biographies are a great way to learn about history.
   - How is this baseball story different from the historical fiction baseball story that we read at our last class?
3. Review the location of biographies.

Types of Literature—Biography

A biography tells the story of a person's life and achievements; an autobiography re-creates the story of the author's own life. Both biography and autobiography are embedded in the time and culture that shaped and was shaped by the subject of the biography. (Galda, Lee, Bernice E. Cullinan, and Lawrence Sipe. 2010. *Literature and the Child.* Belmont, CA: Wadsworth.)

Although biography can be evaluated using the same criteria as nonfiction, some other considerations should also apply:

- The subject chosen should be worthy of note and of interest to children.
- All facts should be grounded in primary source material, as evidenced by the bibliography, source notes, and indexing.
- Portraits should be of real people rather than paragons; it is important that the many human sides of a character be developed.
- Historically accurate depictions of time and place are crucial.
- There should be a balance between fact and story line.

One other category in this classification is collective biography, which is a compilation of biographical sketches, often with a common theme (Dewey classification 920).

Class 3

Say to the students, "The third kind of baseball books in our library is nonfiction. Read the **Non-fiction Anchor Chart** (below). Raise your hand if you have ever played baseball or softball. True books that tell us about these sports and how to play them are nonfiction books. In most cases these books do not tell a story; instead they give facts and information."

1. Read *Baseball in Action*, first explaining its call number.
2. Check for understanding with the following questions:
   - Give an example of one fact about baseball in the book. Ask students to identify other baseball facts from the book.
   - How is this baseball book different from the first two baseball books that we read?
3. Review the location of baseball books in the Nonfiction section, explaining that books in the Nonfiction section are organized by number with books about the same topics having the same number and being shelved together.

Guided Practice/Independent Practice

Encourage students to select historical fiction, biography, and nonfiction books at checkout time.

Assessment

- Assess students' understanding of the differences between these three types of books by doing an "Agree (thumbs up)/Disagree (thumbs down)" activity at the end of each class or at the beginning of the following class with true and false statements about each type based on the anchor charts. The following sentences are sample statements to use for historical fiction books:
  1. The stories in historical fiction books actually happened.
  2. Historical fiction books are found in the Fiction and Everybody sections of the library.
  3. Historical fiction books are based on real events from the past.
  4. Setting is not important in historical fiction books.

Nonfiction Anchor Chart

Nonfiction

Facts and Information

000–099   Generalities

100–199   Philosophy & psychology

200–299   Religion & mythology

300–399   Social sciences

400–499   Language

500–599   Natural sciences

600–699   Applied sciences

700–799   Arts: art, dance, music, sports, etc.

900–999   History, geography, collective biographies

Figure 10.20. Nonfiction Anchor Chart

- Another assessment activity would be to have students select one type of literature (from the three covered in this lesson) that interests them and find a book of that type on the shelf. Begin this activity by reviewing the three anchor charts, especially focusing on location. As students select a book, they show it to the teacher-librarian, stating what kind it is and explaining how they found it. Students can read the books that they found for the remaining class time. The teacher-librarians will clarify and reteach as needed.

Types of Literature—Nonfiction

The term nonfiction describes books of information and fact. Nonfiction or informational books are distinguished from fiction by their emphasis. Both may tell a story and both may include fact. In fiction, however, the story is uppermost, with facts sometimes used to support it; in nonfiction, the facts are uppermost, with storytelling perhaps used as an expressive technique. (Galda, Lee, Bernice E. Cullinan, and Lawrence Sipe. 2010. *Literature and the Child.* Belmont, CA: Wadsworth.)

Through the Eyes of a Child: An Introduction to Children's Literature by Donna E. Norton (New York: Prentice Hall, 1995) lists the following evaluative criteria for informational books:

- All facts should be accurate.
- Stereotypes should be eliminated.
- Illustrations should clarify the text.
- Analytical thinking should be encouraged.
- The organization should aid understanding.
- The style should stimulate interest.

Lesson
Realistic/Multicultural Gender-Fair (MCGF) Fiction
Grades 3–4 (appropriate for grades 5–6 as well)
(Lesson developed by Sarah Latcham, Salina Hemann, and Judith Dickson)

Standard	Benchmark	Objective	EOY Skill
Standard 1: Reads, views, and listens widely both for information and in pursuit of personal interests.	Recognizes different types of literature/genres. Selects a variety of Just Right fiction and nonfiction for independent reading.	Reads different types of literature/genres through reading activities collaboratively planned by the teacher-librarian and the classroom teacher.	Identifies types of literature/genre through activities such as oral literature, reading promotion programs, booktalks, or reading logs. Checks out a variety of Just Right fiction and nonfiction from the library.
Standard 2: Uses inquiry and critical thinking skills to acquire, analyze and evaluate, use, and create information. A. The learner accesses information efficiently and effectively. B. The learner evaluates and extracts information critically and competently. C. The learner uses information accurately, creatively, and ethically.	Understands how call numbers are used to locate books. Uses keywords to initiate an information search.	Uses call number to locate fiction and nonfiction books on library shelves with support. Uses keywords to search library catalog or table of contents.	Uses library catalog to identify and locate materials with support. Locates fiction and nonfiction books on library shelves by call number.

Note: For each Literary Element and Type of Literature, a description of the area and a bibliography of relevant titles are presented at the end of the lesson to assist in planning instruction. A selection of books in addition to those in the printed lists is also located on the website, as is an Excel spreadsheet that can be sorted by literary type, element, grade level, author and a number of other ways.

curriculum/lit/LComponent1.htm
curriculum/lit/LComponent2.htm
bibliographies.htm

Tools and Resources
- Bunting, Eve. *One Green Apple*. New York: Houghton Mifflin, 2006.
- **Realistic Fiction Anchor Chart** (p. 131) (Enlarge or reproduce to post or project.)

Anticipatory Set
Introduce the book by asking if anyone in the class has ever moved and been the "new kid" in the class. Discuss how this feels, and talk about what the new person and the existing class members can do to make the new person feel more at home.

Objectives

Students will:

- Be able to identify realistic fiction as a story that could happen in today's world with characters, setting, and plot that seem convincingly real, and with a theme that is relevant to today's world.
- Recognize that the call number will contain either an E or F.
- Select realistic fiction that they would be interested in checking out and reading.

Input/Modeling/Checking for Understanding

Read *One Green Apple* by Eve Bunting. Discuss how the character not only had to get used to a new class, but a new language, country, and culture as well. Brainstorm a list of ways that students could be welcoming to a new student in their school. (This lesson can be used as an MCGF lesson if this discussion is included.)

Reference the **Realistic Fiction Anchor Chart** (below). Use it as a checklist for the book. Does it have realistic setting, characters, and plot? Is the theme relevant to today's world? Is it shelved with the E or F books by call number? (The authors of this lesson are assuming that students have been introduced to realistic fiction, plot, theme, characters, call numbers, etc., previously. If this is not the case, more background and instruction would have to be done.)

Brainstorm a list of words that the students could use to find similar books using the library catalog. Make sure that the students are clear that "realistic fiction" does not work as a keyword, but that students, school, immigration, etc., would work.

Guided Practice/Independent Practice

Assist students in using the library catalog to find similar books. Depending on the students' level of independence with the library catalog, they could perform keyword searches or an author search, or you could have a visual search button for realistic fiction. Provide the students with a checklist of the realistic fiction criteria and have them practice checking to see if the book they choose fits the criteria.

Assessment

- The students will create a record sheet with the call number, title, and their name on it. First they will use this sheet to locate the book on the shelves. After finding the book, they will show it to the teacher-librarian who in turn will keep the record sheet as an exit sheet so they can record whether or not the students can find a realistic fiction book.

Realistic Fiction Anchor Chart

Realistic Fiction

Story that could happen
in today's world

Characters, setting, & plot seem real

Theme is relevant to today's world

Everybody = E
Fiction = F

Figure 10.21. Realistic Fiction Anchor Chart

Lesson
Types of Literature Review
Grades 3–4
(Lesson developed by Cindy Kunde)

Standard	Benchmark	Objective	EOY Skill
Standard 1: Reads, views, and listens widely both for information and in pursuit of personal interests.	Recognizes different types of literature/genres.	Identifies types of literature/ genres through activities such as oral literature, reading promotion programs, booktalks, or reading log.	Demonstrates increasing understanding of different types of literature.

Tools and Resources

- Aguilar, David A. *11 Planets*. Washington, DC: National Geographic, 2008.
- DiCamillo, Kate. *The Miraculous Journey of Edward Tulane*. Cambridge, MA: Candlewick Press, 2006.
- Knudson, Mike. *Raymond and Graham Rule the School*. New York: Viking, 2008.
- Lewis, J. Patrick. *The World's Greatest Poems*. San Francisco: Chronicle Books, 2008.
- McGill, Alice. *Way Up and Over Everything*. Boston: Houghton Mifflin, 2008.

Note: Make sure that you have these books but leave them on the shelves.

- McKissack, Patricia C. *Abby Takes a Stand*. New York: Viking, 2005.
- Rappaport, Doreen. *Abe's Honest Words*. New York: Hyperion Books for Children, 2008.
- Types of literature **Anchor Charts—Biography** (p. 127), **Fantasy** (p. 124), **Folktales** (p. 134), **Historical Fiction** (p. 126), **Poetry** (p. 120), **Nonfiction** (p. 128), **Realistic Fiction** (p. 131). (Enlarge or reproduce to post or project. All charts are also on the website.)

 curriculum/lessons6.htm

Anticipatory Set

Say to the students, "I like to read and take walks in my free time. What do you like to do? Do we all like to do the same thing? No, and that's good. It would be boring if we all liked the same things. Reading is like that. I like realistic fiction books and am always looking for more books of that type to read. What type of books do you like to read? Do we all like to read the same type of books? No, and that's good. It's good to have a favorite type of books, but reading only one type makes us kind of a 'boring' reader. It's better to be a well-rounded reader who reads a variety of different types of books. Let's learn about the different types of books that you can choose from when selecting books for your personal reading."

Objectives

Students will:

- Be able to identify the characteristics of the seven types of literature (fantasy, historical fiction, realistic fiction, biography, traditional literature, poetry, nonfiction).
- Locate books of each type on the library shelves.

Input/Modeling/Checking for Understanding

Show students the types of literature anchor charts that are posted near the large group meeting area. Explain that the next few lessons will involve going through each type, explaining what it is, showing where those books are located, and reading an excerpt from a sample of that type of book.

Begin with *Fantasy*.

1. Read the **Fantasy Anchor Chart** (p. 124). Write the title and call number of the fantasy sample on the whiteboard (*The Miraculous Journey of Edward Tulane* F/DiC). Review the meaning of the call number and go to the shelf to get the book. Read the first chapter aloud.

2. Give an example of one detail/event in the story that fits the fantasy definition. Ask students to share other examples of details and/or events that fit this definition, too.

3. Remind students that fantasy books are organized by call number in the Fiction and Everybody sections of the library. (They are intershelved with realistic and historical fiction books.) The best way to locate these books is by using the library catalog.

Now move on to *Historical Fiction*.

1. Read the **Historical Fiction Anchor Chart** (p. 126). Write the title and call number of the historical fiction sample on the whiteboard (*Abby Takes a Stand* F/McK). Review the meaning of the call number and go to the shelf to get the book. Review the book's setting—both time and place. Read the first chapter aloud.

2. Give an example of one detail/event in the story that fits the historical fiction definition. Ask students to share other examples of details and/or events that fit this definition, too.

3. Remind students that historical fiction books are organized by call number in the Fiction and Everybody sections of the library. (They are intershelved with realistic fiction and fantasy books.) The best way to locate these books is by using the library catalog.

Now move on to *Realistic Fiction*.

1. Read the **Realistic Fiction Anchor Chart** (p. 131). Write the title and call number of the realistic fiction sample on the whiteboard (*Raymond and Graham Rule the School* F/Knu). Review the meaning of the call number and go to the shelf to get the book. Review the book's setting—both time and place. Read the first chapter aloud.

2. Give an example of one detail/event in the story that fits the realistic fiction definition. Ask students to share other examples of details and/or events that fit this definition, too.

3. Remind students that realistic fiction books are organized by call number in the Fiction and Everybody sections of the library. (They are intershelved with historical fiction and fantasy books.) The best way to locate these books is by using the library catalog.

Next is *Biography*.

1. Read the **Biography Anchor Chart** (p. 127). Write the title and call number of the biography sample on the whiteboard (*Abe's Honest Words* B/Lin). Review the meaning of the call number and go to the shelf to get the book. Read an excerpt from the book.

2. Give an example of one detail/event in the story about Abraham Lincoln's life. Ask students to share other examples of details and/or events in the story that tell us about Lincoln's life.

3. Remind students that biographies are organized by the last name of the book's subject.

The next type is *Folktales*.

1. Read the **Folktales Anchor Chart** (p. 134). Write the title and call number of the folktales sample on the whiteboard (*Way Up and Over Everything* 398.2/McG). Review the meaning of the call number and go to the shelf to get the book. Review the book's setting—both time and place. Read an excerpt from the book and the Author's Note.

2. Give an example of one detail/event in the story that fits the folktales definition. Ask students to share other examples of details and/or events that fit this definition, too.
3. Remind students that folktales are located in the 398 area of the Nonfiction section of the library.

Next is *Poetry*.

1. Read the **Poetry Anchor Chart** (p. 120). Write the title and call number of the poetry sample on the whiteboard (*The World's Greatest Poems* 811/Lew). Review the meaning of the call number and go to the shelf to get the book. Read several poems from the book.
2. Give an example of one detail/event in one of the poems read that fits the poetry definition. Ask students to share other examples of details and/or events from the poems read aloud that fit this definition, too.
3. Remind students that poetry books are located in the 811 area of the Nonfiction section of the library.

The last type of literature is *Nonfiction*.

1. Read the **Nonfiction Anchor Chart** (p. 128). Write the title and call number of the nonfiction sample on the whiteboard (*11 Planets* 523.4/Agu). Review the meaning of the call number and go to the shelf to get the book. Explain aloud how to find the book—using signage, skimming the call numbers of books in that area, etc. Read an excerpt from the book.
2. Give an example of one fact from the section read that fits the nonfiction definition. Ask students to share other examples of facts from the section read aloud that fit this definition, too.
3. Remind students nonfiction books are organized by number, with books on the same topics having similar numbers and being shelved in the same area.

Assessment

- Since this lesson will involve several class periods, do a quick assessment of understanding at the beginning and end of each class period over the types of literature that have been covered so far.
- Using the anchor charts, make several statements about each type of literature (some true and some false), holding up the sample book that was read for that type. Ask students to agree (thumbs up) or disagree (thumbs down) with each statement.

Some sample statements for fantasy would be:

1. A fantasy book *cannot* happen in the real world.
2. A fantasy book does *not* have characters.
3. The world in a fantasy book is *not* believable.
4. Fantasy books can be found in the Fiction and Everybody sections of the library.

- Another assessment activity would be to have students select one type of literature (from the seven covered in this lesson) that interests them and find a book of that type on the shelf. Begin this activity by reviewing the seven anchor charts, especially focusing on location. As students select a book, they show it to the librarian, stating what kind it is and explaining how they found it. Students can read the books that they found for the remaining class time. Clarify and reteach as needed.

Folktales Anchor Chart

Folktales

Old stories from various countries

Folktales, fairy tales, legends

Told long ago to entertain, give advice, or explain the unknown

Parents told their children and their grandchildren

Everybody = E

398s

Figure 10.22. Folktales Anchor Chart

COMPREHENSION STRATEGIES

Lesson
Asking Questions of Text
Grades 5–6
(Lesson developed by Debra Dorzweiler)

Standard	Benchmark	Objective	EOY Skill
Standard 2: Uses inquiry and critical thinking skills to acquire, analyze and evaluate, use, and create information.	Uses questions to understand text.	Asks questions before, during, and after reading. Identifies answers to questions as coming from the text, from the text plus their own thinking, or as needing further research. Identifies questions as closed or open.	Shows increasing skills in finding and using information from print and online sources.

Tools and Resources
- Kajikawa, Kimiko. *Tsunami!* New York: Philomel, 2009.
- Robinson, Sharon. *Testing the Ice.* New York: Scholastic, 2009.
- **"Where Do the Answers Come From?" Activity Sheet** (p. 136)
- **Asking Questions of Text Activity Sheet** (p. 137)
- **Closed and Open Questions Chart** (p. 138)

Anticipatory Set
Say to the students, "When we read a story we are always trying to figure out what is happening. To do this we ask questions before, during, and after reading. Today I will be showing you what my thinking looks like as I am reading a story. I will be asking questions about the story before I start to read, while I am reading the story, and after I have finished reading it."

Objectives
Before the lesson students are able to:
- Ask questions beginning with who, what, when, where, yes or no.
- Ask questions beginning with why, how come, or I wonder.

After the lesson, students will be able to:
- Ask questions before, during, and after reading.
- Identify answers to questions as coming from the text, from the text plus their own thinking, or as needing further research.
- Identify questions as being either closed (or requiring a simple factual answer) or open (or requiring a complicated answer that involves both facts and opinions).

Input/Modeling/Checking for Understanding

Day 1
Use the **Asking Questions of Text Activity Sheet** (p. 137) to record the questions. Tell students that *before* reading they might look at the cover and ask themselves what the story is about. Is this about a real tsunami? When and where did this story take place? What would it be like to experience a

tsunami? While reading the story they might ask questions, such as: How will Ojiisan warn the village about the tsunami? Why does he burn his crops? Will he ever recover his wealth? Then *after* reading ask: Why did the author write this story?

Next look over the questions and decide if they were answered from the story, if there was evidence in the story but you had to think about it, or if the question is still unanswered. You can see that this isn't about a real tsunami because it is a folktale. From the story you can tell that it took place a long time ago in a small village. The story gave some idea about what it would be like to experience a tsunami, but this would also require additional research. The story told us that Ojiisan burned his crops in order to get the attention of all of the villagers. It also said that he never recovered his wealth. We are not sure why the author wrote this story, but he may have wanted to make a point about the difference a person can make when he is willing to destroy everything he has in order to save those he loves.

Show the chart about where answers come from and discuss. For research, you might be able to find the answer by looking at the front or back material in the book or you might need to do some research in an encyclopedia, a book about tsunamis, or on the Internet.

Guided Practice/Independent Practice

Day 2

Hand out an **Asking Questions of Text Activity Sheet** (p. 137) to each student. Tell students that today they will be writing down their own questions. Show them the cover of the book and read the title. Have them write down at least three questions that they have before they hear the story. While reading the story, pause several times to give them a chance to write down some "during reading" questions. Then after reading, have them record some questions that they have after hearing the story. After the students have finished writing down their questions, show them the **"Where Do the Answers Come From?" Activity Sheet** (below) and have them label the questions "T" if the answer came from the story (or text), "T + Me" if there were clues in the text, but I also had to think about the answer, and "R" if the question will require further research.

Ask several students to share their before, during, or after questions. Together label the questions as "T" "T + Me" or "R" questions.

Day 3

Show the **Asking Questions of Text Activity Sheet** (p. 137) that was completed as a class during the previous session. Review the different places that answers come from, from the text, from the text + me, or research is needed.

Where Do the Answers Come From?		
Text (T)	*Text + Me (T+M)*	*Research (R)*
The text answers the question	The text tells *part* of the answer but I figure out the *rest* from what I already know	Additional information is needed

Figure 10.23. "Where Do the Answers Come From?" Activity Sheet

Asking Questions of Text		

Name: _____ Class code: _____ Table: _____

Before	*During*	*After*

T = Text

T + M = Text + Me

R = Research needed

Closed = to clarify or answer a simple question; fact questions; short answers; Who? What? When? Where? Yes or no?

Open = universal concepts or major content areas; answers are usually long and require further research; Why? How come? I wonder?

Figure 10.24. Asking Questions of Text Activity Sheet

Then show the **Closed and Open Questions Chart** (p. 138) to the class. Talk about the difference between closed and open questions. Questions that are closed—or fact questions—only require a short answer. These questions typically begin with who, what, where, or when *or* they require a yes or no answer. These are the kinds of questions that can either be answered from the text, or else the answer may be found quickly from another source such as a dictionary, an atlas, or an encyclopedia. On the other hand, open questions involve ideas and require a much longer answer. These questions typically begin with why, how come, or I wonder. These are usually the kinds of questions that involve a lot of research.

Look again at the questions that were answered last week as a class. Show students which ones would be closed questions, requiring a simple factual answer, and those that are open questions, requiring a complicated fact *plus* opinion answer.

Hand the students' **Asking Questions of Text Activity Sheet** (above) back to them. This time they will be looking over their questions to see if they were "closed" or "open" questions. Ask them to mark whether the question is a closed or an open question. Take the last five minutes to have them share their closed and open questions with the class.

| Closed and Open Questions ||
Closed	**Open**
Facts	Ideas (facts & opinions)
Short answers	Long answers
• Yes or no • Facts (Who What, Where, When)	• How something works (Why or How) • Ideas (Why, How come, I wonder)
Quick and easy to answer	A lot of research is needed

Figure 10.25. Closed and Open Questions Chart

Assessment

Day 2
- Collect the activity sheets and check them to make sure students are able to ask appropriate questions before, during, and after reading. Check informally to see if they seem to understand where the answers come from.

Day 3
- Collect the activity sheets and check them to make sure students seem to understand the difference between closed and open questions.

LITERATURE RESPONSE

Lesson
Author Study: Barbara O'Connor—Writing Stories from Her Heart's Home
Grades 5–6
(Lesson developed by **Stacy Gray, Sarah Latcham, and Cindy Kunde**)

Standard	Benchmark	Objective	EOY Skill
Standard 1: Reads, views, and listens widely both for information and in pursuit of personal interests.	Uses questions to understand text.	Asks questions with support before, during, and after reading literature or informational text. Reads different types of literature/genres through reading activities collaboratively planned by the teacher-librarian and the classroom teacher.	N/A

Note: The two lessons that follow are part of an author study of the work of Barbara O'Connor. Author study is described in detail in Chapter 2, and other author studies are available on the website. Lesson format is different as these lessons are jointly written by teachers and librarians following the Author Study Template, also found on the website. Author study is a collaborative activity, often involving many teachers at a given grade level.

 curriculum/lessons.htm

Tools and Resources
- **Barbara O'Connor Biographical Information** (p. 140)
- Selected books by Barbara O'Connor in multiple copies; see **Books by Barbara O'Connor** (p. 141)

Lessons and Activities

Note: Two sample lessons are presented here. The complete set of six may be found on the website. Each lesson contains questions and activities for a different title.

curriculum/lessons.htm

Fame and Glory in Freedom, Georgia

Type of literature: Realistic Fiction.

Characters:
- Burdette "Bird" Weaver—girl, sixth grade
- Harlem Tate—boy, Bird's friend
- Miss Delphine Reese—Bird's compassionate neighbor
- Mr. Moody—Harlem's caretaker

Setting: Fall in Freedom, Georgia (present).

Barbara O'Connor Biographical Information

Barbara O'Connor was born on November 9, 1950, in Greenville, South Carolina. She was welcomed into the family by her mother and father and her three-year-old sister Linda. Barbara has fond memories of her childhood. She remembers her father as a fun-loving man who enjoyed dogs, car races, and swimming. Her mother was a good seamstress who made yummy chocolate pudding with colored sprinkles on top. Barbara's relationship with her sister was typical—sometimes getting along well and sometimes fighting. They especially enjoyed playing with paper dolls.

Barbara was an independent child who rode her bike everywhere and loved to explore the woods. Other favorite activities were school, board games, reading, singing, and secret things (like secret hiding places and secret diaries with keys). Barbara remembers loving to write as a child; she wrote poems, stories, and even a whole book!

Barbara continued her education at the University of South Carolina, graduating in 1972 with a degree in English. After college, she moved to California and followed a hippie lifestyle. After having a variety of jobs, she married and moved to Duxbury, Massachusetts, where she currently lives with her husband, her son, two dogs, and one cat.

Writing, reading, and children are all things that Barbara loves, so becoming a children's book author is a perfect career for her. She writes both novels and biographies. Barbara loves to write novels because they allow her to let her imagination run wild. Cynthia Rylant is the author who influenced her the most. The strong voice and sense of place in Rylant's *Missing May* are qualities that Barbara works for in her own writing. Barbara develops strong, memorable characters: "I often find myself drawn to the troubled child, the outcast child, the spunky misfit. Those are the kids who find their way into my stories." Barbara enjoys writing biographies because she likes to read about people's lives and likes to research—"I like turning facts about a life into a story about a life."

Barbara especially likes to write about the South because all of her childhood memories come from that part of the country. She advises other writers to write what they feel passionate about and what they know: "That's what writers do. They put little pieces of themselves into their stories—and sometimes their stories take place right in their heart's home."

Barbara gives aspiring writers three final pieces of advice: "1. Read. 2. Never be afraid to write something that's not very good. You can always make it better. 3. Make friends with a librarian."

 http://www.barboconnor.com.   For more information about Barbara O'Connor, visit her website.

Sources of biographical information:
"Barbara O'Connor." *Barbara O'Connor: Children's Book Author.* June 18, 2008. http://www.barboconnor.com/.
"O'Connor, Barbara." *Something About the Author, Volume 154.* Farmington Hills: Thomson Gale, 2005.

Plot: Burdette "Bird" Weaver has two goals in life that she wants to reach, and along the way she learns about the importance of friendship, taking risks, and making sacrifices.

Point of view: First person.

Theme: Reaching your dreams involves taking risks and using the support of your friends.

Prereading and background:
- This book is about a girl who wants to be recognized for doing something important. Have you ever felt this way? What did you want to be recognized for and what did you do?
- Have you ever been in or wanted to be in a spelling bee? Why or why not?
- The setting of this book is in small-town Georgia. Have you ever been to Georgia? Look up information about Georgia and compare it to your state.
- Discuss feeling excluded from a group. How can we help others feel included in a group or friendship?

Books by Barbara O'Connor

Fiction

Beethoven in Paradise. Frances Foster Books, 1997.

Me and Rupert Goody. Frances Foster Books, 1999.

Moonpie and Ivy. Frances Foster Books, 2001.

Fame and Glory in Freedom, Georgia. Frances Foster Books, 2003.

Taking Care of Moses. Frances Foster Books, 2004.

How to Steal a Dog. Frances Foster Books, 2007.

Greetings from Nowhere. Frances Foster Books, 2008.

Nonfiction

Mammolina: A Story about Maria Montessori. Carolrhoda Books, 1993.

Barefoot Dancer: The Story of Isadora Duncan. Carolrhoda Books, 1994.

The Soldier's Voice: The Story of Ernie Pyle. Carolrhoda Books, 1996.

The World at His Fingertips: A Story about Louis Braille. Carolrhoda Books, 1997.

Katherine Dunham: Pioneer of Black Dance. Carolrhoda Books, 2000.

Leonardo da Vinci: Renaissance Genius. Carolrhoda Books, 2002.

Discussion:

- Have you ever wanted a friend as badly as Bird? How did you become friends with someone?
- Why is winning the spelling bee so important to Bird? Think of as many reasons as possible.
- Would you have tried to make friends with Harlem like Bird did? Why or why not?
- Have you ever had a special grown-up in your life like Delphine? What did he or she do to make you feel special?
- Have you ever been to Disney World? What is your favorite thing to do there?
- Bird says, "Miss Delphine had a way of looking through the outside of a person and getting right on in to find the good part—the inside" (p. 48). Do you think this is important? Why or why not? How can we practice looking at the "inside" of a person more often?
- Why was it important for Harlem to win the spelling bee? Have you ever wanted to do something to show others that you can do it well? What was it and how did you do?

Activities:

- Have a classroom spelling bee. See the EducationWorld website.
- Design a brochure to "sell yourself" as a good friend. As a class, brainstorm as many positive qualities as possible about being a good friend, and ask the students to use this list as a guide in designing their brochure.

http://www.educationworld.com/ a_lesson/02/lp282-04.shtml

- Discuss how both Bird and Harlem were excluded from peer groups at their school. Invite the guidance counselor to come and discuss exclusion as a form of bullying and how to handle these situations.
- Investigate the Lion's Club and what they do in your community for people who need eye care. Consider what the school could do to help their cause.
- Make a list of ways to feel good about yourself when you are feeling worried or unsure (e.g., positive sayings, certain clothes to wear to make yourself feel confident, etc.). Take the list out and read it when you need a positive boost.
- Design posters that send positive messages about reaching your life goals (perseverance, courage, etc.) and ask to hang them in the school.
- Using an atlas, plan the route you would take to drive from your hometown to Disney World. Draw the route on a piece of paper and label all of your stops. Calculate how long it would take you to get there traveling 70 miles per hour in a vehicle.
- Visit Barbara O'Connor's website (http://www.barboconnor.com).

Greetings from Nowhere

Type of literature: Realistic Fiction.

Characters:
- Aggie—elderly widow who must sell her run-down motel
- Willow—nine-year-old girl whose father is interested in buying the motel
- Loretta—ten-year-old girl who is traveling with her adoptive parents
- Kirby—troubled boy who is on his way to a special boys' school

Setting: Summer at the Sleepy Time Motel near Shawnee Gap, North Carolina (present).

Plot: Willow, Loretta, Kirby, and their parents all visit Aggie's motel at the same time. During their time together, they develop friendships that change their lives.

Point of view: Third person.

Theme: Friendships help us through difficult times.

Prereading and background:
- Use *World Book Online* to look up information about the Great Smoky Mountains in North Carolina (plants, animals, geography, weather, etc.). How is living in that area of North Carolina different from living in your state?
- One of the main characters is having difficulty at home and has been suspended from several schools. He will now be attending a boys' academy with very strict rules and regulations. Discuss how someone in this situation might feel. How would an academy like this be different from your elementary school?
- One of the main characters is on vacation with her parents during the book. Share memories from summer vacations with your family.
- The book takes place in a rural motel. Use Internet sites such as www.smalltown-america.com, www.lazymeadow.com, and www.route66motels.com to look at pictures of similar rural motels. Share experiences of staying at similar motels, or discuss what it would be like to stay at a motel like this.

Discussion:
- The setting of *Greetings from Nowhere* is so important to the overall story. Describe the setting and discuss how it affects the characters and events.
- Discuss Aggie's decision to sell the Sleepy Time Motel. Why does she later regret that decision?
- Discuss Willow's family situation. Describe how she feels about her mother at various times during the story.
- What does Loretta know about her birth mother at the beginning of the story? How does the trip help Loretta to learn more about this woman?
- Before the story begins and during most of the story, Kirby misbehaves and does things to hurt other people. What do you think are some reasons for his behavior?
- Each of the four main characters—Aggie, Willow, Loretta, and Kirby—lose something during the story. What has each lost and how does each deal with that loss?
- Friendship helps each of the four main characters to deal with problems they are facing. How do these four friends help each other?
- Describe the future plans that the four main characters have made at the end of the story. How do these plans show that they have hope for the future?
- Additional discussion questions are available in the Teacher's Guide for this book on Barbara O'Connor's website.

Activities:
- Write letters from one character to another (such as Loretta to Willow, Kirby to Aggie, Willow to Dorothy) one month and six months after the story takes place.
- Write a story describing what happens the following summer when these four friends reunite.
- Plan a trip to the Great Smoky Mountains. Locate and describe the places you would like to visit. (You can include the places that Loretta visits, but try to find others, too.)
- Aggie loves the Great Smoky Mountains and often describes the beautiful view from the motel. Use Internet sites and print sources to find out what the Great Smoky Mountains look like. Draw a picture of the view that Aggie might see from the motel.
- Use Kidspiration to create a web that portrays the relationships between the main characters.
- Additional activities are available in the Teacher's Guide for this book on Barbara O'Connor's website (http://www.barboconnor.com).

Curricular Ties, Themes, and Awards for Selected Books by Barbara O'Connor				
Title and Selected Awards	**Curricular Ties**	**Type of Literature**	**Annotation**	**Theme**
Fame and Glory in Freedom, Georgia (2003) • Baltimore County Library Great Books for Kids, 2003 • Bank Street College Best Books of the Year, 2003 • Chicago Public Library "Best of the Best," 2003 • Iowa Children's Choice Award Nominee, 2006 • Parents' Choice Gold Award, 2003	Friendship Bullying Popularity Perseverance	Realistic Fiction	Burdette "Bird" Weaver wants to be noticed by other kids in her school. She decides to try to win the state spelling bee and recruits a friend to help her along the way. She soon realizes that fame and glory doesn't necessarily have to come from winning something; it can emerge from finding out what matters in life.	Reaching your dreams involves taking risks and using the support of your friends.
How to Steal a Dog (2007) • ALA Book Links Lasting Connections, 2007 • Bank Street College Best Books of the Year, 2007 • International Reading Association Notable Books for a Global Society, 2008 • NCSS-CBC Notable Trade Book in the Field of Social Studies, 2008 • Parents' Choice Recommendation, 2007 • School Library Journal Best Books of the Year, 2007	Homelessness Family Change	Realistic Fiction	Georgina Hayes has recently become homeless when her father abandons her, her mother, and her brother. They are living out of their car until her mother can get enough money saved up for rent and deposit. Georgina hates living out of the car and it affects everything—her studies in school, her friendships, even her morals. She decides that she is going to steal a dog to claim the reward money and help get a place to live.	Things are not always what they seem. Doing what is right isn't always easy, but it pays off in the end.

Figure 10.26. Curricular Ties, Themes, and Awards for Selected Books by Barbara O'Connor *(Continues)*

Curricular Ties, Themes, and Awards for Selected Books by Barbara O'Connor *(Continued)*				
Title and Selected Awards	**Curricular Ties**	**Type of Literature**	**Annotation**	**Theme**
Greetings from Nowhere (2008) • Parents' Choice Silver Award, 2008	Family Friendship Change	Realistic Fiction	A troubled boy and his mother, a happy family on vacation, a lonely girl and her father, and a recently widowed elderly woman all meet at a run-down motel in the Great Smoky Mountains. During their time together, they share experiences and develop friendships that change their lives.	Friendships help us through difficult times.
Me and Rupert Goody (1999) • ALA Notable Book, 2000 • Bank Street College Best Books of the Year, 2000 • Dolly Gray Children's Literature Award • Kansas City Public Library Best Books, 1999 • School Library Journal Best Books, 1999	Friendship Family Change	Realistic Fiction	Jennalee Helton has a "ton-of-hell" house that she escapes from and goes to Uncle Beau's store. The store is predictable—which is what Jennalee likes—until Rupert Goody shows up. Rupert is an adult who acts like a child and he throws Jennalee's world into chaos, much to her chagrin.	Change is difficult, but learning to love is worth it.
Moonpie and Ivy (2001) • Bank Street College Best Books of the Year, 2002 • Chicago Parent Magazine Best Books of 2001 • Child Magazine Best Books of the Year, 2001 • Massachusetts Book Award, 2002 • Parents' Choice Gold Award, 2001	Family Change Friendship Grief	Realistic Fiction	Pearl feels hurt, confused, and unwanted when her mother takes her to visit her Aunt Ivy (whom Pearl has never met) and then leaves her there. At first Pearl has difficulty fitting in and does hurtful things to those around her. But through her interactions with Ivy and a neighbor boy and his grandmother, Pearl finds hope by learning how it feels to be accepted and loved.	Feeling loved and accepted will help one to find hope in difficult situations.
Taking Care of Moses (2004) • Bank Street College Best Books of the Year, 2004 • Iowa Children's Choice Award Nominee, 2008 • Parents' Choice Award Winner, 2004	Family Friendship Courage Honesty Helping Others	Realistic Fiction	Randall Mackey is holding on to a big secret. He knows who left the baby at the local church and he cannot tell anyone in order to keep others from getting in trouble. He has to decide what needs to be done so the townspeople stop fighting and an old friend can stay at home.	It may not always be easy, but when it comes to making important decisions it is essential to do the right thing.

Figure 10.26. Curricular Ties, Themes, and Awards for Selected Books by Barbara O'Connor

11

Sample Lessons: Inquiry Model

> Throughout this book, you will find sidebars featuring the small link icon shown here with either a full or abbreviated URL. The full URLs lead to items referenced in the text; the shorter ones are for the ICCSD website that contains actual lessons and other information. The webpages for the short URLs begin with http://www.iccsd.k12.ia.us/library/. Once you have bookmarked the main site, you will have no difficulty finding the specific tool you wish to access.

OVERVIEW

In this chapter, we present a sampling of lessons that are a part of the inquiry portion of our curriculum. The lessons are presented in a standardized lesson design format. These lessons and a variety of other lessons may also be found on the website.

They are arranged according to the elements of the inquiry model presented in Chapter 9. Handouts, activity sheets, visuals, and/or assessments accompany most lessons. **Boldfaced** type indicates that an item is printed with the lesson; page numbers are included too for ease in locating the materials.

curriculum/lessons.htm

Lessons in Chapter 11

DEFINE THE INFORMATION NEED

Lesson
Developing an Understanding of Your Topic
Grades 9–10
(Lesson developed by Jill Hofmockel, Jim Walden, and Beth Belding)

Standard	Benchmark	Objective
Standard 1: Reads, views, and listens widely both for information and in pursuit of personal interests. Standard 2: Uses inquiry and critical thinking skills to acquire, analyze and evaluate, use, and create information.	Connects ideas to personal interests and previous knowledge and experience. Applies critical thinking skills when reading, viewing, and listening. Recognizes and refines the need for information. Uses a variety of print and electronic tools to find information.	Explores topics of interest. Formulates essential questions based on information needs. Develops purpose or thesis statement.

Note: This lesson is part of a major unit titled "Symposium" that is completed by all ninth-grade students in their Language Arts class. In this project, students prepare and present a symposium on an issue of interest. Students are guided step by step through this process, with frequent checkpoints. The unit appears in Chapter 12 and on the web.

 https://sites.google.com/site/icwest library/home/class-links/language-arts

Tools and Resources
- Selection of books on topics students have chosen (multiple copies)
- Document camera or overhead
- **Topic Selection for Symposium Form** (p. 147)
- **Getting Started on Research Handout** (p. 148)

Anticipatory Set
Say to the students, "In class, you completed your topic selection form (Figure 11.1), and that form has been returned to you by your teacher. Now, you know what your symposium issue will be. Today, we will begin work on building background knowledge on your symposium topic, so that you can begin to focus on your final research topic."

Objectives
Students will:

- Begin to focus their symposium topic.

Input/Modeling/Checking for Understanding
Say to the students, "You are going to begin your research today with a book that has information on your topic. Later, you will use a variety of resources including our online databases and the web. Books are a good place to start. Can anyone give some reasons for this?" (authoritative, focused, can use table of contents and headings).

Topic Selection Symposium 2011

Name: _____ Period _____ Points _____

We challenge you to choose a symposium topic that is timely, rigorous, and interesting to you.

Use this sheet to brainstorm your top five topic ideas, based on the following criteria and in-class discussion.

Topics may include:
- Human rights issues/abuses
- Social and policy controversies within our country or abroad
- Unresolved conflicts
- Social issues in America

List your ideas in the following table. Please give a thorough topic idea summary. You might include potential research questions you might like to research. There is a sample topic idea to help you.

	Topic Ideas
Ex.	The effects of advertising on children. How does it influence small kids?
	Should it be limited? Are any groups working to make any changes? How?
1.	
2.	
3.	
4.	
5.	

Your teacher and librarian will evaluate these ideas and suggest the top two ideas for you to choose as your symposium topic.

Figure 11.1. Topic Selection for Symposium Form

Have students access the **Getting Started on Research Handout** (p. 148) from their symposium packet. Walk them through the questions on the handout. Tell them that this will be completed and handed in at the end of the day. Remind them of the use of the table of contents, chapter headings, index, glossary, etc. Tell them these text features save time and allow them to skim most of the information, and then read carefully the sections that directly pertain to their topic.

Tell students that their goal for today is to begin to focus on the specific area that they will research. In order to do that, they will need to read and build background on the topic.

Have students access a book from the cart provided. The librarian and the teacher should assist with this process.

Guided Practice/Independent Practice

Students should have the majority of the period to read and answer the questions on the "Getting Started" handout. The librarian or teacher should check with every student at least once to be sure they all understand their topics and the issues on the "Getting Started" handout.

Assessment

- When about 10 minutes remain in the class, remind students to complete the "exit" assessment (Question 5 on the "Getting Started" handout).
- The "Getting Started" handout will be turned in and checked by the librarian prior to the next class.

Getting Started Symposium 2011

Name: _____ Teacher: _____ Pd: _____ Points: _____

Start working toward a better understanding of your symposium topic. Use the elements of your library book (table of contents, chapter titles, index, etc.) to help you identify which sections of your book you should be skimming and which sections you should be reading more closely when you begin note taking.

This is a preliminary organizer. You may or may not end up using all of the ideas on this worksheet, but it should give you a great start on your research.

1. What is the main focus of your symposium research? _____
   _____
   _____
   _____
   _____

   Best section(s) of my library book for this info: _____

2. What are some of the possible causes of this problem or situation? What things are contributing to the problem?
   _____
   _____
   _____
   _____

   Best section(s) of my library book for this info: _____

3. What are some of the possible effects (on individuals, families, communities, nations, etc.) of this problem or situation?
   _____
   _____
   _____
   _____

   Best section(s) of my library book for this info: _____

4. What are some of the possible solutions to this problem or situation? What could be done to prevent this problem from taking place? How can this situation be fixed once it has taken place? _____
   _____
   _____
   _____
   _____

   Best section(s) of my library book for this info: _____

5. What is one interesting fact or personal story that you read today? (Be sure to write down the page number from your book so you can find it later for your notes.)
   _____
   _____
   _____
   _____

Figure 11.2. Getting Started on Research Handout

LOCATE INFORMATION

Lesson
Using Keywords to Find Online Information and Choosing
Appropriate Sources
Grades 5–6
(Lesson developed by Debra Dorzweiler)

Standard	Benchmark	Objective	EOY Skill
Standard 2: Uses inquiry and critical thinking skills to acquire, analyze and evaluate, use, and create information.	Uses technology to locate information. Identifies information need. Uses keywords to initiate an information search.	Uses selected online resources to locate information. Selects appropriate resources from a results list obtained from an electronic search. Identifies keywords to guide information search. Uses keywords to search library catalog or index.	Shows increasing skills in finding and using information from print and online.

Tools and Resources
- Computer with Internet connection, multimedia projector, and screen
- **Research Planning Sheet** (p. 151)
- **Research Planning Sheet Example** (p. 151)

Anticipatory Set
Say to the students, "Have you ever tried to find something very small that you knew was in your desk drawer? That happened to me the other day—I was looking for a cooking utensil that I knew was in the kitchen drawer, but I couldn't find it! What do you think I did to find it? I had to empty out the entire drawer until I was able to find the right utensil.

"That same kind of thing happens when you are looking for information in a nonfiction book or on the Internet. It wouldn't be practical to read the entire book to find just a short section in it, and it wouldn't be possible to read everything on the Internet to find just one thing. Today we will talk about a strategy that helps to narrow our search for specific information in a nonfiction book or on the Internet. That strategy is called a keyword search."

Objectives
Before the lesson, students are able to:

- Launch Internet browser.
- Log in to netTrekker or other student-friendly search engine.

After the lesson, students will be able to:

- Develop a list of keywords from information topic or questions.
- Conduct a "wildcard" search.
- Perform a keyword search in a student-friendly search engine.
- Choose an appropriate article to answer their information need.

Input/Modeling/Checking for Understanding

<table>
<tr><td>

Note: This lesson could be adapted to any collaborative unit.

</td></tr>
</table>

Day 1

Say to the students:

I am trying to find some information about channels for the unit on land-forms. I could enter the name of my topic and use that as a keyword. However, there might be several other words that I could use to help me find just the right information about my topic. In order to do that, I need to spend a little time planning my research before I start looking for information.

My topic is channels. There are different kinds of channels, so I want to be sure to limit my search to channels that have to do with landforms. Also I need to think about the questions that I have about channels. Here is my planning sheet. After I have identified my topic, I need to think of some possible fact questions, or questions that will be answered easily in one or two sentences. This information will come directly from the author. These questions often begin with words such as "who, what, where, and when." Then I need to think of some possible inference questions. This information will come from the author and from my own thinking about the topic, as I try to understand it. These are questions that often begin with the words "how" or "why."

After I have a list of questions I can now think of some possible keywords to use. The keywords usually come from my questions. I read over my questions to find important words. These are words that are unique to my topic, so I will ignore words like "are" and "do." The keywords are what I will use to help me find information online. It is important to spend some time thinking about the best words to use because this will save me time in my search. If my topic could be either singular or plural (channel or channels), I can use the wildcard so that results matching either one of these keywords will be found. For my topic that would be channel*.

If students need more guidance, complete a research planning form together as a class. Choose a topic that nobody in the class will be researching. Figure 11.4 (p. 151) is an example.

Ask students to review the important things they need to remember when searching by keyword: correct spelling is important, a wildcard search with the asterisk (*) immediately after the word will expand the search options, and they must sort through the list to see which of the results might actually be on their subject.

Day 2

Say to the students:

Once I know what information I want to find I am ready to begin an online search. Today we will be using netTrekker to find information about our landforms. After I have logged into netTrekker, I begin by entering one of my keywords. When I enter the term "channel*" with a wildcard, there are five pages with articles that match either the keyword "channel" or "channels." But after looking at the first article, I notice that it is about television "channels" and not the landform. I may be able to get better results by entering "channels landforms." This time I get only two articles, but these both match my topic. I try different keywords from my keyword list until I find an article that will work for my project. An article titled "Ohio Stream Management Guide" has a whole section on channels that works perfectly. It even tells me about different types of channels. This is something that I hadn't found in any of my other sources.

Guided Practice/Independent Practice

Day 1

Have students work on the **Research Planning Sheets** (p. 151) in pairs.

Research Planning Sheet

Name: _____ Class code: _____

My topic is: _____

Here are some FACT questions I have about this topic:

Who _____?

What _____?

Where _____?

When _____?

Yes or No _____?

Here are some INFERENCE questions I have about this topic:

How _____?

Why _____?

Here are some possible KEYWORDS that will help me find information about this topic:

_____   _____

_____   _____

_____   _____

_____   _____

_____   _____

Figure 11.3. Research Planning Sheet

Day 2

Have students work with their partners to search for information using netTrekker that will work for their projects. After they find the article they should save it as a text file in their project folder. Later they will use this article to take notes for their research project.

Assessment

Day 1

- Check the **Research Planning Sheets** (above) and provide feedback as needed before students continue on to the next step in the research process.

Day 2

- Check the article saved in the students' project folders to make sure that it is appropriate for their project.

Research Planning Sheet Example

Name: _____ Class code: _____

My topic is: <u>Channels</u>

Here are some FACT questions I have about this topic:

Who first discovered channels?

What are channels used for?

Where are channels found?

When do channels occur?

Here are some INFERENCE questions I have about this topic:

How are channels made?

Why are there channels?

Here are some possible KEYWORDS that will help me find information about this topic:

channels

channels as landforms

history of channels

how channels are made

channel* (wildcard)

Figure 11.4. Research Planning Sheet Example

Lesson
Basic Searching in the Library Catalog
Grades 3–4
(Lesson developed by Debra Dorzweiler)

Standard	Benchmark	Objective	EOY Skill
Standard 2: Uses inquiry and critical thinking skills to acquire, analyze and evaluate, use, and create information.	Understands how call numbers are used to locate books.	Uses call number to locate fiction and nonfiction books on library shelves (with support). Uses library catalog to identify and locate materials (with support).	Demonstrates increasing skills in use of library catalog to locate materials.

Note: While we use the Follett Destiny Catalog in our libraries, this lesson is concept based and may be easily modified for other systems. Lessons for keyword and visual searching are available on the website.

curriculum/lessons10.htm

Tools and Resources
- Access to Destiny Catalog (or other electronic library catalog)
- Computer with Internet connection, multimedia projector, and screen
- **Basic Search Call Slip for Assessment** (p. 155)

Anticipatory Set
Say to the students, "We have enjoyed finding books in the Destiny Catalog with the Visual Search buttons. Sometimes there isn't a Visual Search button available for the books we are looking for. This is when we will want to do a 'Basic Search.' This will allow us to look for books by a favorite author, by the book title, or by the subject. We will learn how to do this during the next few class sessions."

Objectives
Before the lesson, students are able to:
- Identify the different sections of the library.
- Locate a book in the library using the call number.
- Use the Visual Search buttons in the Destiny Catalog to find a book.

After the lesson, students will be able to:
- Use the Basic Search buttons in the Destiny Catalog to find a book by author, title, or subject.
- Find the book's call number in the Destiny Catalog.
- Review finding the book on the library shelves.

Input/Modeling/Checking for Understanding

Note: This lesson may take several days the first time it is introduced.

Author Search
Show students how to access the Destiny Catalog from the desktop. When the Destiny Catalog opens up, show the Basic Search screen. Identify the "Find" box and the search buttons for the students. The catalog may be searched by:

- Keyword
- Title
- Author
- Subject
- Series

Say to the students, "Today we will be using three of these buttons to find books by author, title, and subject." Demonstrate how to search by author. For example, to find books by author Barbara Park, type her name into the "Find" box. Then click on the "Author" button. The Destiny Catalog will show a list of all the books by Barbara Park that we have in the library. Other examples might be to look for books by Suzy Kline, Dr. Seuss, or Mary Pope Osborne.

Show (or review) how to look through the results list and find the title, author, and call number in the record. Ask students what information they will need to find the book on the shelf.

When looking for books by the author, there are some important things to remember:

1. Words do not need to be capitalized.
2. Correct spelling is <u>essential</u>!
3. Click on the "Author" button to search only by the author.

Ask students to review the important things they need to remember when searching by author: the words in the author's name must be spelled correctly and the "Author" button must be selected before doing the search.

Title Search

Say to the students, "Today we will be looking for books by the title of the book. To find a book by the title, type in the first part of the book's title." Show students how to find a book, such as *Hansel and Gretel*. Type the title into the "Find" box, then click on the "Title" button.

Show students what to do if they aren't sure how to spell a word in the title. They only have to type in the first part of the title and then click on the "Title" button. The same list will appear. Emphasize that if they spell a word wrong in the title, the Destiny Catalog will not find *any* results!

Show students an example of a book title that begins with "A," "An" or "The" since these words do not need to be typed. The Destiny Catalog will look for the second word of the title instead.

Review how to look through the results list and find the title, author, and call number in the record. Remind students that they will need to find the call number before they can find the book on the shelf.

When looking for books by the title, there are some important things to remember:

1. Words do not need to be capitalized.
2. Correct spelling is essential!
3. The words in the title need to be in the correct order.
4. Click on the "Title" button to search only by the title.
5. It is okay to type in only the first part of the title.
6. You can skip the first words of a title if they are "A," "An" or "The."

Have students review the important things to remember when searching for a book by title—words do not need to be capitalized, the title must be spelled correctly, the words must be in the correct order, and the word "title" must be selected. It is okay to type in only the first part of the title and the words "A," "An" and "The" can be skipped if they are the first word in the title.

Subject Search

Say to the students, "Sometimes we want to find a book on a specific subject. For example, I might want to find a book about soccer. To do this I will want to search by subject, or what the book is about. I will type in the word "soccer" and then click on the subject search button. The Destiny Catalog will show me a list of all of the books that we have on soccer. I can choose one from the list that looks just right for me."

Review how to look through the results list and find the title, author, and call number in the record. Remind students that they will need to find the call number before they can find the book on the shelf.

When looking for books by the subject, there are some important things to remember:
1. Words do not need to be capitalized.
2. Correct spelling is essential!
3. Use as few words as possible (show an example of trying to do a subject search for "playing soccer," which results in 0 hits).
4. Type in all of the word.
5. Click on the "Subject" button to search only by the subject.

Guided Practice/Independent Practice

Author Search

Have students brainstorm a list of possible authors they might want to look up. Write these on the board so students won't have to figure out the spelling on their own.

Have students choose an author from the list and write it down on their "Author Search Call Slips" (p. 155). Have them practice an author search in the Destiny Catalog.

Title Search

Have students brainstorm a list of possible titles they might want to look up. Write these on the board so students won't have to figure out the spelling on their own.

Have students choose a title from the list and write it down on their "Title Search Call Slips" (p. 155). Have them practice a title search in the Destiny Catalog.

Subject Search

Have students brainstorm a list of possible subjects they might want to look up. Write these on the board so students won't have to figure out the spelling on their own.

Have students choose a subject from the list and write it down on their "Subject Search Call Slips" (p. 155). Have them practice a subject search in the Destiny Catalog.

Assessment

Author Search

- Have students complete an "Author Search Call Slip" (p. 155) for an author search using the Destiny Catalog. Ask them to find the book on the shelf and turn it in with their completed call slip tucked inside.

Title Search

- Have students complete a "Title Search Call Slip" (p. 155) for a title search using the Destiny Catalog. Ask them to find the book on the shelf and turn it in with their completed call slip tucked inside.

Subject Search

- Have students complete a "Subject Search Call Slip" (p. 155) for a subject search using the Destiny Catalog. Ask them to find the book on the shelf and turn it in with their completed call slip tucked inside.

Basic Search Call Slip for Assessment

Name: _____ Class code: _____

Basic Search by Author

Author: _____

Title: _____

Call Number: _____

_____

Name: _____ Class code: _____

Basic Search by Title

Title: _____

Call Number: _____

_____

Name: _____ Class code: _____

Basic Search by Subject

Subject: _____

Title: _____

Call Number: _____

_____

Figure 11.5. Basic Search Call Slip for Assessment

Lesson
Navigating Websites without Getting Lost
Grades 7–8
(Lesson developed by Susie Corbin-Muir)

Standard	Benchmark	Objective
2A: The learner accesses information efficiently and effectively.	The learner uses a variety of print and electronic tools to find information.	The learner uses resource-specific navigational features to access information.

Teen Health & Wellness
http://www.teenhealthandwellness.com/

Mayo Clinic
http://www.mayoclinic.com/

Centers for Disease Control and Prevention
http://www.cdc.gov/

MedlinePlus
http://www.nlm.nih.gov/medlineplus/

The World Health Organization
http://www.who.int./en/

Tools and Resources
- LCD projector and computer (possibly a SMART Board, if available)
- Computers: at least two per group
- List of possible websites (see sidebar)
- **Website Navigation: How to Navigate a Website without Getting Lost** (p. 158), one or two per group
- **Online Research Exit Card** (p. 159)
- Poster paper for listing strategies for navigating websites

Anticipatory Set
Say the following to the students:
- "Have you ever gotten lost? What did you do to get back on track?" (Allow time to share.)
- "Have any of you ever gotten lost in cyberspace? Have you ever done a search and gone to a website and eventually lost track of where you really are? Or gone to a website that should have the information you need but you can't seem to find it? What did you do?" (Allow time to share.)
- "Just as there are tools, signs, and people in our real world that help us find our way, there are devices that website developers use to help the users find their way to the information they need. Some websites are easier to use than others, but hopefully we'll come up with some things that websites have that can make our jobs easier."
- "Today, your group will be assigned a specific website or online database for which you will become the expert navigators. You will then act as that website's GPS to keep us all from getting lost in cyberspace."

Objectives
Students will:
- Navigate a website, identifying and using various navigation tools and features.

Input/Modeling/Checking for Understanding
Say the following to the students.:
- "What are some features you use in books that help you get around and find the information you need?" (List on overhead, whiteboard, or on the screen using an LCD projector.)
- "What features do websites often use to help you navigate? When you first get to a website, what do you do to help yourself get around?"

Key Vocabulary for This Lesson	
article	navigation tools
homepage	online database
icons	reliable

- "Let's navigate the KidsHealth website together. We are going to identify useful tools that you need to look for as you get to a website's homepage. Then we will ask your group to do the same for some other websites that we will be using for research this year."

  http://www.kidshealth.org/

- "How can you tell if you are at the homepage? Why might you want to start there?" (KidsHealth is an interesting website because it provides information at three levels: parents, kids, and teens.)
- "Let's go into the Teen Health & Wellness site. Look around this homepage. In the next two minutes, you and your partner should try to find the answers to the following questions:
  1. Can you tell who is hosting this website? How? Do you think that they can be trusted? What is their purpose for providing this information?
  2. How can you look for specific information on this website? Is there more than one way? If so, which do you prefer?" (Share responses.)
- "Some websites provide a page of information about the sponsor of the website. It may be a link at the top of the page or a brief statement at the bottom of the page. Often you can tell a little about the sponsor by the website address: .gov, .org, .com, etc."
- "Some ways to find information include a search window and list of articles by subtopics. You will notice tabs at the top right of the page you are on. You will see that you can also look at the information for parents or for kids. Sometimes you will get more information in these portions of the site."
- "Let's look at the article on the common cold in the parent section. Once you find this article (a piece of writing about a topic), take a look around. Are there any new features? Can you tell if you are seeing the entire article on the first screen? If not, how did you know? How can you get to the other screens? Is there a "table of contents" or listing of what this article will cover? Are there arrows at the bottom of the screen to get you to the next section? Does the website allow you to save, print, or e-mail the article? If so, where did you find this information? Did they use any special icons (or pictures) to let the reader know these features were available? Is it possible to print the entire article? If so, can you tell how long the entire article is (how many pages will print out)?"
- "Are there any other features that would help a reader with navigation or comprehension? Examples would include options to have the text read aloud, hypertext to definitions of words in the article, or a glossary."
- "Does KidsHealth provide links to other websites that may have additional information on your topic? Where did you find this?"
- "Let's fill in this **Website Navigation** sheet (p. 158) and see what we've learned." (Using the LCD projector, ask students to provide answers to the prompts on this worksheet.)

Guided Practice/Independent Practice

Say to the students, "Your group has been assigned the website at the top of the Website Navigation sheet you have been given. You will need to work together to become experts. You will share your knowledge with the rest of the groups at the end of class today or at the beginning of class tomorrow. Take notes on the Website Navigation sheet. Tomorrow, after we hear from all groups, we will develop strategies for becoming better users of online information sources."

> Note: As students share, use the poster paper to create a list of navigational strategies and devices. These can be posted for students to refer to as they do individual research at a later date.

Assessment

- Collect the **Website Navigation** sheets (p. 158) from the groups to check that they understood what they were looking for.

Website Navigation: How to Get Around a Website without Getting Lost!

Your group has been assigned the website listed below. Your job is to discover the tools that the website designer has given you that help you find and understand the information you need to answer health-related questions.

Group Members	
Website	
Homepage navigation tools	
Article navigation tools	
Options for printing, saving, or e-mailing articles	
Links to other websites	
Features that help readers with comprehension	
Special icons or symbols used in this website	
How do you know this website is reliable?	
What do they tell you about the group who is hosting this website?	
Rate this website for ease of use from 1–10. Explain your answer.	Very Easy ⟵⟶ Very Difficult 1 2 3 4 5 6 7 8 9 10
Favorite feature(s)	
Problems we had in navigating this website	

Figure 11.6. Website Navigation: How to Navigate a Website without Getting Lost

- Evaluate the group's ability to share what they learned from their website exploration activity with the other students.
- Students will apply what they learned this lesson the following week during a research project. There will be **Online Research Exit Cards** (below) for them to fill out at the end of the research day. A sample is included in Figure 11.7.

Online Research Exit Card

Name _____ Class Period _____

Today, I chose to use this website: _____

_____

_____

Navigation tools I used include:

_____

_____

_____

Will you use this website again tomorrow?   Yes   No   **Why or why not?**

_____

_____

_____

_____

_____

Figure 11.7. Online Research Exit Card

PROCESS INFORMATION

Lesson
Evaluating Sources of Information
Grades 9–12
(Lesson developed by Andrea Frederickson)

Standard	Benchmark	Objective	EOY Skill
The learner evaluates and extracts information critically and competently.	Determines accuracy, relevance, authority, and suitability.	Applies evaluative criteria to determine the relevancy, suitability, authority, objectivity, and currency.	N/A

Tools and Resources

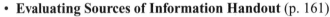

curriculum/lessons.htm

- LCD Projector and computer
- **Evaluating Sources of Information Handout** (p. 161)
- Poster—Evaluating Sources of Information (on the website)

Anticipatory Set

Say to the students, "You've all chosen your research topics. You also have a list of guiding questions. You'll be using the databases SIRS and EBSCO first and then the Internet to locate information on your topic. You will need to evaluate all information that you find before you use it. You'll be using an evaluation tool that will help you sift through articles and information and find things that are best suited to you and your specific research project."

Objectives

Students will:

- Understand and apply the five criteria for evaluating information and choosing appropriate sources of information for a research project.

Input/Modeling/Checking for Understanding

Distribute the **Evaluating Sources of Information Handout** (p. 161). Go over all bullets on the sheet and explain the importance of each. Point out the poster on the wall with the same basic information.

Using the LCD projector, go to SIRS and display a sample article. Using the handout, all students will fill in the information in the first evaluation table as you evaluate the article together. An important part of the modeling is to show students examples of appropriate explanation in complete sentences. After reading the short article, students will help to determine which of the sample guiding questions are answered. Next they'll discuss the reading level of the article. After that they will talk about the reliability of an article from a database like SIRS versus the Internet. They will also discuss whether the article is fact or opinion. Next, students will look at the publication date and decide whether it is acceptable considering the topic. Students will have an opportunity to ask questions as you go over all five criteria.

Guided Practice/Independent Practice

Students will find their own SIRS article and fill out the evaluation boxes with appropriate explanations in complete sentences. The classroom teacher and teacher-librarian will circulate around the room and okay the evaluation. Then students can begin taking notes on their first article.

Assessment

- Students will evaluate each source of information used for their research project.
- Each article evaluation will be checked before students print and/or use articles.
- The evaluation sheet will be submitted with the final project.

Evaluating Sources of Information

Use the following five criteria!

Is your article:

→ *Relevant*   **How pertinent is the information to the topic?**
- Does this source answer most of my guiding questions?
- Is it something I can really use?
- Does it provide enough information or detail?

→ *Readable*   **How suitable is this source for me?**
- Does the Lexile level match my reading ability?
- Is this something I can read and understand? Is it too hard, too easy, or just right?

→ *Reliable*   **How reliable is the information?**
- Is there any information available about the author and his/her expertise on the subject?
- Has a recognized editor/publisher been involved in the publication process?
- Is this from a subscription database where articles are reviewed?

→ *Relatively Free from Bias*   **How balanced is the information?**
- What is the author's purpose in presenting this information?
- Is the information free from bias?
- Is the information backed by facts or is it merely opinion?

→ *Recent*   **How current is the information?**
- When was the item published?
- Does the publication date matter in terms of my topic?

Now analyze an article you find by completing the following chart. You must write a one-sentence explanation of your assessment.

Article title: _____

	Yes	No	Don't Know	Explanation (complete sentence)
Relevant				
Readable				
Reliable				
Relatively Free from Bias				
Recent				

Figure 11.8. Evaluating Sources of Information Handout

Lesson
Using Nonfiction Text Structures to Improve Comprehension
Grade 7
(Lesson developed by Sue Richards)

Standard	*Benchmark*	*Objective*
1: Uses a variety of reading comprehension strategies to understand literature and informational text.	Applies critical thinking skills when reading, viewing, and listening.	Reads widely and fluently to make connections with self, the world, and previous reading.
2B: Evaluates and extracts information critically and competently.	Selects and records information relevant to the problem or question at hand.	Uses appropriate techniques such as highlighting or paraphrasing to extract and record information from resources.
3: Seeks multiple perspectives, shares information and ideas with others, and uses information resources ethically.	Participates and collaborates as a member of a team of learners.	Contributes to the exchange of ideas within and beyond the learning community.

Note: This lesson is a follow-up to the study of text structures in a literacy class. It is an introductory lesson in a social studies unit on global issues and could be used in a number of subject areas.

Tools and Resources
- Document camera and projector
- Magazine articles from EBSCO or another online database on the topic of child labor at a variety of Lexile levels; see **Suggested Child Labor Articles Listed by Lexile** (p. 163).
- Post-It Notes and highlighters
- D'Adamo, Francesco. *Iqbal*. New York: Simon and Schuster, 2007.
- Article: Price, Sean. 2007. "Lost Childhoods." *Junior Scholastic* 109, no. 11: 10.
- **Using Nonfiction Text Structures to Improve Comprehension** (p. 164)
- **Child Labor Note-Taking Sheet** (p. 165)

Anticipatory Set
Say to the students, "In literacy class you read the book *Iqbal*, which was about a child laborer's life in Pakistan. That book was fiction but was based on a true story. Who can summarize what happened to Iqbal? Today we are going to read a magazine article about child workers in Africa. As we read the article, we will review the nonfiction text features and structures that you learned about in literacy class earlier this year. When we are done analyzing this article together, you and a partner will receive another magazine article to read and analyze. Finally, you will answer questions about the article to show how well you understand the issue of child labor."

Objectives
Students will:

- Evaluate and extract information critically and competently using appropriate techniques.

Input/Modeling/Checking for Understanding
Project the first page of the article "Lost Childhoods" using the document camera. Ask: "What is the title of this article? What is the subtitle? Based on this information, what do you think the article is going to be about?"

Suggested Child Labor Articles Listed by Lexile

Current Events. "Working for Change: India Strengthens Child Labor Laws." December 1, 2006, 1–3. Lexile Reading Level: 1000.

Dunn, Deborah. "Is it Fair to Eat Chocolate?" *Skipping Stones*, November/December 2008, 22–23. Lexile Reading Level: 980.

El Nabli, Dina. "Too Young to Work." *Time for Kids*, April 1, 2005, 4–5. Lexile Reading Level: 860.

Farish, Terry. "Fisher Boys." *Faces*, May/June 2009, 27–29. Lexile Reading Level: 920.

Ganguly, Meenakshi. "On a Crusade for Kids." *Time for Kids*, March 8, 2002, 6. Lexile Reading Level: 820.

Harvey, Mary. "Stolen Childhoods." *Scholastic Scope*, February 9, 2004, 15–17. Lexile Reading Level: 740.

Kowalski, Kathiann M. "Not at All Sporting." *Faces*, April 2006, 14–16. Lexile Reading Level: 920.

Maki, Reid. "Children Working Long and Hard." *Faces*, April 2006, 34–37. Lexile Reading Level: 1120.

Palmer, James. "Iraqi Children Join Labor Force." *World & I*, June/July 2006, 32–32. Lexile Reading Level: 1020.

Smith, Steph. "Lost Childhoods." *Scholastic News—Senior Edition*, November 15, 2002, 4–6. Lexile Reading Level: 850.

Stalcup, Ann. "India's Child Labor." *Faces*, September 2003, 8–12. Lexile Reading Level: 1060.

Stehling, Susan. "A Painful Problem." *Faces*, April 2006, 18–21. Lexile Reading Level: 1070.

Tortora, Jason. "Child Laborers in India Unionize to Support Families." *New York Amsterdam News*, August 7, 2003, 18. Lexile Reading Level: 700.

Upadhyay, Ritu. "Hard at Work." *Time for Kids*, January 24, 2003, 4–6. Lexile Reading Level: 890.

Use the technique of "reading around the text" to look at text features such as pictures, captions, and text boxes. Instruct students to look at the picture and read the text box on page 1. Ask: "What does the picture tell you about this boy? How does he feel about his job?"

Project page 2. Read the box called "About Our Cover." Remind students that one text structure is *description*. This describes one of the jobs children do in diamond mines. It also contains an example of another text structure, *sequence*, which deals with time or the order of events. Ask: "Who can find the example of sequence in this text? What is the cue word?" (Kamwala and his brothers cannot return to school *until* their fees are paid.)

Read the text boxes at the bottom of page 2. The quote from Linda Golodner is an example of another text structure, *compare/contrast*, which explains how things are alike or different. Ask: "What two things are being compared? What are the text cues?" (children's and adults' wages; *as much as*)

Show page 3. Read the quote by Guy Thijs. Ask: "What text structure is this?" (*cause/effect*)

Look at the picture of children making mats. Ask: "What does this picture tell you?"

Read the text box called "Teen Diary: A Report from Morocco." This contains examples of all five text structures you learned earlier. Review them. Ask: "How would you *describe* the chores a domestic worker does?" (household jobs such as cooking, doing dishes, cleaning, making beds, washing windows, laundry)

Say to students: "Zahra's employers could have made her job easier. Instead, they made it harder. Find the example of *compare/contrast*." (They had a washing machine, but they made me wash by hand.) Ask: "What is the text cue for this structure?" (*but*)

Ask: "What text structure is being used when you see the cues *10 years ago, when she was 17*?" (*sequence*). "What is another example of *sequence* in this box?" (*I woke up at 6:30 or 7 a.m. and got to bed at 11 p.m.*)

Say to students, "Another text structure is *cause/effect*, which explains why something happens or the consequences of some event." Ask: "What is an example of *cause/effect* in this box?" (her job performance and the employer's abuse) "What is the text cue?" (*if*)

Using Nonfiction Text Structures to Improve Comprehension

Name: _____ Period: _____

Name of article: _____

DESCRIPTION (facts that create a mental picture or support a big idea)

Big idea: The life of a child laborer is difficult and often dangerous.
Details: Describe the jobs done by child laborers, their lives, or working conditions.

SEQUENCE (deals with time)

At what age do children start working? When and for how long do they work?

CAUSE/EFFECT (why something happens or the consequences of a situation)

What causes children to work?

What are the negative effects of child labor?

PROBLEM/SOLUTION (identifies a problem and tells what can be done about it)

Child labor is a worldwide problem. What can be done to solve this problem?

COMPARE/CONTRAST (how things are alike or different)

In one of the articles Senator Tom Harkin from Iowa compared child labor to slavery.
How are they similar?

Contrast your jobs, chores, wages, or allowance to those of a child laborer.

Child laborers do not have much time to study, relax, or play. What are some things that you get to do that they do not?

Figure 11.9. Using Nonfiction Text Structures to Improve Comprehension

Say to students, "The final text structure you learned about is *problem/solution*." Ask: "What was the solution to Zahra's problem?" (A human rights group helped her leave her job.)

Guided Practice/Independent Practice

Read the article aloud or ask students to take turns reading the article. Use Post-It Notes to note text structures and cues. Record notes by paraphrasing.

Pair students with a partner. Give each team a follow-up article at an appropriate Lexile level. The handout on p. 163 contains 14 articles from EBSCO. Give each student the sheet called **Using Non-fiction Text Structures to Improve Comprehension** (p. 164). Direct students to do the following:

1. Read the questions so they know what information to look for in the article.
2. Read the article silently.
3. Go back and read the article again, either silently or aloud. Code the text structures using (D) for description, (S) sequence, (C/E) cause/effect, (P/S) problem/solution, and (C/C) compare/contrast.
4. Highlight text cues and information that will help answer the questions.
5. Record answers briefly in their own words.
6. Discuss with partners.

Assessment

- Observe students working with partners.
- When all groups are done, have the class discuss their articles and responses.
- Although the articles discuss child labor in a variety of countries, ask students to identify similarities and record them on the **Child Labor Note-Taking Sheet** (below).

Child Labor Note-Taking Sheet	
Name: _____	Period: _____
Big idea	**Descriptive details and sequence**
Cause of child labor	**Effects of child labor**
Problem	**Solution**
Compare to slavery	**Contrast with your life**

Figure 11.10. Child Labor Note-Taking Sheet

Lesson
Note Taking
Grades 3–4
(Lesson developed by Sarah Latcham)

Standard	*Benchmark*	*Objective*	*EOY Skill*
Standard 2: Uses inquiry and critical thinking skills to acquire, analyze and evaluate, use, and create information.	Begins to extract information from text based on need.	Uses note-taking strategies to record information with support.	Shows increasing skills in extracting information from print and online.

Note: The major difference between this lesson and the note-taking lesson for fifth and sixth grades (on the website) is that in this lesson, the teacher or librarian is responsible for finding appropriate sources and provides them for the students. In the fifth and sixth grades version, the students are more actively involved in finding the sources of information.

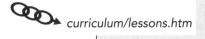

curriculum/lessons.htm

Tools and Resources
- Articles for note-taking set for students/transparency/SMART Board
- Chart paper, overhead, or SMART Board
- Pencils
- Transparency pens
- Introductory books
- **Rules for Note Taking—Grades 3–4** (p. 167)
- **Note-Taking Checklist—Grades 3–4** (p. 167)
- **Note-Taking Rubric—Grades 3–4** (p. 168)

Anticipatory Set
Introduce note taking by reading a book/article that will pique students' interest and lend itself to creating some guiding questions. Some suggestions include: picture book biographies, *Owen and Mzee* by Isabella Hatkoff, or natural disasters. After reading the introductory story, lead the students in a discussion of the book. Ask them to generate a list of further questions that they have. Record the questions on chart paper, transparency, or SMART Board.

Objectives
Students will:

- Be able to answer a question using note-taking strategies with an article provided by the teacher.

Input/Modeling/Checking for Understanding
Depending on how in-depth you would like to get, you can then review the questions and select several that are easier to answer with the class. This promotes the students' thinking about the subject. Some questions are difficult to answer (What was _____ thinking when that happened? This is hard to answer unless you can locate a primary document, for example.) If you don't have the time to do this, you can preselect several questions for the class to answer. Model skimming an article to

see if the answer to the question is found in that article. Read for understanding the article/paragraph that answers the question. You can model "chunking" the article using sticky notes to help students focus. Finally, reread to take notes. The notes that the students write down should follow the guidelines for note taking that you have posted. It is hard for students to not write a sentence. Liken this to texting in that they want to convey their ideas, but be as short as possible. The notes need to be understandable and answer the question.

Guided Practice/Independent Practice

Repeat with additional articles/questions, gradually releasing the responsibility to the students for writing the notes and finding the answers. At the end of the session, have students share their "best" notes. Discuss why they are good (referring to **Rules for Note Taking—Grades 3–4**, below) and how they could be improved. Students could also place their notes by the questions on chart paper or using a SMART Board. This would lead to how to organize notes to create a final project.

Assessment

- Use the **Note-Taking Checklist/Rubric** (pp. 167, 168) to review the students' notes that have been taken independently.

Rules for Note Taking—Grades 3–4

Skim information and examine visuals.

Read information in chunks.

Reread to take notes.

Use own words (no copying).

Record notes you understand.

Write notes, not sentences.

Record notes that answer questions.

Figure 11.11. Rules for Note Taking—Grades 3–4

Checklist for Note Taking

Name _____

_____ Notes are not complete sentences.

_____ Notes are written in student's own words and are not copied.

_____ Notes are short.

_____ Notes are understandable.

_____ Notes answer the question.

Figure 11.12. Note-Taking Checklist—Grades 3–4

Self-Evaluation of Research Process			

Name _____ Topic _____

	RESEARCH STUDENT (needed a *LOT* of help)	RESEARCH APPRENTICE (needed a *LITTLE* help)	RESEARCH EXPERT (needed *NO* help)
I reread information in CHUNKS.			
I recorded only information that answered research questions.			
I recorded information that I understand in notes.			
I recorded NOTES, not sentences.			
I used my own words.			

One thing that is good about how I took notes is:

_____

_____

_____

One thing I would do better next time I take notes:

_____

_____

_____

The hardest thing for me in taking notes was:

_____

_____

_____

The most interesting thing I learned about _____ **[insert topic] is:**

_____

_____

_____

Figure 11.13. Note-Taking Rubric—Grades 3–4

Lesson
Two-Column Note Taking
Grades 6–8
(Lesson developed by Julie Larson)

Standard	*Benchmark*	*Objective*
Standard 2: Uses inquiry and critical thinking skills to acquire, analyze and evaluate, use, and create information.	Selects and records information relevant to the problem or question at hand.	Uses appropriate techniques such as highlighting or paraphrasing to extract and record information from resources.

Tools and Resources
- Document camera or overhead
- Informational text sample with clear headings, one per student. Text should be related to the topic they will be researching.
- **Two-Column Note-Taking Form** (p. 170)

Anticipatory Set
Say to the students, "We have talked about how headings and subheadings in text that you read can help you find information. Today we are going to use a note-taking method that is based upon the idea of topics, subtopics, and details."

Objectives
Students will:

- Learn a two-column note-taking method based upon identifying topics and details in nonfiction text.

Input/Modeling/Checking for Understanding
1. Provide students with an article or other text sample. Model the note-taking process for students using the first two headings of the article. Discuss the following:
   - The section headings represent topics or big ideas, and the sections (paragraphs) contain details.
   - If the heading does not contain a suitable topic name, read the first few sentences to determine the topic.
   - Record the topic in the first column, the details in the second.
2. Have students draw a two-column note-taking form on notebook paper or duplicate the **Two-Column Note-Taking Form** (p. 170) for students.
3. Have students write the source of the information in the space provided on the form, reviewing citation rules discussed earlier.
4. Have students write each topic on the left side of the line, and to the right of the line make a bulleted list of supporting details mentioned in the text. Remind students to write details in their own words, using as few words as possible. Model the first topic with details for students, then have them complete listing topics and details from the text provided.

Guided Practice/Independent Practice
After students have completed the activity (15 minutes), have them work with a partner and compare the topics and details they have recorded. Students will use the two-column method for a variety of note-taking activities.

Assessment

- Circulate as students write their topics and details. Help them identify big ideas and details, as necessary.

Two-Column Note-Taking Form

Name: _____

Topic: _____

Source of your information: _____

_____

Big Idea/Topic	Details

Figure 11.14. Two-Column Note-Taking Form

CREATE AND COMMUNICATE

Lesson
Note Taking and Citation Using Index Cards
Grades 9–10
(Lesson developed by Denise Rehmke)

Standard	*Benchmark*	*Objective*	*EOY Skill*
Standard 2: Uses inquiry and critical thinking skills to acquire, analyze and evaluate, use, and create information.	Selects and records information relevant to the problem or question at hand. Organizes information for practical application. Respects intellectual property rights and understands the need for documenting sources.	Employs a systematic method of organizing extracted information. Respects others' intellectual property by avoiding plagiarism and observing copyright guidelines. Cites sources in a properly formatted bibliography.	N/A

Technology has made it easier to extract information from resources, particularly the growing number of electronic resources. Most of us are very proficient with the prevalent "copy/paste" technique. While this can be an efficient means to extract information, the danger is that the temptation to plagiarize is so strong. Requiring the use of note cards in the research process has several advantages:

- Taking notes on note cards, if done correctly, facilitates paraphrasing, as opposed to word-for-word copying, the hallmark of plagiarism.
- Paraphrasing on note cards requires that the researcher read, digest, analyze, and reflect on the readings. This does not always happen when using the copy/paste technique.
- Coding note cards to properly prepared bibliography cards facilitates more accurate attribution and bibliographic citation.
- Using note cards enables the researcher to organize ideas and information more easily, another important step in the research process.
- The tactile experience of writing notes, then handling and sorting the cards, puts the emphasis on thinking.

Note: This lesson is part of a large research unit completed by ninth-grade students. The complete unit, "Symposium," is found in Chapter 12. While we believe the use of note cards is still a sound means for students to acquire note-taking and citation skills, the lesson could be modified to prepare notes electronically using Microsoft OneNote, NoodleTools, or some similar application.

Tools and Resources
- Document camera or overhead to project sample
- 3 × 5 note cards
- **Sample Bibliography Card** (p. 173)
- **Sample Note Cards** (p. 173)
- **Note Card Evaluation** (p. 175)

Anticipatory Set
Say to the students, "Who can define the term plagiarism?" (Taking someone else's words and passing them off as your own without giving credit to the original source.) "Plagiarism has been an issue for centuries, but because of technology it is becoming even more prevalent. How does technology make plagiarism easier?" (First, information is even more readily accessible to anyone and everyone, primarily because of the Internet. And the ability to copy from one electronic source,

capturing digital text or images, then pasting it into a new document makes it far easier than ever to plagiarize.) "And is plagiarism just something that high school teachers rant about?" (No! Find some recent articles about Stephen Ambrose and Doris Kearns Goodwin, two well-respected, contemporary writers. Both have been accused of plagiarism, which has changed the direction of their careers.) "And perhaps you heard about the recent law school graduate. He was accused and found guilty of plagiarizing several papers while he was in law school, one of which he had published in a law review journal. He lost his job with the firm that had hired him. His law degree was revoked. Talk about a life-altering mistake! And we've had some recent cases here at our school." (Cite local examples.) "So plagiarism is a problem!"

Objectives
Students will:

- Learn note taking with index cards keyed to bibliographic citation.

Input/Modeling/Checking for Understanding
Say to the students, "Avoiding plagiarism involves two key steps. The first is to paraphrase, rather than copy word for word from your sources. The second is to properly cite the sources, giving credit to the original authors. During the next two days, we're going to learn and practice taking notes and citing sources. I must warn you the technique we're going to use is very low-tech! But because it is low-tech, your focus will be on what you're reading and thinking, which is exactly where your focus needs to be!

"At this stage of your research, there are three basic steps: (1) identify relevant, valuable resources; (2) prepare a bibliography card for each of these resources; and (3) prepare note cards to record relevant information from each of the sources." (Give students the following instructions.)

Step 1: Identify Relevant, Useful Resources
1. Skim and scan to determine the value of the article or book. With books, read the table of contents. Note the chapter titles and headings. With articles, read the headings and subheadings. Read the first and last paragraphs of relevant-sounding chapters. Read the first and last sentences of each paragraph in a promising chapter.
2. If the information is relevant, valuable, and useful, prepare a **Sample Bibliography Card** (see, for example, p. 173) for that resource.

Step 2: Prepare a Bibliography Card
1. Record the bibliographic information for each resource on a separate card following the format specified by our Bibliography Style Sheet. (Each student has a copy of this in his/her school-provided planner). Prepare one bibliography card for each useful resource. Do not take notes on the bib cards. Do not put more than one bibliographic citation on each card.

 *curriculum/lessons/bibliography/ H-BibStyle2010.pdf*

2. Assign a bibliography code to each bib card. Write the bib code in the upper right corner of the bib card. The first resource will have the bib code of 1, the second resource will have the bib code of 2, etc.
3. In the lower left, record where the resource was found, particularly for books. For example: West Lib 362.29 Hur. (The location code is not absolutely necessary, but recommended; it makes things much easier if you need to find the material again.)

Step 3: Prepare Note Cards
Project **Sample Note Cards** (p. 173) or use transparencies. Samples are shown in Figure 11.16 and on the website, but you will want to develop your own tailored to specific assignments. Model the following for students:

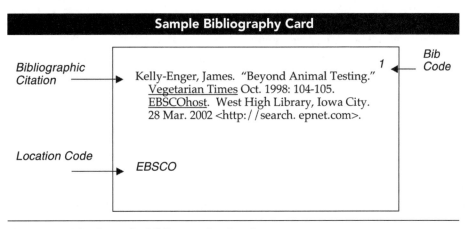

Figure 11.15. Sample Bibliography Card

1. After a resource has been identified as relevant, appropriate, and useful, and a bib card for it has been completed, *begin taking notes.*
2. *Record the appropriate bib code* in the upper right corner of the card. This code corresponds to the bib code assigned to this resource on its bib card.
3. *Record the page number(s)* the information is on in the lower right corner of the card.
4. In the upper left corner, *record a tag*, or at least leave an open space for a tag. A tag is a single word or short phrase that describes a subtopic of your main research topic. (Sometimes, the subtopics aren't clearly evident until a fair amount of reading and thinking is done. In that case, just leave a space for the tag and add it later.)

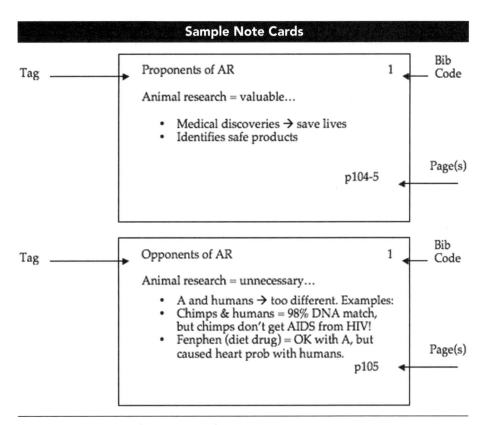

Figure 11.16. Sample Note Cards

5. *Read a passage.* Think about the main point or idea of the passage, and some of the supporting details. Think about how one could explain this point to someone else. Write that explanation on a note card. This is paraphrasing. Here are some *paraphrasing* tips:
   - Don't use complete sentences (unless quoting). Use brief phrases instead.
   - Use abbreviations.
   - Use familiar words and expressions.
   - Record the main point. Then record the supporting details (bulleted list).
   - Record just one main idea and its supporting details on each note card.
   - Only write on one side of each card.

6. *For each relevant resource* (book, article, interview, etc.), *create one bibliography card and from one to many content note cards.* Most of the note cards will have information that has been paraphrased from the original sources.

7. It might be tempting to copy word for word onto note cards and promise oneself to write it "in my own words" later. This is not recommended! If you delay putting your thoughts about the information into your own words, you are much more likely to plagiarize—intentionally or unintentionally! *Translate or paraphrase the information and ideas into your own words immediately upon reading it!*

8. A strategy that helps some researchers with note taking is to highlight first, then translate and paraphrase onto the note cards. Photocopy pages from print sources, or work with printouts from electronic sources. As you read passages, *highlight the main ideas and the important supporting details.* Then fill out the note cards as described earlier.

9. *Occasionally, a quote is desirable;* one needs to extract word for word from a particular source.

10. Or *perhaps there is a relevant statistic or some data* that would be helpful to include.

11. If passages are copied verbatim, *place the quotation in quotation marks.* If it is a quote from someone other than the author, clearly *record the name of the individual whose words they are.*

12. For statistical information or data, *include the source of the data* (e.g., U.S. Census Bureau, American Cancer Society, PETA).

13. In general, keep the "quoting" to a minimum. *Do more paraphrasing than quoting!*

Guided Practice

Show transparencies of various bib cards and note cards. Ask students if the cards are correctly done, or if there are errors or omissions. Poll the class with some examples; call on individual students with others.

Independent Practice

Homework: Students each complete a bib card and at least three note cards for one of the sources they have found so far.

Day 2 begins with a recap of the elements of a bib card and note cards, and a reminder of the note-taking tips. Students continue to work on cards during this period while the teacher and the librarian check the progress of each student by looking over their bib cards and note cards, making suggestions, and identifying a few outstanding examples. Make transparencies of some of the outstanding examples to show in this class.

Assessment

- The bundles of cards are assessed by the librarian using the score sheet shown in Figure 11.17; points are counted in the students' overall grade for the assignment.

Note Card Evaluation

_____ out of 15 points

Name _____

Topic _____

_____ Has minimum of 15 note cards.

_____ Notes contain complete, relevant information for your topic positions.

_____ Notes do not contain enough complete relevant information for your topic positions.

_____ Written well in your own words or documented with quotations. No copying (plagiarism)!

_____ Needs to be done more in your own words.

_____ Well organized with proper labels and tags.

_____ Needs to be organized and labeled better.

Comments or questions:

Figure 11.17. Note Card Evaluation

Lesson
Creating a Beginning Bibliography
Grades 5–6
(Lesson developed by Sarah Latcham)

Standard	Benchmark	Objective	EOY Skill
Standard 2: Uses inquiry and critical thinking skills to acquire, analyze and evaluate, use, and create information.	Cites information sources.	Locates bibliographic information in a source. Creates bibliography with support.	Demonstrates increasing skills in creating a bibliography.

EasyBib
http://www.easybib.com/

Palomar
http://www.palomar.edu/dsps/actc/mla/

Citation Machine
http://citationmachine.net/

KnightCite
http://www.calvin.edu/library/knightcite/index.php

Noodle Tools
http://www.noodletools.com/

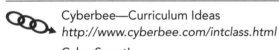

Cyberbee—Curriculum Ideas
http://www.cyberbee.com/intclass.html

CyberSmart!
http://cybersmartcurriculum.org/mannersbullyingethics/

Tools and Resources
- Assorted nonfiction books
- Access to the library catalog
- Access to online databases such as EBSCO, SIRS
- Access to a bibliographic tool such as EasyBib, Palomar, Citation Machine, KnightCite or NoodleTools (see sidebar)
- **Sample Bibliography Graphic Organizer** (p. 177)
- **Bibliographic Citation Assessment Form** (p. 177)

Anticipatory Set
This lesson would be best done as part of a collaborative project between the classroom teacher and the librarian. If so, the anticipatory set may be done by the classroom teacher and the bibliography is being created as part of a larger research project. If this is not the case, discuss with the students the importance of giving credit to the sources used in a project. There are several good websites with teacher ideas/lessons on copyright and plagiarism (see sidebar for additional ideas). Tell students that when they create an original expression of an idea, they also are entitled to copyright protection, so we want to extend that same courtesy to the authors of the sources of information that they are using. One way to do this is by taking good notes. Another way is to cite all sources in a bibliography.

Objectives
Students will:

- Recognize the need to create a bibliography.
- Create a bibliographic citation for several different types of sources.

Input/Modeling/Checking for Understanding
Choose which type of source you are interested in having your students cite. Taking them through multiple types of sources will take several class sessions. The type of source will probably depend on the type of research happening in the classroom. If you are not teaching this lesson in collaboration with the classroom teacher, you will want to visit each type of source in turn. Post or discuss the checklist with students so they know the criteria that you will be assessing them on.

Each student should have a Bibliography Graphic Organizer. You can copy a paper version for each student or use one digitally on computers. A **Sample Bibliography Graphic Organizer** for a book is shown in Figure 11.18 (below). A complete set of organizers for commonly used sources appears on the website.

curriculum/lessons/bibliography/ H-BibGraphicOrganizer.pdf

Begin by looking at a real nonfiction book. Model where to find the bibliographic information on the verso page. If you have been teaching the "librarian information" page to your students with parts of a book, they might be familiar with this page. Show them that the information can also mostly be found on the title page (author, title, publisher), but they will need the verso for copyright date and location of the publisher. Model filling out the graphic organizer using the actual book.

The bibliographic information for books is also available from the library catalog. Model using the library catalog to copy and paste the bibliographic information. First, show the students how to search and create a list using My List in Destiny or a similar tool in other catalogs. From Resource Lists, click on My List. There is a "Citation View" here. If you click on this, the citation is available. Model copying and pasting each piece of the citation from the library catalog to the graphic organizer.

As you teach additional sources, such as reference books or online databases, include how to cite the source in your lessons. Some electronic sources, such as World Book Online, include the bibliographic information at the bottom of the article. Practice copying and pasting this information. It doesn't need to be put into the graphic organizer unless that is the goal of your lesson.

Guided Practice/Independent Practice

Provide time for students to create their own bibliographies for each type of source. After assessing their ability to create a bibliography independently, you may want to introduce them to bibliographic websites such as those listed earlier. At the time of this writing, all of the websites listed previously have free versions available.

Assessment

- Collect one sample of a bibliography citation from each student to assess using the checklist shown in Figure 11.19.

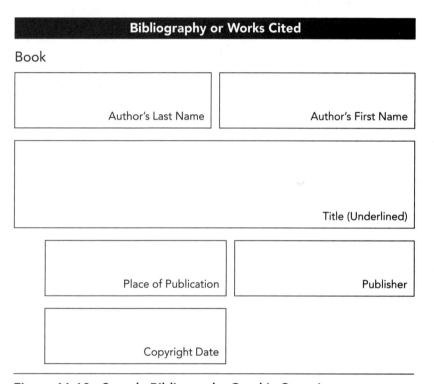

Figure 11.18. Sample Bibliography Graphic Organizer

Bibliography or Works Cited

Name_____

_____ Is able to identify the type of source used

_____ Is able to locate the bibliographic information for the source

_____ Is able to fill out the graphic organizer or use an online citation tool to create a bibliography

_____ Understands that sources need to be cited

Figure 11.19. Bibliographic Citation Assessment Form

Lesson
Producing a "New Directions" Movie
Grades 5–6
(Lesson developed by Sheryl Vitosh)

Standard	Benchmark	Objective	EOY Skill
Standard 2: Uses inquiry and critical thinking skills to acquire, analyze and evaluate, use, and create information. The learner uses information accurately, creatively, and ethically.	Uses technology appropriately to create and share information. Cites information sources.	Uses technology appropriately to create and share information. Cites information sources.	Demonstrates appropriate technology skills such as keyboarding and word processing (EOY). Cites information sources.

Note: This lesson is part of a collaboration with a language arts teacher done at the beginning of the school year. The unit had several goals, including introducing the writer's workshop process, focusing the students on their school's theme for the year ("Moving in a New Direction" [MIND]), and reviewing and improving technology skills. Prior to this lesson, students have selected appropriate clip art for their presentations and created a storyboard using the **Storyboard Illustration** template (p. 179), including slide titles and a script for the narrative portion of the show. This lesson begins the process of importing clip art into the movie and labeling slides according to the storyboard. Successive lessons deal with adding the narrative and audio. Completed projects are posted to StoryTube. More information about this unit may be found on the web.

http://www.iccsd.k12.ia.us/ Schools/Shimek/Library/ MovinginaNewDirection.htm

Tools and Resources
- Computers with network access
- Photo Story for Windows (may also be done in iMovie or other presentation product)
- Clip art selected in previous classes and stored in the student's folder
- "How to Do It" guides created by the librarian so that students can work independently (see previous sidebar)
- **Storyboard Illustration** (p. 179) and a storyboard created in class
- **Photo Story Rubric** (p. 181)

Anticipatory Set
This unit will have been initiated by the showing of a sample video created by the librarian that illustrates the idea of "Moving in a New Direction" and incorporates good design and content elements. Remind students of that movie and that today they will start to assemble their own movie.

Objectives
Students will:

- Begin to assemble their movie from clip art selected and stored in their network folders following the storyboard developed previously.

Storyboard Illustration

Give students a template for creating their storyboard based upon the model below. One or two slides per page works well; the number of slides will depend upon project requirements. Provide a large square for describing or sketching the clip art for each slide, and a space for the title of each slide to be written. Include questions to be "answered" by the slide, depending upon the topic of the presentation. These questions can be brainstormed and decided upon by the class. The storyboard provides a plan for the project and should be completed before students begin using the computer.

Instructions for the student:
For each slide, draw a sketch of your clip art for that slide, and write a title or text on the lines provided. Use complete sentences except for the title and summary slide. Simple words work best!

(Describe picture or clip art here)	(Describe picture or clip art here)
(Slide 1) Title	**(Slide 4) Answer this question: What is one difficulty you foresee? How will you overcome this difficulty?**

(Describe picture or clip art here)	(Describe picture or clip art here)
(Slide 2) Fair use statement. Same picture as first slide. You will type the "Fair Use" statement on this slide. Some of the material in this presentation is covered under the Fair Use Guidelines of the copyright Law, Title 17, U. S. Code	**(Slide 5) Answer this question: How will you know when you have "Moved in a New Direction," or accomplished your goal?**

(Describe picture or clip art here)	(Describe picture or clip art here)
(Slide 3) Answer this question: In what way do you want your life to move in a new direction? Use the list we brainstormed in class to write a complete sentence below:	**(Slide 6) Summary slide. Add the source credit for your clip art to this slide.**

Figure 11.20. Storyboard Illustration

Input/Modeling/Checking for Understanding

1. Beginning the project
   - Instruct students in how to begin a new project using Photo Story or other program.
   - Have students save the project—Rename and save to their MIND Folder.
   - Be sure students have their completed storyboard in front of them, and follow the design they have previously created.
   - Give instructions for importing clip art from the location where it is stored.
   - Have students import clip art for each slide.
   - Remind students to save frequently.
2. Adding titles to slides
   - Have students go to their student folders and open (double-click) saved Photo Story.
   - Instruct students in how to add titles to their slides.
   - Add the title to the first slide—make sure it doesn't cover up important parts of your picture.
   - Add the Fair Use Statement to slide 2—you can give this one an "effect" (this provides a nice opportunity to discuss copyright and citation).
   - Add the iCLIPART credit (or other clip art source credit) to slide 6 (the speech bubble).
   - Save project—remember to say "yes" to "replace existing project?"!

Successive lessons will allow students to add narrative to the slide show, following the script they have written on their storyboards.

Guided Practice/Independent Practice

Continue this process until all slides are created and titled.

Assessment

- The **Photo Story Rubric** (p. 181) is given to students as they begin their project. When the project is completed, students evaluate their own projects in pencil. Then the teacher and librarian evaluate in pen.
- Videos can be posted on SchoolTube, a free site for educators, and a time can be set aside for students to view one another's shows.

 *http://www.schooltube.com/*

	"Moving in a New Direction" Photo Story Rubric

Please evaluate your work below using a pencil. Your librarian and teacher will evaluate using a pen.

Title of Photo Story: _____   <u>Score</u>____ /27

	3	2	1	0
Choosing	• Writing territories are explored when choosing subject for PS. • Subject is appropriate to Shimek Theme, "M.I.N.D." • Subject is meaningful to author.	Includes at least two requirements.	Includes at least one requirement.	No attempt/ incomplete.
	3	**2**	**1**	**0**
Drafting	• Planning template is used in drafting PS. • Template includes ideas for photos/graphics. • Questions are answered using complete sentences.	Includes at least two requirements.	Includes at least one requirement.	No attempt/ incomplete.
	3	**2**	**1**	**0**
Revising	• PS contains no misspellings or grammatical errors. • Constructive peer feedback is given throughout the revising process. • Changes are made to PS in order to improve overall effectiveness.	Includes at least two requirements.	Includes at least one requirement.	No attempt/ incomplete.
	3	**2**	**1**	**0**
Content	• PS contains all of the required slides. • Story maintains a clear purpose so that audience gains an adequate understanding of the subject. • PS shows originality and creativity.	Includes at least two requirements.	Includes at least one requirement.	No attempt/ incomplete.
	3	**2**	**1**	**0**
Pictures/ Graphics	• Are clear and in focus. • Are appropriate for the topic; i.e., they help tell the story. • Are used with permission; i.e., fair use statement has been included.	Includes at least two requirements.	Includes at least one requirement.	No attempt/ incomplete.
	3	**2**	**1**	**0**
Transitions	• Are smooth. • Appropriate to the subject matter. • Add to the overall flow of the PS.	Includes at least two requirements.	Includes at least one requirement.	No attempt/ incomplete.
	3	**2**	**1**	**0**
Narration	• Speech is distinct and understandable throughout the entire PS. • Is loud enough to be heard. • Shows enthusiasm and expression.	Includes at least two requirements.	Includes at least one requirement.	No attempt/ incomplete.
	3	**2**	**1**	**0**
Music	• Is appropriate for the subject. • Can be heard on all slides. • Does not interfere with the narration.	Includes at least two requirements.	Includes at least one requirement.	No attempt/ incomplete.
	3	**2**	**1**	**0**
Saving Work	• PS is saved in M.I.N.D. folder on Vol.1. • Saved as wmv file in preparation for being uploaded on SchoolTube. • Artifacts containing evidence of the writing process are included.	Includes at least two requirements.	Includes at least one requirement.	No attempt/ incomplete.

1. What is one thing you enjoyed about creating your Photo Story?
2. What is one thing you would like to improve in your Photo Story?
3. Will you create a Photo Story during Writer's Workshop in the future?
   Below, please include any comments that might make planning for future students helpful.

Figure 11.21. Photo Story Rubric

12

Collaborative Inquiry Units

OVERVIEW

In this chapter, we present three inquiry units, each developed by librarians and classroom teachers working collaboratively to address the standards and learning objectives of the curricular area and the library curriculum. Each of these units includes an overview which articulates the content-area curriculum and library curriculum standards addressed, the understandings and essential questions, the assessment evidence, and the teaching activities involved. Also included in this chapter are selected lessons, activities, and assessments that accompany each unit. All of the lessons, student packets, activity sheets, rubrics, and assessments for each of the units are available on the website; a sampling of these documents is included in this chapter.

Units in Chapter 12

Beta Biographies—Language Arts, Grades 3–4

Third- and fourth-grade students (Beta Team) at Shimek Elementary complete a collaboratively developed and taught inquiry unit designed by the librarian and classroom teachers. The unit addresses several key standards of the language arts curriculum as well as numerous aspects of the inquiry standards, benchmarks, and objectives of the library curriculum. The students learn about biographies and then select a subject of interest for their biographical research. As a class, they brainstorm ideas and characteristics of individuals and develop categories of information to guide their research: childhood and education; challenges; contributions and accomplishments. While these are fairly typical subtopics of biographical research, this project additionally asks the students to interpret and use insight to determine the character trait that their subject has exemplified in his or her life. They learn to access information in several different types of print and electronic resources. Note-taking techniques and bibliographic citation are primary focus areas, with instruction, modeling, and frequent checks. They learn and practice public speaking techniques and present their findings accompanied by slides they have created. To help them be attentive listeners, they record facts from their classmates' presentations that are incorporated into a game later. This unit incorporates many research and production skills and strategies for elementary students.

Invisible Invaders: Infectious Disease Research Project—Science, Grade 7

The Invisible Invaders: Infectious Disease Research Project is integrated into the seventh-grade science curriculum in our district, and is taught collaboratively by the librarians and science teachers in each junior high school. The lessons vary somewhat. One employs the SQR3 method of note taking (survey, question, read, recite, review), while others use the "Trash-'N-Treasure" method from Barbara Jansen (see Further Reading sidebar), with the students using note cards. There is a focus on evaluating resources and there is a key lesson and activity addressing evaluative criteria. There is also a focus on bibliographic citation—why and how. In one school, all of the students create brochures as the end product to communicate their findings; in another school, students are given a menu of end product choices from which to select. This collaborative unit has become a core unit in the seventh-grade science curriculum for the content standards addressed, as well as the library inquiry standards.

> **Further Reading**
>
> Jansen, Barbara A. 1996. "Reading for Information: The Trash-'N-Treasure Method of Notetaking." *School Library Media Activities Monthly*, February: 29–32.

Symposium—Language Arts, Grade 9

The symposium unit has been integrated into the ninth-grade language arts curriculum for nearly thirty years. It has clearly evolved over the years: topics and issues have changed; tools and resources have changed; strategies and techniques for accessing and extracting information have changed. But some aspects of this research project have remained constant: the need to instruct and give guided practice to note-taking skills, analysis, deep reading and comprehension, organization and synthesis of ideas, and drawing conclusions. Certainly, technology has significantly impacted, facilitated, and enhanced some elements of the inquiry process, but technology hasn't changed every aspect of this project. The higher order thinking skills required by this project still challenge students. This month-long unit is taught collaboratively with language arts teachers; however, the librarians are the lead teachers, doing most of the instruction, and responsible for most of the assessment of student work, except for the final presentation. Because the main objectives of this unit have to do with research and communications skills, the focus is on the inquiry process, and a significant portion of the grades students earn for the month is based on the work they perform each day in this project.

BETA BIOGRAPHIES—LANGUAGE ARTS, GRADES 3–4

 Unit
Beta Biographies—Language Arts
Grades 3–4
(Unit developed by Sheryl Vitosh)

Desired Results

Established Goal(s)
- Library Standard 1: Reads widely both for information and in pursuit of personal interests.
- Library Standard 2A: The learner accesses information efficiently and effectively.
- Library Standard 2B: The learner evaluates information critically and competently.
- Library Standard 2C: The learner uses information accurately, creatively, and ethically.
- Library Standard 3: Seeks multiple perspectives, shares information and ideas with others, and uses information and resources ethically.
- Language Arts: Reading—engage in reading by applying effective strategies for comprehension.
- Language Arts: Inquiry—access information to define, investigate, and evaluate questions, issues, and problems.
- Language Arts: Communication—listen, speak, view, and create to communicate for authentic purposes.

Understandings
- An individual's life story can be examined by looking at common elements.
- Biographical information may be located in a variety of resources.
- Character traits may be synthesized and ascribed by examining various aspects of an individual's life.
- There is a process for moving from selecting a topic through information gathering, analysis, synthesis, and communication of ideas to others.

Essential Questions
- What is a biography?
- How are biographies arranged in the library?
- What are the common elements that comprise an individual's life story?

Students will know:
- What a biography is.
- The process for locating, extracting, processing, analyzing, organizing, synthesizing, and presenting information.

Students will be able to:
- Locate biographies in the library.
- Identify/classify information.
- Access information from a variety of sources (book, encyclopedia, EBSCOhost).
- Take notes by paraphrasing.
- Organize and synthesize information from notes.
- Properly cite sources.
- Create PowerPoint slides.
- Locate and import graphics.
- Use techniques of effective speaking.
- Self-assess (**Biography Project Student Rubric**, p. 193).

Assessment Evidence	
Performance Task(s) • Select a subject of interest. • Locate a biography (book) about the individual. • Take notes using proper techniques. • Locate biographical information in other sources: encyclopedia, EBSCOhost. • Meet with librarian or teacher daily to check on progress. • Cite sources properly. • Prepare a presentation effectively communicating information regarding the subject (individual). • Incorporate effective use of technology to enhance the presentation. • Share with parents.	**_Other Evidence_** • Participation in class.

Teaching and Learning

Learning Activities

(**Boldfaced** type indicates that an item is included in the book; other lessons and resources are accessible on the website.)

- **Biography Project Schedule** (p. 187)
- Locating biographies
- **Biography Classification Graphic** (p. 188)
- Selecting research subject (biography)
- **Biography Project Student Rubric** (p. 193)
- Modeling note taking
- **Biography Note-Taking Sheet** (p. 189)
- Using the encyclopedia
- Note taking
- Using EBSCOhost
- Introduction of PowerPoint **Biography Planner Slides** (pp. 190–192), as graphic organizers for notes
- Modeling effective speaking
- Creating PowerPoint slides
- Locating and inserting graphics in PowerPoint
- **Biography Trivia Contest Worksheet** (p. 194)
- Parent PowerPoint
- Parent Presentation and Viewing

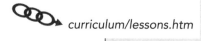
curriculum/lessons.htm

More information about the project and timeline may be found on the web.

Biography Project Schedule	
Where to Find a Biography	The students review what a biography is and how biographies are shelved in the library. Each student checks out a biography.
Classifying What I Want to Know	Kidspiration is used to help brainstorm what information to look for when taking notes. It will also help to classify the information into topic areas.
Selection of Biography	The students select a person to research, identifying their top three choices.
Introduce Rubric	The student rubric will be explained.
Model Taking Notes	The class will be guided through the note-taking process. The grading rubric for content will be reviewed.
Note Taking	Students begin taking notes from their book, focusing on childhood and education. Notes are checked.
Note Taking	Students continue taking notes focusing on challenges. Notes are checked.
Note Taking	Students continue taking notes focusing on accomplishments. Notes are checked.
Using the Encyclopedia	Introduce print encyclopedias. Students find the encyclopedia with their person, and put Post-It Notes at the beginning and end of the article.
Note Taking	Students take notes from the encyclopedia article. Notes are checked.
Note Taking	The students will be instructed on the use of an online source, EBSCOhost, to find biographical information. Notes are checked.
Introduce PowerPoint Planner	PowerPoint planner is introduced and modeled as an organizer for notes. The students will be taught the skill of moving from notes to complete sentences. The grading rubric is reviewed.
PowerPoint Planner	The students will use their own notes to write complete original sentences for their slides. When completed, students will self-edit and have their slide plan checked by a teacher.
PowerPoint Planner	Share the character trait listing to help the kids think of a meaningful character trait that describes the research person. Model writing a character trait with a supporting detail. Students will use their own notes to write sentences for their character trait slides. When completed, students will self-edit and have their slide plan checked by a teacher.
PowerPoint Planner	Model writing bibliographic information from the note-taking sheet. Students will complete their student rubric for content. Teacher will complete the teacher rubric for content.
Model Effective Speaking	Demonstrate effective eye contact and voice quality for character trait videotaping using video of librarian/teacher for students to grade.
Picture for Title Page	Model creating the title page, importing photos (from WorldBook).
Completion Day	Students will share with a partner and get feedback. Students will complete their student rubric for proofreading. Teacher will complete the teacher rubric for proofreading.
Student PowerPoint Viewing—Two sessions	Today the students will present to the class, using PowerPoint slides to enhance the presentation. The class will be taking notes on their fact sheet to be used during tomorrow's trivia contest.
Biography Trivia Contest	The students will work in teams to create a question about each team member's research person. The answer to the question must be the name of the researched person. The questions will then be read aloud by the teacher, and the teams can work together using their notes from the previous days' presentations to figure out the answers.
Parent PowerPoint Parent Presentation and Viewing	The parents are invited to the presentation and the individual viewing of their student's biography PowerPoint. The process involved in the research, the resources used, and the PowerPoint slides will be displayed.

Figure 12.1. Biography Project Schedule

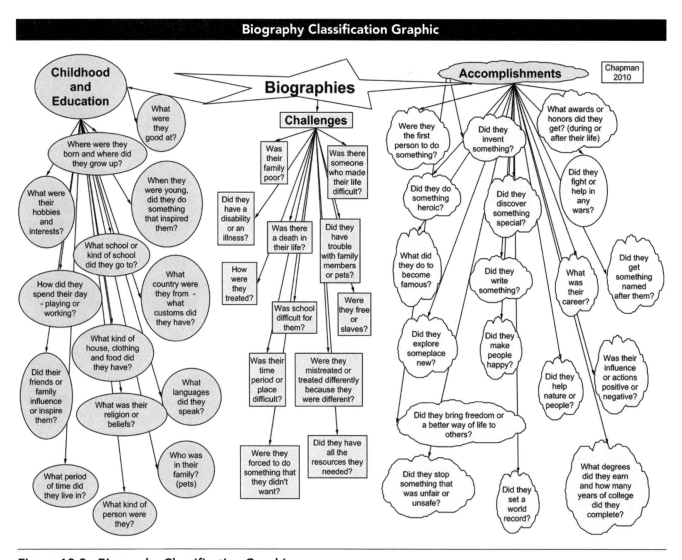

Figure 12.2.   Biography Classification Graphic

Biography Research Notes

Facts about his/her childhood and education:	What challenges did this person encounter?	What accomplishments make this person important in history?

BOOK

Title: _____ Author: _____ Copyright Date: _____

Slide 2	Slide 3	Slide 4

ENCYCLOPEDIA

Encyclopedia: _____ Article Title: _____

Author: _____ Copyright Date: _____

Slide 2	Slide 3	Slide 4

ONLINE SOURCE

http://search.epnet.com   Database: EBSCOKids   Article Title: _____

Copyright Year: _____

Slide 2	Slide 3	Slide 4

Figure 12.3. **Biography Note-Taking Sheet**

Biography Planner Slide 1

Name of Person_____

by Your Name_____

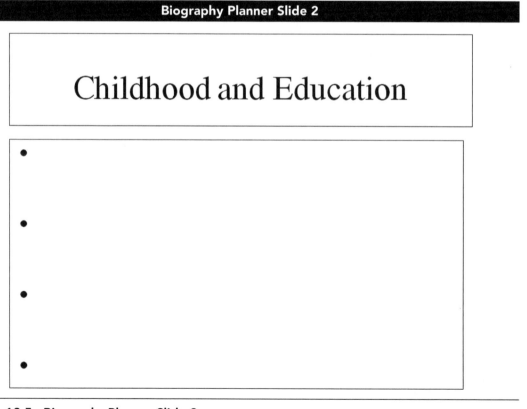

Some of the material in this presentation is
covered under the Fair Use Guidelines of
the copyright Law, Title 17, U. S. Code.

Figure 12.4. Biography Planner Slide 1

Biography Planner Slide 2

Childhood and Education

-
-
-
-

Figure 12.5. Biography Planner Slide 2

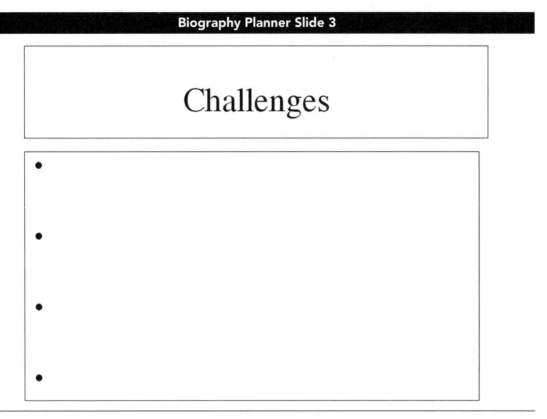

Figure 12.6. Biography Planner Slide 3

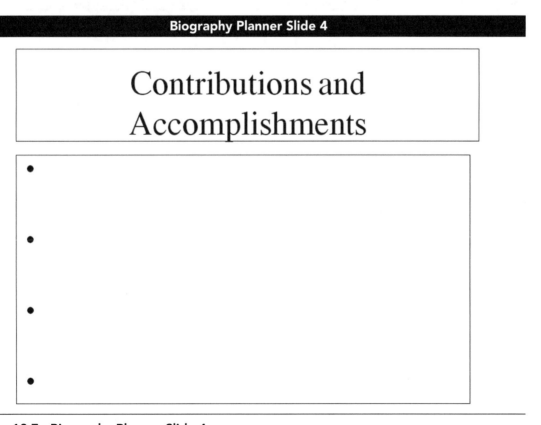

Figure 12.7. Biography Planner Slide 4

Biography Planner Slide 5

What Character Trait Did This Person Exemplify?

Double click to add
media clip

Write what you will say
on the video here.

•

Figure 12.8. Biography Planner Slide 5

Biography Planner Slide 6

Bibliography

- ## Book
  Last Name, First Name. Title of Book. Copyright.

  •

- ## Encyclopedia
  Last Name, First Name. "Title of Article." Encyclopedia Name. Copyright.

  •

- ## Online Database

  Write "Title of Article." Copyright.

  - http://search.epnet.com EBSCOKids.

Figure 12.9. Biography Planner Slide 6

Biography Rubric—Student

Scoring Rubric Total _____ / 39

	3	2	1
CONTENT Total _____ / 18	Use of important words in note format	Some use of important words in note format	Little or no use of important words in note format
	Organized notes in correct categories	Organized some notes in correct categories	Organized little or no notes in correct categories
	Chose most important notes for sentences	Chose important notes for sentences	Chose notes of lesser importance for sentences
	Use of complete sentences on slides	Some use of complete sentences on slides	Little or no use of complete sentences on slides
	Use of complete information in bibliography	Some use of complete information in bibliography	Little or no use of complete information in bibliography
	Character trait is insightful and well supported.	Character trait is somewhat insightful and supported.	Character trait lacks insight and support.
	3	**2**	**1**
PROOFREADING Total _____ / 9	Correct spelling is transferred from first draft to slide show.	Most correct spelling is transferred from first draft to slide show.	Little or no correct spelling is transferred from first draft to slide show.
	Correct capital letters are transferred from first draft to slide show.	Most correct capital letters are transferred from first draft to slide show.	Little or no correct capital letters are transferred from first draft to slide show.
	Correct punctuation is transferred from first draft to slide show.	Most correct punctuation is transferred from first draft to slide show.	Little or no correct punctuation is transferred from first draft to slide show.
	3	**2**	**1**
POWERPOINT Total _____ / 12	The title slide is attractive, easy to read, and contains an appropriate photo.	The title slide is somewhat attractive, easy to read, and contains a photo.	The title slide is difficult to read, and has no photo.
	The background color is attractive, and highlights the text well.	The background color is somewhat attractive, and highlights the text.	The background color makes the text difficult to read.
	Appropriate use of eye contact	Some appropriate use of eye contact	Little or no use of eye contact
	Voice is spoken clearly with appropriate pace.	Some voice is spoken clearly with appropriate pace.	Little or no voice is spoken clearly with appropriate pace.

Figure 12.10. Biography Project Student Rubric

Biography Trivia Contest

As you watch your classmates' biography presentations, record the researched person and student who gave the presentation. Then choose important facts that are interesting and unique to the researched person.

Researched Person	FACTS
	1.
Student	2.
	3.

Researched Person	FACTS
	1.
Student	2.
	3.

Researched Person	FACTS
	1.
Student	2.
	3.

Researched Person	FACTS
	1.
Student	2.
	3.

Figure 12.11. Biography Trivia Contest Worksheet

INVISIBLE INVADERS: INFECTIOUS DISEASE RESEARCH PROJECT— SCIENCE, GRADE 7

Unit
Invisible Invaders: Infectious Disease Research Project—Science
Grade 7
(Unit developed by Sue Richards, Susie Corbin-Muir, and Elizabeth Schau)

Desired Results

Established Goal(s)
- Science Standard 2: Design and conduct investigations using appropriate methods and tools.
- Library Standard 1: Uses a variety of reading comprehension strategies to understand informational text.
- Library Standard 2A: The learner accesses information efficiently and effectively.
- Library Standard 2B: The learner evaluates and extracts information critically and competently.
- Library Standard 2C: The learner uses information accurately, creatively, and ethically.

Understandings
- Infectious diseases are similar/different in terms of symptoms, treatment, prevention, transmission, incidence, and location.
- Why are some infectious diseases declining in incidence while others are on the rise?

Essential Questions
- What causes infectious diseases?
- How are infectious diseases treated?
- How are infectious diseases prevented?
- How do I locate information efficiently?
- How do I determine what information is more relevant and accurate?
- How do I effectively communicate information to my audience?

Students will know:
- Key terms associated with infectious diseases (i.e., transmission, virus, bacteria, vector, epidemic, pandemic, vaccine).
- That infectious diseases are transmitted from person to person, from animal (a vector) to person, or via contact with contaminated food or water.
- How infectious diseases affect the human body, how they are treated and/or prevented, and ways to limit the spread of an infectious disease.
- That environmental and economic factors affect the spread of infectious disease.
- Strategies and skills for locating, evaluating, and using a variety of sources of information.

Students will be able to:
- Access information from a variety of sources.
- Evaluate information sources, take effective notes, organize and synthesize information, and properly cite sources of information.
- Use desktop publishing skills to create a brochure that conveys current accurate information to a specific audience.

Assessment Evidence	
Performance Task(s) <ul><li>Select a topic, locate and read information on the topic.</li><li>Take notes using proper paraphrasing.</li><li>Cite all sources used.</li><li>Summarize information.</li><li>Organize information; create a storyboard.</li><li>Develop a bibliography.</li><li>Locate images to enhance the written text.</li><li>Create a brochure or another product to communicate findings.</li></ul>	**Other Evidence** <ul><li>Activity worksheets.</li><li>Observation.</li><li>Checkpoints (note cards, bibliographies).</li><li>Rubrics.</li></ul>

Teaching and Learning

Learning Activities

(**Boldfaced** type indicates that an item is included in the book; other lessons and resources are accessible on the website.)

- Introduction to unit; selection of topics; description of end product; brainstorming contents and design features; reviewing packets, and evaluation rubric.
  - **Disease Research Overview and Timeline** (p. 197)
  - **Disease Research Project Options** (p. 207)
  - **Disease Research Project Evaluation** (p. 198)
  - **Disease Research Bibliography Rubric and Brochure Contents** (p. 206)
- Note taking—creating note cards.
  - Lesson: Note taking with the SQR3 strategy
  - Lesson: Note taking with the Trash 'N Treasure strategy
- Evaluating and citing sources.
  - Lesson: **Evaluating and Citing Sources of Information** (pp. 199–202)
  - Activity: **Disease Research Evaluating and Citing Sources Activity** (p. 203)
- Summarizing/synthesizing.
  - Activity: **Disease Research Summarizing Notes Worksheet** (p. 205)
- Storyboarding.

Production

- Locating, saving, and citing images/graphics.
- Creating and formatting a bibliography.
- Creating a brochure (Microsoft Word).
  - **Disease Research Bibliography Rubric and Brochure Contents** (p. 206)
- Assessing brochure/refining use of checklist.
- **Disease Research Project Options** (p. 207).

Infectious Disease Research Project

The CDC and the WHO are agencies that provide health information to the public and advisories for international travelers. One of these agencies has hired you to join their publications department, which produces brochures about a number of infectious diseases. They need high-quality, accurate information to promote public health. You will be creating a brochure on a specific disease for one of these agencies. **These brochures are to be written for a teenage reader.**

OBJECTIVES

Each student will:
1. Study one infectious disease in depth;
2. Practice research skills including:
   - Accessing information using a variety of print and online sources
   - Note taking and paraphrasing information in one's own words
   - Organizing information in a cohesive, creative manner
   - Citing sources of information;
3. Learn the basics of desktop publishing and importing images;
4. Produce a brochure that conveys current knowledge about the disease;
5. Learn about other diseases from classmates.

EXPECTATIONS:

You will be expected to come to class prepared and use your time efficiently. You will be on task and not disrupt others. You will be respectful of the resources in the library and computer lab. You will meet all deadlines set by the teacher or librarian.

EVALUATION:

You will use *at least* **four** sources to gather information. At l**east two** of the sources must be **print** (a book, encyclopedia, etc.). You will record *all* your research notes on **note cards.** You will record the sources of your information and graphics on **"bib cards."** You will produce a brochure intended for readers ages 12–18 that conveys current knowledge about your disease. It will be presented in an attractive and well-organized format, including a title and at least **two graphics** with **captions**.

DISEASE UNIT TIMELINE

Day 1 Classroom
- Students pick topics. Process choices.

Day 2 Classroom
- Intro. DCD and WHO. Hired to make brochure for teens.
- Brainstorm contents. Brainstorm design features. Show samples.
- Assign students to read over evaluation rubric.

Day 3 Library
- Hand out diseases article. Put name, period and #1 on top. Put name of disease on packet cover.
- Examine title page and model bib card.
- Bib card due by end of period. (5 pts.)
- Assign—read and highlight article.

Day 4 Classroom
- Signature due (5 pts.). Collect bib cards that didn't get done previous day.
- Model note taking/note cards using killer flu article. Explain code.
- Work on note cards. Five cards due tomorrow.

More information about the project and timeline may be found on the web. *curriculum/Lessons.htm*

Figure 12.12. Disease Research Overview and Timeline

Evaluation for Disease Research Project			
SPECIFIC REQUIREMENTS		**Possible Points**	**Points Earned**
Cause and Transmission	• The reader would understand what microbe causes this disease and how it is transmitted or spread	5	
Organ or Organ Systems	• The reader would understand how this disease affects the body	5	
Symptoms	• The reader would be able to spot the signs of this disease (e.g., How soon do they develop? How long do they last?)	5	
Treatment or Cure	• The reader would understand what a doctor would do or recommend	5	
Prevention	• The reader would understand how to avoid getting this disease with medicine and/or through personal behavior	5	
Incidence	• The reader would know quantitative information about this disease	5	
Location	• The reader would know where in the world this disease is most likely to occur	5	
Layout/Design	• Title conveys content of brochure and grabs reader's attention • Shows correct formatting of columns, text, images and captions • Includes at least two relevant images • Captions included for each image in body text and serve to complement the text	10	
Total Points for Brochure		45	
Additional Project (by choice, scored with rubric)		5	
Total for Project		50	
Additional Points			
Bibliography	• Cited **ALL** sources of information **AND** graphics • Used at least four sources; including two print sources • Accurately followed bibliography style sheet	10	
Work habits and conduct		20	
Checkpoint assessments		40	
Storyboard (rough draft)		20	
Grand Total		140	

Figure 12.13. Disease Research Project Evaluation

Lesson
Evaluating and Citing Sources of Information
Grade 7
(Lesson developed by Sue Richards)

Standard	Benchmark	Objective
Standard 2: Uses inquiry and critical thinking skills to acquire, analyze and evaluate, use, and create information. B. The learner evaluates and extracts information critically and competently. C. The learner uses information accurately, creatively, and ethically.	Selects and records information relevant to the problem or question at hand. Practices ethical behavior with regard to information and information technology.	Applies evaluative criteria to determine the appropriateness of the information with respect to: relevancy, suitability, authority, objectivity, and currency of the information. Observes copyright guidelines by recording sources using a standard format. Creates a properly formatted bibliography.

Tools and Resources
- Computer for each student; projector for teacher computer
- **Disease Research Evaluating and Citing Sources Activity** (p. 203)

Anticipatory Set
Say to the students, "You have had an opportunity to locate some basic information on your disease topic using print resources. Now that you have some basic information, another source you could try is the Internet. There is a great deal of information out there, but there is also a lot of 'junk.'

"It is important for you to carefully evaluate the sources of information you find on the web. When we looked for magazine articles using EBSCOhost, we talked about five criteria to consider when evaluating sources. The same five criteria should be used to evaluate websites.

"We will review those five criteria as we examine some online resources. This will help you locate useful information on your research topic. I will also show you how to cite online resources for your bibliography. At the end of the period you will be given an activity sheet to complete to demonstrate your ability to evaluate sources of information."

Objectives
Students will:

- Learn to locate, evaluate, and cite online resources.

Input
Say to the students, "Log on to the computer using your student login and password. Launch Internet Explorer."

Search Engines/Directories on the Web
Ask: How many of you like to do research using the Internet? Why? (Fast, easy, get lots of information.) That's the good news.

Ask: What problems have you had using the Internet? (Sometimes you can't read the information, may not be on your topic, a personal website by someone who doesn't know what he is talking about, etc.)

Ask: When you use the Internet, what is your favorite search engine? (Google.) How many of you use Google?

Evaluating Sources of Information

Go to Google. Search rabies. Point to CDC—Rabies.

Ask: Who remembers what CDC stands for? (Centers for Disease Control and Prevention.)

Ask: What makes you think you can trust the information from this site? (It's a government agency that distributes health information. Point out .gov URL.)

Review the evaluative criteria of *AUTHORITY* (#3 in Figure 12.14). *Is the information reliable? What do you know about the author? Is he/she an expert?*

Ask: What is the purpose of CDC? (To keep citizens informed so they can be safe and healthy.)

Review the criteria of *OBJECTIVITY* (#4). *What is the author's purpose in presenting this information? Is the information backed by facts or is it merely opinion?* If possible, try to determine if the author's purpose is to inform, persuade, or sell something. Try to detect whether the information is factual or just an opinion.

Go to the *CDC* site. Look at *"Rabies Basics."*

Ask: Which of these do you think could be useful? Why? (When to get medical attention, care, symptoms, how transmitted, diagnosis, prevention, because these are topics that should be covered in the brochure.)

Review the evaluative criteria of *RELEVANCY* (#1). *Is the information on target for my research topic? Is it relevant? Is it something I can really use?*

Ask: Which topics are not relevant? Why? (Risk for pets, prevention in pets, because you are researching diseases in humans, not animals.)

Click on the U.S. map. Look at the section called *"Cost of Rabies Prevention."*

Ask: Is this a required topic? (Point out that it is not required, but "economic impact" is one of the optional topics. See Figure 12.16.)

Go back to the *Rabies homepage.* In the article, find *"rabies virus"* and click on the link. Start reading the first paragraph.

Ask: Is this information useful? Why? (No, it is hard to read; it is not at a suitable reading level.)

Review the evaluative criteria of *SUITABILITY* (#2). *Can I read and understand the information or is it too advanced or specialized?*

Ask: Who is the target audience for your brochure? (Teens ages 12–18) Could the audience for my brochure read and understand it?

Go back.

Ask: Do you see a part of the website that might be more suitable? ("Rabies and Kids.") Show that part of the site.

Point out that *Rabies—Medline Plus* is another .gov. Show what nlm.nih stands for.

Go back to results. Point out *WHO*.

Ask: What does that stand for? What makes you think that this site would be authoritative and objective? (They are health experts whose job it is to distribute information to keep people healthy.)

Look at the last date updated (Sept. 2010).

Ask: What does this tell you? (It's up-to-date, current.)

Review the criteria for *CURRENCY* (#5).

Start to read the article.

Ask: Is this written at a suitable reading level?

Go back to search results. Point out *Wikipedia*.

Ask: How many of you use Wikipedia? What do you know about this site? (It is a free encyclopedia and anyone can contribute or edit articles at any time. This means it can be updated constantly, keeping it current.)

Remind students that *CURRENCY* is only one of the criteria for evaluating information.

Point out the alert—"This article may require cleanup to meet Wikipedia's quality standards."

Ask: I don't think I should use this article. Why? (I don't know anything about the qualifications of the people editing. *AUTHORITY*?)

Ask: If you use information from Wikipedia, how can you be sure it is objective, factual and not just someone's opinion? (Find out if it is backed up by other sources.)

Go back to the article and assess the *SUITABILITY*.

Go to *"Rabies"* from KidsHealth.org.

Ask: Who maintains this website? (An organization.)
Ask: What do you need to know before you take their information? (Who are they?)
Explain: Some .orgs may be useful; some may not. It depends on who is posting the information.

Go to the site. It is called *KidsHealth*. Look at "What's in this article?" Have students raise their hands for each topic that is required in the packet.

Scroll down to the end of the article.

Ask: Who reviewed this article and when? What does this tell you? (A doctor so it is authoritative and it's fairly current.)

We need to know more about the organization responsible for this website. Click on *KidsHealth* at the top of the screen. Point out that they have sections for Parents, Kids, and Teens.

Ask: Why would this be useful? (More readable.)

Click on *"About KidsHealth."* This explains what this organization is and who provides their information.

Go to the site *Rabies—What You Need to Know*.

Point out that KidsHealth was a useful .org site. Not all .orgs are useful.

Ask: Whose web site is this and what is their area of expertise? (It is the Cat Fanciers' Association. They are experts on cats and cat shows.)

> Ask: What would be a more authoritative source for medical information? (CDC, WHO, a hospital, a university, a doctor, a state department of health, etc.)

While searching the web we turned up some good information, but we also found some "junk." It took time to evaluate each site to find relevant, reliable, objective, current information at a suitable reading level. Let me show you a shortcut.

Go to the *NW homepage*, and click *"Library"* then *"Science 7 Resources."* Here you will find links to websites for *Infectious Diseases*. All of these have been evaluated by your teacher and librarian.

> Ask: Which websites do you recognize? (CDC, KidsHealth, Medline Plus.)
>
> Explain: The Mayo Clinic is a well-respected medical clinic. Two websites are maintained by state departments of health (IL and NY). They are like the CDC, except at the state level, and they provide easy-to-understand fact sheets. Medline is an online medical encyclopedia. Rather than doing random Google searches, we encourage you to use these sites.

Go back to the Library page. Remind students that netTrekker is another search engine to try besides Google. It has teacher-recommended websites.

Point out Teen Health & Wellness, an online service provided by the AEA that covers some disease topics. (*If time permits, try Lyme disease.*)

- *Both netTrekker and Teen Health can be accessed remotely, but will need a username and password.*

Remind students that they must *cite* the sources of their information. Refer to the Bibliography Style Sheet for the correct format. Point out that under *Online Resources* there are examples for the recommended websites. Model how to write a bibliographic citation for the CDC website.

curriculum/lessons/bibliography/ H-BibStyle2010.pdf

Remind students not to include Google in a citation.

> Ask: Why do you not put Google in a bibliography? (It's a search engine, not a website.)

Checking for Understanding
Checking for understanding is built into the modeling in the form of questions to ask.

Guided Practice
As students research their chosen disease topics, the teacher and librarian will provide guidance, assistance, and remediation, as needed.

Independent Practice
Students may access the Internet from home or independently in the library.

Assessment
The teacher and librarian will informally assess students' ability to navigate the web and print appropriate information. The students' ability to evaluate and cite sources will also be assessed using the **Disease Research Evaluating and Citing Sources Activity** (p. 203) that has been designed jointly by the teacher and librarian. The librarian will also assess the ability to properly cite sources by evaluating the students' final bibliographies.

Evaluating and Citing Resources

Name _____   Period _____   Points _____

When you are researching, an important skill is being able to select the BEST information—that which is most appropriate for your particular need. As you examine sources of information ask yourself the following questions to help you evaluate and select the best information to meet your research need.

☐ 1. Relevancy   *How relevant is the information to the topic?*

   Is this source appropriate (on target) for my research topic?

☐ 2. Suitability   *How suitable is this source for me?*

   Is this something I can read and understand or is it too sophisticated or advanced?

☐ 3. Authority   *How reliable is the information?*

   Is there any information available about the author? Can you tell if he or she is an expert on the subject?

☐ 4. Objectivity   *How balanced is the information?*

   What is the author's purpose in presenting this information? Is it fact or is it merely opinion?

☐ 5. Currency   *How current is the information? Is that important?*

   When was the item published? Is it up-to-date enough for my topic?

Practice applying these evaluative criteria. Here is the research topic you are investigating:

Explain the cause, transmission, prevention, and treatment for the disease anthrax.

Answer these questions about the Internet search results on the separate page. Make sure that you look at the website's **address** (URL) and the brief **description** about each site. After you *circle* a letter, <u>explain</u> your answer on the lines below each question. **DO NOT USE A LETTER MORE THAN ONCE!**

Which website is **least relevant** to the research topic?   A B C D E F G H   *circle one*

_____

_____

_____

Which website is the **least suitable** for you?   A B C D E F G H   *circle one*

_____

_____

_____

Which website has the **least authority** for the topic?   A B C D E F G H   *circle one*

_____

_____

_____

Which website has the **least current** information?   A B C D E F G H   *circle one*

_____

_____

_____

Now, from the remaining four websites, select the one site you think would be the best, the most appropriate for gathering information on the research topic.

I think the best site would be: _____ *(indicate letter)*

Figure 12.14. Disease Research Evaluating and Citing Sources Activity   *(Continues)*

Evaluating and Citing Resources *(Continued)*

Now, analyze this website by completing the chart below. Put a **checkmark** in one of the three boxes labeled **Yes**, **No**, or **Don't Know** next to each of the five evaluative criteria listed. Then provide a reason for your checkmark in the box labeled **Explanation**.

	Yes	No	Don't Know	Explanation
Relevancy				
Suitability				
Authority				
Objectivity				
Currency				

Another website that I think would be useful is: _____ *(indicate letter)*

Complete the chart just as you did with the one above.

	Yes	No	Don't Know	Explanation
Relevancy				
Suitability				
Authority				
Objectivity				
Currency				

Citing Online Resources—Practice

When researching, cite the sources you used to find all of your **information**.

On December 12, 2010, a student did a search for measles on the Internet and found a website called **Epidemic and Disease Control Program**. The student used the site to take notes.

Look at the six bibliography samples below. **One** is correct; the others contain mistakes. *CIRCLE* the citation that is correct. Under each of the others, explain **all** of the mistakes you found.

"Measles." Web. <http://www.edcp.org>

Measles. *Epidemic and Disease Control Program* Web 12 Dec. 2010 <http://www.edcp.org>

"Measles." *Google*. Web. 12 Dec. 2010. <http://www.google.com>.

"Measles." *Epidemic and Disease Control Program*. Web. Dec. 12, 2010. <http://www.edcp.org>.

"Measles." *Epidemic and Disease Control Program*. Web. 12 Dec. 2010. <http://www.edcp.org>.

"Measles." *Epidemic and Disease Control Program*. Web. 12 Dec. 2010. <http://www.edcp.org>.

Figure 12.14. Disease Research Evaluating and Citing Sources Activity

Note-Taking Summary

Do NOT write in complete sentences!
Use this to organize the information on your note cards.

Enough	Need More	
		What microbe **causes** the disease?
		How is the disease **transmitted** or **spread**?
		What **organs** are affected by this disease? What does it do to your body?
		What **symptoms** are associated with the disease? How soon do they develop? How long do they last?
		How is the disease **treated** or **cured**? How does it clear up?
		How is this disease **prevented**? How can you avoid getting it?
		What **incidence** information did you find out about your disease?
		In which **locations** of the world is the disease **most often** found?

- What are other similar or related diseases?

- What is the historical significance of the disease?

- Who discovered the cause of the disease?

- Who was instrumental in the treatment and/or cure of the disease?

- What is the economic impact of this disease?

- What recent breakthroughs have occurred in regard to the disease?

- What does the future hold with regard to the disease?

- What other interesting information did you find about your particular topic?

Figure 12.15. Disease Research Summarizing Notes Worksheet

Bibliography Rubric

A. FORM AND CONTENT   (**U** = Unacceptable; **A** = Acceptable; **O** = Outstanding)

U	A	O		
❐	❐	❐	1.	Listed alphabetically (1 pt.)
❐	❐	❐	2.	Used correct punctuation (2 pts.)
❐	❐	❐	3.	Used correct indentation (1 pt.)
❐	❐	❐	4.	Included correct information per entry (3 pts.)
❐	❐	❐	5.	Used a variety of sources, print and online (1 pt.)

B. NUMBER OF SOURCES   Required 4 _____ (1 pt.)   Over 4 _____ (2 pts.)

GRADE/SCORE _____ **/10 pts.**

Disease Brochure Contents

Each brochure **MUST** contain:
- ❏ Title
- ❏ Body text
- ❏ Two graphics (with captions)
- ❏ Bibliography

Each brochure **MUST** address the following required questions:
- ❏ What microbe **causes** the disease?
- ❏ How is the disease **transmitted** or spread?
- ❏ What **organs** or **organ systems** are affected by this disease? What does it do to your body?
- ❏ What are the **symptoms** associated with the disease? How soon do they develop and last?
- ❏ How is the disease **treated** or **cured**? How does it clear up?
- ❏ How is this disease **prevented**? How can you avoid getting this disease with medicine and/or through personal behavior?
- ❏ What **incidence** information can you find about this disease?
  - ○ Who is most often affected?
  - ○ How many cases of this disease were reported in recent years?
  - ○ How many deaths were reported?
  - ○ Is this disease on the rise or on the decline?
- ❏ In which locations of the world is the disease **most often found**?

Other questions you should try to address, **if possible**, include:
- ❏ What are other similar diseases?
- ❏ What is the historical significance of the disease?
- ❏ Who discovered the cause of the disease?
- ❏ Who was instrumental in the treatment and/or cure of the disease?
- ❏ What is the economic impact of this disease?
- ❏ What recent breakthroughs have occurred in regard to the disease?
- ❏ What does the future hold with regard to the disease?
- ❏ What other interesting information did you find about your particular topic?

You must include **ALL** of the required elements and answers to the required questions above to earn maximum points. See the Project Evaluation page for more information on grading.

Figure 12.16. Disease Research Bibliography Rubric and Brochure Contents

Infectious Disease Project Options

This menu of project options is based on ideas about differentiation from Diane Heacox, described in her book *Differentiating Instruction in the Regular Classroom* (Free Spirit Press, 2002).

- All students will complete enough tasks to equal ten points.
- Students will contract with their teachers for the projects they want to complete.
- A bibliography and notes will be turned in by each student.

2-Point Options (you may do up to three of these two-point projects)

You work at the CDC and your boss needs the following graphics; pick one or more to create:

- A chart or other graphic to highlight the deadliest infectious diseases that includes statistics about how many people die from each disease.
- A map that shows where a specific disease is most prevalent (common). Color-code the map to show the severity of the problem.
- A poster that explains the spread of a specific disease.
- A timeline of important dates in history related to a specific disease. This could include epidemics as well as milestones in the understanding and treatment of the disease.

4-Point Options

You work for an organization that focuses on public health. Please identify the organization you work for and choose one of the following tasks to complete for your job there. Examples of organizations include the World Health Organization, the Red Cross, and Rotary International.

- Create a public service campaign that educates parents about the need to vaccinate their children or a public service campaign about how to prevent the spread of disease.
- Interview a public health official and write an article for the local newspaper.

Another four-point option

- Pretend you are a bacterium, virus, or other disease pathogen. Create a comic strip, rap, or other way to inform your audience about how you are spread. Be sure to teach your audience how you can be defeated.

6-Point Options

- Create a brochure for a doctor's office about a specific disease.
- You are a reporter for the Weather Channel. Create a report for your station about a natural disaster and how it is creating conditions favorable for an outbreak of a specific disease such as cholera.

10-Point Options

- You are an epidemiologist. Create a presentation asking for funding to eradicate a disease in a specific area of the world.
- You are a teacher and want to create a fun way for your students to learn about staying healthy and avoiding infectious diseases (you may choose to focus on one disease or a variety of related diseases). You choose to create a game for them to play. Be sure that the game helps them learn about the disease(s) you have selected.
- You are a health worker and have just returned from a country where there are a significant number of cases of a specific infectious disease. Create a scrapbook/journal or website/blog about your two weeks in this country and what you learned about the disease that is having an impact on that country.

Figure 12.17. Disease Research Project Options

SYMPOSIUM—LANGUAGE ARTS, GRADE 9

Unit
Symposium—Language Arts
Grade 9
(Unit developed by Denise Rehmke, Beth Belding, Jim Walden, and Jill Hofmockel)

Desired Results

Established Goal(s)
- Library Standard 2A: The learner accesses information efficiently and effectively.
- Library Standard 2B: The learner evaluates information critically and competently.
- Library Standard 2C: The learner uses information accurately, creatively, and ethically.
- Library Standard 3: Seeks multiple perspectives, shares information and ideas with others, and uses information and resources ethically.
- Language Arts: Reading—engage in reading by applying effective strategies for comprehension.
- Language Arts: Inquiry—access information to define, investigate, and evaluate questions, issues, and problems.
- Language Arts: Communication—listen, speak, view, and create to communicate for authentic purposes.

Understandings
- Many issues (e.g., human rights, social issues, conflicts) can be analyzed in terms of the problem (cause and effect)/solution paradigm.
- To develop a comprehensive position on an issue, a wide range of information and information sources must be consulted.
- Navigation techniques and search strategies facilitate the location of information.
- There are logical steps in the research process for locating, evaluating, organizing, and communicating information to make a point.

Essential Questions
- What is the main focus of my research?
- What are some causes of or contributing factors to the problem?
- What are some of the effects (on individuals, families, communities, nations, etc.) of this problem or situation?
- What are possible solutions to this problem?
- What could be done to prevent this problem?

Students will know:
- The general range of content, structure, and features of a wide variety of information sources.
- How to select authoritative sources for formal academic research based on established evaluative criteria.
- The process for locating, extracting, processing, analyzing, organizing, synthesizing, and presenting information.

Students will be able to:
- Use specific features of individual databases to better search and access information.
- Apply evaluative criteria to select the best available sources for a research topic.
- Properly create bibliographic citations for sources, take notes using note cards, use strategies for organization of note cards, and create a formal outline.
- Articulate the cause, effect, and solution of issues surrounding their topic.
- Use multimedia/technology to effectively enhance the presentation of information to an audience.

Assessment Evidence	
Performance Task(s)	**Other Evidence**
• Select a topic that is timely, significant, and interesting. • Effectively use the catalog to locate books and media items on the topic. • Access a wide variety of databases. • Use searching/navigating skills to find relevant information. • Apply evaluative criteria to select sources to support research topic. • Create perfectly formatted bibliographic citations for sources. • Properly paraphrase/quote on note cards. • Recap with librarian or teacher to check understanding of content and research progress. • Create a formal outline. • Develop a bibliography. • Create a 5–7-minute presentation effectively communicating information regarding the topic. • Incorporate effective use of technology to enhance the presentation.	• Pre-activity: Topic selection activity, discussion, (worksheet). • Locate and check out relevant books. • Refine topic (worksheet). • Select and print articles from SIRS, Opposing Viewpoints, CQ Researcher. • Properly created note cards and bib cards. • Idea organizer (graphical outline). • Work ethic.

Teaching and Learning

Learning Activities

(**Boldfaced** type indicates that an item is included in the book; other lessons and resources are accessible on the website.)

- **Symposium Project Overview** (pp. 210–211) and **Symposium Project Timeline** (p. 212) (full packet is accessible on the website).
- Lesson: Topic selection discussion/activity (see **Developing an Understanding of Your Topic**, pp. 146–148, in Chapter 11).
- Lesson: Using the library catalog.
- Lesson: Review SIRS; introduce CQ Researcher and Opposing Viewpoints databases.
- Lesson: Bibliographic citations, note-taking strategies (see **Note Taking and Citation Using Index Cards**, pp. 171–175, in Chapter 11).
- Lesson: **Symposium Project Idea Organizer** (p. 213).
- Lesson: Review various EBSCOhost databases; introduce Teen Health & Wellness.
- **Symposium Project Research Recap** (p. 214): Meet individually with librarian or teacher to discuss topic and research process.
- Lesson: Create a **Symposium Project Formal Outline** (p. 215).
- Lesson: Review bibliography.
- Lessons: Create effective visuals to enhance a presentation.

Symposium Project 2011

Name _____ Teacher _____ Period _____

Symposium Project 2011

A symposium is a gathering or meeting in which a group of individuals deliver short addresses on a topic.

In this project, students will prepare and present a symposium. Each student will select an issue of interest and research that issue using a variety of information resources. Each student will present information addressing the issue: giving background, then describing the problem and the possible solutions.

REQUIREMENTS/GRADING CRITERIA

Required Resources

You must use a minimum of six resources. You must use at least:

- ❏ One book
- ❏ One article from SIRS
- ❏ One article from EBSCO-MAS
- ❏ Two articles from any other West High databases (CQ Researcher, Teen Health & Wellness, Opposing Viewpoints, EBSCO-Newspaper Source, Academic Search Elite, ERIC, etc.)

For the sixth resource, you may use another book, another database article, or any of the following:

❏ print or electronic reference tools	❏ surveys
❏ articles from print magazines or newspapers	❏ interviews
❏ free websites	

You may certainly use more than six resources!

POINTS TO EARN DURING RESEARCH   _____ out of 125

Topic Selection Worksheet	_____ out of 10	2 Bib Cards	_____ out of 10
Book Checkout	_____ out of 5	Idea Organizer	_____ out of 5
Getting Started Worksheet	_____ out of 10	Research Recap	_____ out of 5
Book Bib Card	_____ out of 5	Note Cards (Minimum: 6 bib + 50 notes)	_____ out of 20
2 Bib Cards	_____ out of 10	Outline	_____ out of 15
Note Cards (Minimum: 3 bib + 15 note)	_____ out of 20	Bibliography	_____ out of 10

WORK ETHIC   _____ out of 20

Everyone is expected to make full use of class time each and every day; this means staying on task. Take responsibility for doing your work; if you need help, ask for it. Be mature, respectful, and cooperative at all times.

Figure 12.18. Symposium Project Overview   *(Continues)*

Symposium Project 2011 *(Continued)*

Symposium Presentation

Introduction   _____ out of 10

Speaker presents an interesting and relevant introduction that captures the audience's attention through an anecdote, an image, a question, etc.

Content   _____ out of 50

The speech is convincing and has adequate factual information to support its position. The information is logically organized. Speaker is well prepared and has done extensive research. He or she can readily cite the source of any information that is used.

Language   _____ out of 5

The language used is clear and easy to follow. Excessive slang and verbal fillers are avoided. Most of the information is paraphrased and explained in the speaker's own words. Direct quotations are properly identified.

Articulation/Voice   _____ out of 10

The speaker articulates sentences clearly, expressively, and with sufficient volume. Pronunciation and voice tone are appropriate, and pitch is varied.

Eye Contact/Gestures/Physical Presence   _____ out of 10

The speaker stays focused throughout the presentation. He or she does not slouch, fidget, or use distracting movements. Hand gestures are used when appropriate. The speaker maintains good eye contact with the audience and does not rely heavily on notes. He or she appears comfortable and confident.

Conclusion   _____ out of 10

Speech concludes with an easily identified conclusion. An effective conclusion reviews the main points of the argument. The conclusion should make a memorable impression on listeners and leave the audience with something to think about.

Timing   _____ out of 10

Speech limits are five to seven minutes. The speaker stays within those limits.

Visual Aid   _____ out of 10

Speaker enhances presentation by using visual aids to highlight or present supporting evidence. Visuals should be visually pleasing (not distracting) and easy to view and follow.

Outline   _____ out of 10

Final typed outline follows proper formal outline format. Information is arranged logically. Main points are supported with plenty of facts and details.

Final Bibliography   _____ out of 5

Final typed bibliography follows proper bibliographical format. Bibliography contains at least five resources which were obtained from a variety of sources.

Symposium Total Points   _____ out of 275

Figure 12.18. Symposium Project Overview

Symposium Project Schedule

	Date	Topic/Activity	Site	Turn in or show us . . .
0	Feb 23	☐ Topic selection discussion/activity.	Class	☐ Topic Selection worksheet due at **start** of next class. (10 pts.)
1	March 2	☐ Lesson: Using library catalog. ☐ Locate, evaluate, and select at least one book.	Lab	☐ Check out at least one relevant book and show us. (5 pts.)
2	March 3	☐ Pre-reading, identifying main ideas.	Class	☐ Getting Started worksheet due at end of class (10 pts.). 8 pts. max. if turned in next day.
3	March 4	☐ Review: Review **SIRS**. Using **CQ Researcher** and **Opposing Viewpoints**. ☐ Locate, evaluate, and select at least two articles.	Lab	☐ Print out two articles.(1-SIRS, and 1-CQ Researcher or Opposing Viewpoints)
4	March 7	☐ Lesson: Bibliographic citations, note-taking strategies. (*Bring books and articles with you to class.*) ☐ Idea Organizer introduced.	Class	☐ Bib card for book due at **end** of class. (5 pts.) ☐ Bib cards clipped to two above articles due at **end** of class. (10 pts.)
5	March 8	☐ Work day.	Class	
6	March 9	☐ Work day.	Class	☐ At least **15** note cards due at end of class. (15 pts.)
7	March 10	☐ Lesson: Review **EBSCO-MAS**, Academic Search Elite, ERIC, Newspaper Source, Business Source, or Health Source. Using **Teen Health & Wellness**. ☐ Locate, evaluate, and select at least two articles.	Lab	☐ Print out two articles. (1-EBSCO-MAS, 1-Teen Health & Wellness, or another EBSCO database) ☐ Idea Organizer due at **end** of class. (5 pts.)
8	March 11	☐ Work day. Locate, evaluate, and select additional relevant articles.	Lab	☐ Bib cards clipped to yesterday's two articles due at **start** of class. (10 pts.) ☐ Note cards returned.
9	March 21	☐ Work day/recap.	Class	☐ Consult with teacher/librarian. (5 pts.)
10	March 22	☐ Work day/recap.	Class	☐ Consult with teacher/librarian. (5 pts.)
11	March 23	☐ Work day/recap	Class	☐ Consult with teacher/librarian. ☐ Finished note cards due at **end** of class: at least **6** bib cards and at least **50** note cards. (20 pts.)
12	March 24	☐ Lesson: Outlining.	Class	☐ Idea Organizer returned.
13	March 25	☐ Work day.	Class Lab	☐ Draft outline due at beginning of class. ☐ Note cards returned.
14	March 28	☐ Lesson: Formatting a bibliography.	Lab	
15	March 29	☐ Work day. Outline and bibliography.	Lab	
16	March 30	☐ Work day: work on final product.	Lab	☐ Outline and Bibliography due at beginning of class. (15 + 10 pts.)
17	April 1	☐ Work day: work on final product.	Lab	
18	April 4	☐ Work day: work on final product.	Lab	

Figure 12.19. Symposium Project Timeline

Symposium Project—Idea Organizer/Outline Organizer

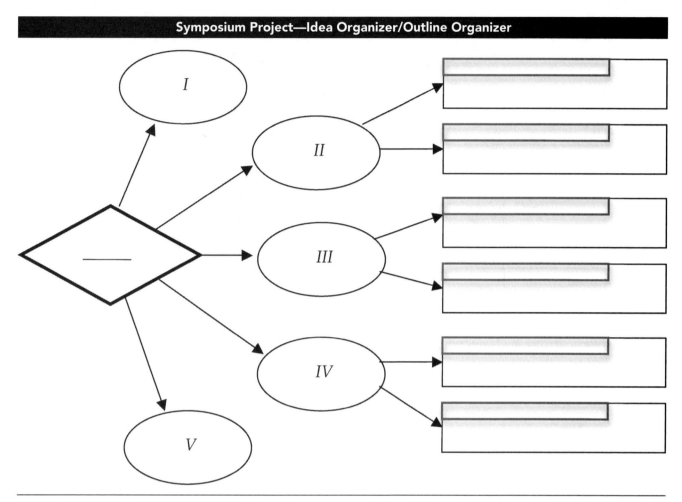

Figure 12.20. Symposium Project Idea Organizer

Research Recap (5 points)

Topic: _____

Complete your **Idea Organizer** and this form prior to your meeting with the librarian. **Bring both with you.**

Research Tool	# of Useful Resources Found	Type of Resource (e.g., book, magazine or newspaper article, pamphlet, webpage)	Where accessed (school or home)
Library Catalog			
SIRS			
EBSCO			
Opposing Viewpoints			
Other databases			
Websites			

Be prepared to discuss the following:

1. In two minutes, explain what you know about your topic. Address each of the subtopics briefly.

2. Do you have thought-provoking ideas for your introduction and conclusion?

3. Which resource has been the most valuable to you so far in helping you understand your topic? Why?

4. What has been the most difficult step in this research process?

Figure 12.21. Symposium Project Research Recap

Symposium Project-Formal Outline

Your **Idea Organizer** will be helpful in developing the outline. Consult it!

When developing an outline, note the following:

1. **Content:**   Keep comparable headings parallel.

2. **Format:**   To divide, there must be at **least two** parts. There can never be an **A** without a **B**, a **1** without a **2**, an **a** without a **b**, etc.

3. Use **Roman numerals** for the main topics: I.   II.   III.   IV.

   Subtopics are given **letters** and **numbers** as follows:

   - capital letters   A.   B.   C.   D.
   - Arabic numerals   1.   2.   3.   4.
   - lower case letters   a.   b.   c.   d.
   - Arabic numerals in parentheses   (1)   (2)   (3)   (4)
   - lowercase letters in parentheses   (a)   (b)   (c)   (d)

4. **Indent** subtopics so that all letters or numbers of the same kind will come directly under one another in a vertical line.

5. Begin each topic line with a **capital letter**. Do not capitalize words other than the first unless they are proper nouns or proper adjectives.

6. There must **never** be a lone subtopic under any topic; there must be either two or more subtopics or none at all. Subtopics are divisions of the topic above them. **A topic cannot be divided into less than two parts.**

Figure 12.22. Symposium Project Formal Outline

Index

About the Authors

Mary Jo Langhorne served as Library Coordinator for the Iowa City Community School District from 1994 to 2002, following 18 years as a teacher-librarian at Northwest Junior High and City High School. She was an adjunct faculty member in The University of Iowa School of Library and Information Science from 1999 to 2010, working with students who were pursuing careers as school librarians.

Denise Rehmke is the current Library Coordinator in the Iowa City Schools. She was the librarian at West High School from 1991 to 2008, and was at South East Junior High prior to that. She has been an adjunct faculty member at the University of Iowa School of Library and Information Science. As the current Library Coordinator, she directed the most recent library curriculum review for the district.

About 12,000 students attend **Iowa City Community School District (ICCSD)** schools. The district has nineteen elementary schools, three junior highs, two comprehensive high schools, and one alternative school. The district covers 130 square miles and serves the communities of Iowa City, Coralville, Hills, North Liberty, University Heights, and the surrounding rural areas. The University of Iowa, located in Iowa City, contributes to the diversity of the community and to its strong expectations for high-quality schools.

The ICCSD Library Program has been strongly supported by the district for over 30 years, as evidenced by its receiving national school library awards on three different occasions, most recently in 1997. The district maintains full-time teacher-librarians with support staff in all schools except for the two smallest, which have half-time librarians. There are currently 30 librarians employed in the schools, including a professional cataloger and the district library coordinator. The Superintendent of the Iowa City Community School District is Stephen Murley. David Dude is the Director of Information Services.

The following teacher-librarians currently working in the Iowa City Community School District have contributed to this guide:

Elizabeth Belding
West High School

Patricia Braunger
Grand Wood Elementary School

Kelly Butcher
Lemme Elementary School

Jenahlee Chamberlain
Kirkwood Elementary School

Susie Corbin-Muir
North Central Junior High School

Ernie Cox
Twain Elementary School

Joan DePrenger
Horn Elementary School

Judith Dickson
Weber Elementary School

Debra Dorzweiler
Penn Elementary School

Andrea Frederickson
City High School

Kristi Harper
Garner Elementary School

Salina Hemann
Lincoln Elementary School

Jill Hofmockel
West High School

Anne Marie Kraus
Roosevelt Elementary School

Cindy Kunde
Wickham Elementary School

Julie Larson
South East Junior High, Tate High School

Sarah Latcham
Van Allen Elementary School

Dolores Madden
Hoover Elementary School

Connie McCain
Lucas Elementary School

Michelle Morey
Longfellow Elementary School

Jeff Morris
City High School

Devin Redmond
Coralville Central Elementary School

Denise Rehmke
Library Coordinator

Susan Richards
Northwest Junior High School

Elizabeth Schau
South East Junior High School

Michael Schlitz
Mann Elementary School

Chelsea Sims
Hills Elementary School

Sheryl Vitosh
Shimek Elementary School

Jim Walden
West High School

The following individuals who have retired or moved from the district also contributed to this curriculum:

Barbara Becker

Suzanne Bork

Jean Donham

Becky Gelman

Jean Gerig

Ann Holton

Mary Jo Langhorne

Mary MacNeil

Deborah McAlister

Lynn Myers

Jennifer Olson

Karen Parker

Lisa Petrie

Cathy Schiele

Joel Shoemaker

Barbara Stein

Victoria Walton

Nancy Weber

Susan Wells

Nancy Westlake